LOVE SONGS
OF
ARNHEM LAND

LOVE SONGS OF ARNHEM LAND

Ronald M. Berndt

THE UNIVERSITY OF CHICAGO PRESS

The University of Chicago Press, Chicago 60637
Thomas Nelson (Australia) Limited

Published 1976
University of Chicago Press edition 1978

82 81 80 79 78   5 4 3 2 1

ISBN: 0-226-04389-4
LCN: 77-83828

Printed in Singapore by Times Printers Sdn Bhd

To my wife
Catherine Helen

CONTENTS

Appendixes
The Interlinear Texts

ILLUSTRATIONS

Diagrams

PREFACE

The original version of this volume was assembled early in the 1950s, but I decided to withdraw it from the publisher who had accepted it. This was partly because I wanted to reorganize it, but also because I was not sure that its frankness and its erotic content would be appreciated by non-Aboriginal readers. Then other matters intervened and the manuscript was left to gather dust for over two decades. During that time my wife (Dr Catherine Berndt) and I wrote *Sexual Behaviour in Western Arnhem Land*, which was published in 1951. This remains the only full-scale study on Aboriginal sexuality. It focuses on myth, songs and actual sexual behaviour in traditional western Arnhem Land. The present volume looks at the subject from the regional perspective of north-eastern Arnhem Land. And it concerns three song cycles that were commonly sung in 1946–47 at Yirrkalla among people from the surrounding country who made that their base for varying periods.

These three song cycles say something about attitudes towards erotic phenomena. But they do so in a particular way, by projecting the situational contexts dealt with in the songs outside the home area of the 'composers' or songmen themselves. In one sense, what they offer is an image of local sexual relations, presented *as if* it related to the people of the regions that are broadly suggested in the names sometimes attached to two of the sequences, 'Goulburn Island' on one hand, 'Rose River' on the other, on the western and south-eastern perimeters of north-eastern Arnhem Land. The exotic, as it were, has been pre-digested and put within a local, traditional frame of reference, providing an aura of verisimilitude that has (or had in the 1940s) a direct bearing on contemporary views about sexual relationships. The song

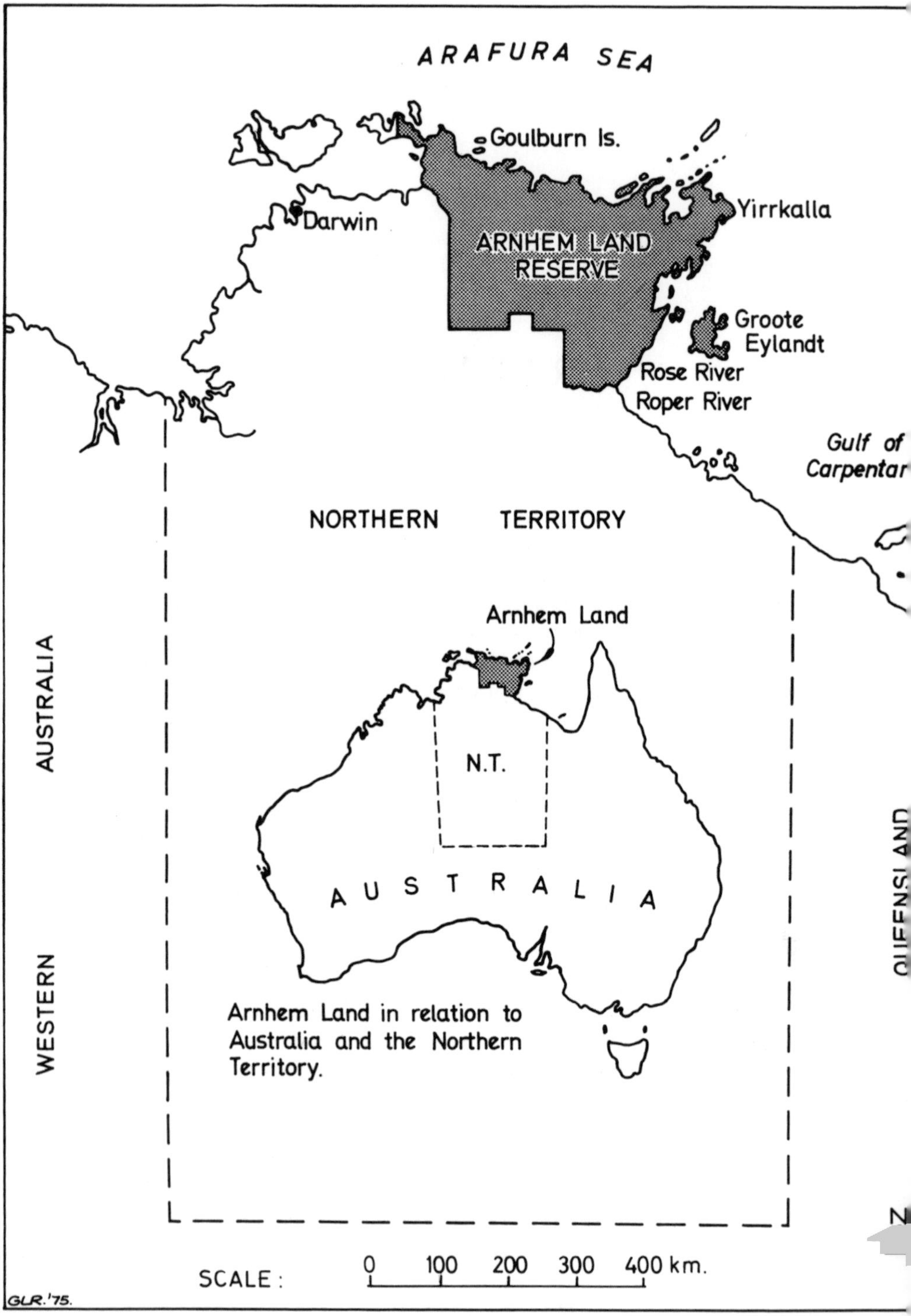
ARAFURA SEA
Goulburn Is.
Darwin
Yirrkalla
ARNHEM LAND RESERVE
Groote Eylandt
Rose River
Roper River
Gulf of Carpentar
NORTHERN TERRITORY
WESTERN AUSTRALIA
QUEENSLAND
Arnhem Land
N.T.
AUSTRALIA
Arnhem Land in relation to Australia and the Northern Territory.
SCALE: 0 100 200 300 400 km.
GLR.'75.

language conveys the message in the local idiom of symbolism and imagery which are in turn linked to a generalized pattern of socio-cultural values. In other words, although the songs claim to deal with events and characters outside the home area of the singers, they are actually phrased in familiar terms—in ways that the listeners can identify and respond to.

Songs of sexual love, and of events leading up to and surrounding the ultimate act of coitus, show differences as well as some similarities throughout Aboriginal Australia—in structure, in frankness and explicit detail, and in the ways such elements are wrapped up symbolically. Like stories, graphic art, drama and dance, stylized joking and so on, the songs illustrate a range of variations on a basic theme—the theme, in this case, being heterosexual relationships as a normal, and normative, aspect of human life.

The distinctiveness of north-eastern Arnhem Land 'cultural style', for instance, can be seen by comparing the underlying significance of the three song cycles presented here with those from western Arnhem Land. These two regions were very similar in some respects. They had, traditionally, broadly the same sort of religious orientation, and shared many of the same premises about socio-economic life in general. Also, they suffered the erosive effects of European invasion and conquest—though less drastically, to begin with, than in more closely settled regions: the partial protection of the Arnhem Land Reserve from the 1930s to the early 1950s gave them the illusion of continuing to own the land and resources which had 'always' been theirs. (Land and natural resources were not prizes to be contested and fought over in Aboriginal Australia. They were 'god-given', and emotionally inseparable from the people with whom they were linked through mythological charter and social inheritance.) The differences between the two regions become most marked when one considers their social organizational and cultural emphases (see R. and C. Berndt 1970). In the Goulburn Islands, Oenpelli and the Liverpool River regions pre- and extra-marital liaisons were a recognized feature of life in the near past and, so it would seem, the more distant past as well, expressing a local concern with achieving sexual satisfaction in a direct physical way. The reasons for this were complex. The impact of the outside world brought a weakening of marital ties, and the emergence of an arrangement for legitimizing pre- and extra-marital liaisons. Along with this went a relaxation of prohibitions that had restricted sexual relations between certain close or classificatory relatives.

In north-eastern Arnhem Land, the crisis was less acute and there were more opportunities for traditional ideas and practices to continue in a shape that the local people acknowledged as *their* way of looking at things, in contradistinction to other ways. Reference to sexual matters, although it was often direct and frank—as in the case of some of the songs—was, and is, usually surrounded by symbolic allusion, expressed through the beauty of traditional poetry. This does not necessarily mean that less attention was paid to the physical expressions of sex and to its emotional components. It is simply that the conventional approach took a different form. The circumstances will become clearer as we proceed. Before we do so, I should mention that the secular *djamalag* (sweetheart) ceremony of the Goulburn Islands and Oenpelli (see R. and C. Berndt 1951: 142–6; R. Berndt 1951*b*: 156–76) appeared to eastern Arnhem Landers unduly sensual and even crude. Where, they asked, was the subtlety of love-magic, of symbolic imagery, of gradual stimulation through the building-up of tension—a kind of prolonged savouring of an inevitable consequence?

Conversely, western Arnhem Landers who had seen the elaborate ritual which ordinarily accompanied traditional and public expressions of love in the north-eastern region, or those who had listened to one song after another and to the relatively indirect erotic references, wondered why it was necessary to spend so much time on extraneous matters when the sexual appetite could be assuaged much more easily and without such conventional preliminaries. Basically, this is really a question of aesthetics. It could well be argued that if the sex object, and/or the whole erotic sequence for that matter, is to be attractive and desirable to those embarking upon such an experience, certain expectations must be fulfilled. To put it another way, in traditional Aboriginal terms, while the aim of the exercise was coitus, it was rarely simply that. Verbal stimulation, especially in song, was usually considered a necessary prelude, and here we are unmistakably in the realm of aesthetic appreciation. It is this, the art of love, with which we are really concerned in this volume.

In western Arnhem Land, whatever might be said in general terms, the focus in the late 1940s was not on the gross achievement of coitus without such trimmings. Erotic expression took several forms, including a number of stories that children as well as adults found hilariously funny; but the most popular at that time were what I have called 'Gossip' songs (see R. and C. Berndt 1951: 211–40). Not all of the songs had erotic overtones, but that was their most typical feature. Their favourite topic was sweetheart relationships, but they were interested in husbands and wives too. Some were sentimental, but many emphasized quite heavily the physical aspects of sex. No esoteric significance was implied; and most of the songs were direct, outspoken, and ostensibly served to stimulate erotic feelings. Each song, complete in itself, referred to a specific event. Also, each song concerned actual persons who were not named: each encapsulated, as it were, a small interpersonal situation. It was left to listeners to speculate upon just who the participants really were. Because the society was relatively small and privacy at a minimum, the difficulties surrounding the guessing game were easily overcome. In contrast to north-eastern Arnhem Land songs, which are arranged as song cycles, these people in the west capitalized on contemporary social relations. This feature is almost entirely lacking in songs from the north-eastern side. Further, western Arnhem Land songs provide poetic images of events which were anticipated or had already taken place. This means, in effect, that sexual stimulation was both sought and achieved through re-living or re-thinking the adventures of others. Reliance on others, on the social dimension, was of paramount importance to them.

In north-eastern Arnhem Land, the love songs have a semi-religious or sacred aura. In Aboriginal Australia, speaking generally, it was not unusual for such love cycles to have mythic sponsorship, without themselves being necessarily mythic statements. Additionally, projecting a series of what are regarded as eternally relevant issues on to the screen of the Dreaming provides legitimation. These north-eastern Arnhem Land songs, however, also purport to treat actual situations—even though those situations are outside the local area. They are not concerned with mythic beings. Nevertheless, they do refer constantly to mythic symbolism and are closely correlated with religious ritual. By this means, a content that is related to ordinary behaviour is transmuted into something different—into the sphere of religious implication. Sexual activity is thus seen as more than a pleasant means of stimulating and gratifying personal desire. It is that, certainly, so the songs suggest. But that mundane relevance is considered to be of secondary importance, as something set within a complex patterning having further connotations. The broader picture primarily expresses the thesis that sexual union is an eternal principle in nature which is reflected in universal fertility and natural continuity.

The beauty of the song imagery provides an exotic setting that is easily identified by the people, and the actions portrayed in the songs fall within their range of expectation. What we have is a kind of illusory screen which appears to heighten sexual attractiveness, but in doing so strengthens religious feeling. In their setting, the signals that are provided not only enhance the physical appetite but implicitly support religious ideology and values.

North-eastern Arnhem Land society had no traditional institutionalization of pre- and extra-marital associations. Where they did occur, from all accounts they were carried out surreptitiously or (occasionally) within a ritual context. By comparison, western Arnhem Land appears to have been, thirty years or so ago, almost hedonistic. That view, of course, is somewhat deceptive since it is actually the compartmentalization of differing social activity which is relevant in the west. In north-eastern Arnhem Land, religion permeated and integrated all aspects of living and, in the circumstances, one would not expect it to exclude sexual manifestations.

The three song cycles discussed here demonstrate that north-eastern Arnhem Landers had an outward-looking orientation, at least up to a point: that they maintained communication with Aborigines on their fringes and took an interest in the mixture of sameness and difference they attributed to these not-quite-strangers. There is no information on how the processes of accommodation and innovation operated in the far-distant past; but certainly in the near past, up to the end of World War II, the north-easterners were quite selective in what they accepted into their own frameworks, flexible as those frameworks were. They seem to have adopted this kind of approach in their dealings with Indonesians as well.

The coastal people of western Arnhem Land were visited by Malayan and 'Macassan' traders over a very long (but still unspecified) period. This was followed by intensive Japanese and, especially, European impact. When I was writing my introduction to the original draft of this manuscript in 1950, I observed that one conspicuous feature in that area was the weakening of traditional codes of morality. Since then, the trend has accelerated.

North-eastern Arnhem Land also came under strong pressures from the outside world. But until very recently it was more remote from the main population centres and also much more inaccessible by road. It is hard to gauge what effects this contact may have had on the patterning of sexual behaviour—and on the song cycles themselves. Certainly, in the late 1940s there appeared to be fewer changes than might have been expected. In both spheres there was a distinctiveness which people acknowledged as being *their* regional style in contrast to others. It could be, perhaps, that longer exposure to alien contact resulted in a more balanced accommodation of new ideas—or conversely, in a greater degree of conservatism. And this was true, up to the early 1950s. Over a long period, the north-easterners were able to adjust gradually to alien influences, to come to terms with them and to develop an inner core of resistance, a resistance that enabled them to maintain basic features of their indigenous life and beliefs. They did this, it seems, by channelling such features in particular ways, categorizing and labelling them and conventionalizing their place in the local scheme by allocating them predominantly to one of the two moieties (in this case, to the *dua* moiety). This meant achieving not only compartmentalization but also integration, since the moieties are essentially interdependent and complementary. In the process, it left what was defined as indigenous, or non-alien, virtually untouched, providing a positive role for introduced themes and simultaneously cloaking them with traditional validity. It is not my intention to demonstrate this here, except to say that the moiety responsible for assimilating and transmuting non-Aboriginal elements (the *jiridja*, or yiridja, moiety) has also sponsored the great 'Macassan' song cycle, among others. However, that same moiety is responsible for its own repertoire of characteristically Aboriginal traditional features, which cannot be traced to non-Aboriginal origins.

North-eastern Arnhem Land society was able to cope fairly well with alien influences, in this quite ingenious fashion, largely because of its religion. This provided a complex patterning which infiltrated, both intellectually and ideologically, at the level of belief and values, into all areas of social activity.

Since the 1950s the situation has changed to an extent that the north-eastern Arnhem Landers of those days could not have envisaged. The Yirrkalla area has come to be the centre of large-scale developments of local bauxite resources (see R. Berndt 1964; R. Berndt (ed.) 1971: 35–7), which have changed the entire face of the countryside. The Gove dispute, as it turned out to be, came to a head in 1963 and has not yet been satisfactorily resolved in the interests of the Aborigines involved. Despite protests by themselves and others, the township of Nhulunbuy was established and has grown in size—spatially and in terms of its population of non-Aborigines, resident on traditional 'tribal' land and on what was, since 1931, ideally an inviolable reserve.

For the local people, this momentous and pervasive alien contact has presaged the ultimate destruction of their culture. In spite of pious governmental pronouncements on the desirability of preserving traditional Aboriginal rights and socio-cultural identity, it has proved virtually impossible to stem the tide sweeping towards cultural obliteration. Government sponsorship of local art forms, including bark paintings and other items made for general sale, and dance and drama 'tidied up' largely for the urban public, do not effectively counter the overall trend. The 'core of resistance' I mentioned, which the local people had developed sensibly and thoughtfully over many years, could not withstand the force of such catastrophic events. Whole areas of traditional life have been pushed aside in an effort to cope with unprecedented experiences and impinging non-Aboriginal attitudes. One can interpret the current situation as an encroaching ugliness, a diminution of aesthetic appreciation and awareness based on something more than commercial considerations. This is nowhere more apparent than in what remains today of their traditional oral literature and song-poetry.

I recorded these love songs in 1946–47. Since then, my wife, Catherine Berndt, and I have revisited north-eastern Arnhem Land on several occasions. However, I have not been able to re-record these songs—although my wife has obtained further, fragmentary excerpts. I would not go so far as to say they have been lost from the memory of these Aborigines; but there is no doubt that it would virtually be impossible now to re-create the sequences in the same form as they are given here.

In 1950, when the first version of this manuscript was completed, I noted that European contact, with the opportunities for increased mobility, had the effect of bringing north-eastern Arnhem Land Aborigines into closer intimate association with other non-adjacent Aboriginal groups. I continued by saying that one result of this was a weakening of existing traditional authority, and that another was the modification of existing patterns of sexual behaviour. Today, I would not emphasize those aspects: the real devastation really occurred later than this.

Also, at that time I suggested that the three cycles to be discussed here were of alien Aboriginal origin—that they had been introduced into north-eastern Arnhem Land. I went on to say, then, that such 'foreign' themes had been correlated with local traditional knowledge and belief. This I now consider was *not* the case. The Goulburn Island and Rose River cycles, although they are focused on non-local situations, were and are of indigenous (or local) inspiration. The underlying themes are traditional, defined in local terms, and the songs themselves are arranged in the verse style that is typical of this area. On the other hand, the Djarada (which will also be discussed) was considered to be definitely 'foreign' in style, even though the themes it treats were not necessarily atypical from the standpoint of local opinion.

In the characteristic songs of north-eastern Arnhem Land, word order and word form are not fixed and invariant. There is room for limited flexibility, with no sanctions to enforce strict conformity. What *is* important is that each song should include the appropriate 'names'—the sets of ordinary and singing names of the characters and environmental features and sites that make up its basic content. Everything of significance in the north-eastern Arnhem Land socio-cultural world has a 'name' (*jagu-miri* or yagu-miri, 'name-with'), and it is in the songs that all of these names are stored.

The original field research from which the three song cycles are derived was carried out in north-eastern Arnhem Land between August 1946 and July 1947. In this book I have restricted myself to this earlier material from Yirrkalla without bringing in later material from shorter visits up to 1971 to this and other places. During 1946–47, Aborigines from virtually all parts of the north-eastern Arnhem Land socio-cultural bloc were present from time to time—people from the English Company's and Wessel Islands, from Arnhem Bay and Elcho Island, and from even as far west as Milingimbi in the Crocodile Islands. On the south-eastern side, they came from Blue Mud and Caledon Bays—and a few even from Groote Eylandt, which is outside this cultural-linguistic area. My research was carried out mainly in the Riradjingu and Gumaidj dialects, with men who at that period understood little or no English. Men of other dialectal units and clans were also present, and made up a regular, changing circle (series of circles) of 'owners' who were in a position to provide the specialized knowledge required. During this period, men of all ages and affiliations living in the Yirrkalla camps (as they were then) were drawn within my orbit of interaction for purposes of discussion. The overall population was then a little over 200. By the beginning of 1970 this figure had increased to 800 or so (see C. Berndt 1970*a*: 30–3). (More recently, for reasons I won't go into here—the Gove developments, among others—much of the population has again been dispersing, into a number of outlying settlements and camps.) Because my wife and I were anthropologists, with even at that time considerable field experience behind us, we were able to adapt ourselves reasonably well to their community life as a family unit. In that way we gained a more detailed and intimate insight into a wide range of activities than would have been possible had either of us carried out this research separately. My only regret is that we had no mechanical recording aids (no tape recorders) which would have ensured the preservation of many songs (i.e., of music-plus-words) that even by the early 1960s were no longer remembered.

It is important to add, in view of the present upsurge of interest among people of Aboriginal descent generally in questions relevant to the Aboriginal heritage, that local Yirrkalla people made it clear to us that they were tremendously interested in what we were doing. They went out of their way on almost every occasion to help us at all levels of enquiry. The majority of the older men were well aware that unless we recorded all aspects of their life, in the form in which we saw it at that particular point in time, it would be irretrievably lost. They recognized that we were, in effect, recording this material for future generations. That awareness was most marked in this area, where the people had a healthy respect for and pride in their own traditional background—respect and pride which, in spite of trends to the contrary, continue to exist in a modified form today. At that time, too, we made friendships which continue on through changing circumstances. Some of the older men and women who played a vital and major role in our work then have since died—but many of the younger ones remain: no longer young, of course—we have grown older together.

It is, therefore, appropriate to acknowledge the great help and patience of our Aboriginal friends in this region. It was a mutual undertaking, a kind of reciprocal arrangement. Compensation—over and above the essential remuneration which is or should be an accompaniment of all anthropological field research—exists for them in the production of this and other works on their area. For myself, the compensation is of the same order.

Although this study concerns sexual behaviour and attitudes primarily from men's point of view, it is not unreasonable to suggest that these did not differ radically among women. Certainly, this is the case with the songs themselves, since they have to do with both men and women, and were sung openly in the main camps. And my wife has several versions of the Goulburn Island cycle, including a sequence of songs that diverges from the one I set out here (though I have recorded other sequences as well). Nevertheless, my discussion does not pretend to convey female perspectives on or attitudes towards sexual activity, or on other matters. My wife worked exclusively with women, as I did, exclusively, with men.

Apart from two orientation chapters—one on a general view of Aboriginal sexuality and the other on the socio-cultural background of north-eastern Arnhem Land—the entire focus of this volume is on the songs themselves. All are translations from original texts recorded by myself. These songs are presented in interlinear form in three appendixes at the end of the book: the serious student is advised to compare my translations with the texts. A fuller, more widely comparative study of sexuality must wait for the presentation and analysis of a great deal of detailed material—not only on songs, but on actual cases and dreams and local discussion of these, as well as on religious beliefs and rites.

Finally, I wish to acknowledge the kind co-operation of the Methodist Overseas Mission of Northern Australia (now the United Church in North Australia). In 1946–47, this organization was under the liberal guidance of its chairman, the Rev. Arthur Ellemor. The original version of this study was written at the Department of Anthropology, University of Sydney, when Professor (now Emeritus Professor) A. P. Elkin held the chair. In this context, I recognize his indispensable help and encouragement during the period when my wife and I worked under the auspices of the (then) Australian National Research Council, the Research Committee of the University of Sydney, and that University's Department of Anthropology. The actual writing of the first version was carried out while preparing material for publication under grants from the Commonwealth Research Committee, administered by the University of Sydney. The present revised version has been completed in the normal course of my research activity at the University of Western Australia.

This study is dedicated to my wife. She has been and continues to be my constant companion on all our fieldwork: she has assisted me considerably—first in the preparation of the original version of this work, as in many others, and now in its revised form.

Ronald M. Berndt
Department of Anthropology
University of Western Australia

one

BACKGROUND TO THE SONGS

I

A PERSPECTIVE ON ABORIGINAL SEXUALITY

I do not propose to embark here on a detailed consideration of sexual manifestations in Aboriginal Australia, either generally or specifically. My main concern is with three love song cycles and not with the overall patterning of Arnhem Land sexuality. Nevertheless, these songs appear to reflect, at least to some extent, the reality of traditional life in that area, particularly within the sphere of values and attitudes. Because of that, it is necessary to provide a perspective which I hope will aid in the appreciation of this traditional life, as well as emphasizing the underlying significance of the songs.

In the self-consciously permissive society of today, it is difficult to appreciate that as recently as in 1952, in a review of my volume *Kunapipi* (1951*a*), Leonhard Adam (1952: 82) took me to task for not using Latin to describe 'certain details [of a sexual nature] which, quite apart from their unsavoury character, are hardly necessary for the understanding of the Kunapipi cult'. It was not unusual in anthropological works of the last century to record in Latin entries that were considered to be explicitly of a sexual nature. Roth (1897: 169–84), perhaps more outspoken than some, entitled a chapter in one of his works 'Ethno-pornography', and warned readers that what followed was 'not suitable for perusal by the general lay reader'. It is a matter of wonder, now, to read what was included under Roth's heading: material on male and female initiation, marriage, pregnancy, babyhood, menstruation and even 'foul' language, among other things. To some extent, his 'frank' approach was unusual, even then, although in some respects it was symptomatic of the times. Today, explicit sexual detail and frank discussion of sexual matters are more or less accepted as the current fashion. Simultaneously, sexuality has increasingly been phrased in pornographic terms, which means that it is often treated as something essentially obscene. While this development seems to be relevant to Australian–European society, among others, it was not the case as far as Australian Aborigines were concerned—not traditionally. The material I treat here is of a sexual nature, relating to events leading up to and surrounding the sexual act *per se*. To refer to this I have used the term 'erotic', since the songs concern love in emotional terms as well as sensuality where the issue of sexual enjoyment is dominant.

Australian Aborigines were fully aware of the fundamental issues relating to physical survival. This involved recognition of the important part sexual activity may play in both personal and social adjustment and in the ultimate happiness of men and women. Normal sexual expression, regularized through the conventional channels, bore no relation to what is sometimes called 'shame'. Gratification of the sexual appetite was acknowledged to be a natural urge, like taking food to satisfy hunger. Sexual maturity in men and women was a desirable quality, a necessary concomitant of physical and mental development—and initiation rites for youths and girls emphasized this, among other matters.

Religious life over much of Aboriginal Australia centred on procreation, on the renewal of human beings and of the natural species, and on the continuity of family and community life through mythic intervention and guidance. The basic concept was one of spiritual and material fructification, with sexual intercourse either directly or symbolically implied as an essential element stimulating or activating this process. The most obvious examples are to be found in the great fertility cults of Arnhem Land and of the western-central region of the Northern Territory: but such emphases are no less apparent in many other areas (see R. Berndt 1974). This ideological background underlines Aboriginal acceptance of sexual sequences as entirely natural manifestations—as ordinary facts of living.

Although sex was associated with religion, this does not mean that it was considered a mystery. The biological-physiological aspects of human life were well understood, in a general way, as they were for the natural species within their environment. Human beings were regarded as part of nature, with the same life essence as other natural species. This is not a matter of relegating man to the status of an animal. Rather, it expresses the idea of an empathy existing between them, the assumption that all belonged to an overall divine scheme or pattern. It was also a matter of humanizing the natural environment, making it social, and viewing sexual expression as one of the significant keys to understanding its meaning.

Traditionally, Aborigines went naked, or almost so. Occasionally some covering or decoration was worn, but not necessarily to hide the genitals (see R. and C. Berndt 1964: 103–4). Nudity or near-nudity was normal for people of both sexes and all ages, and did not in itself arouse sexual feeling. For the unclothed human body to assume sexual attractiveness, or to be singled out for that purpose, some change in ordinary posture or carriage was considered to be necessary: a man might swagger with buttocks protruding or penis erect; a woman might sway her hips, coyly 'flash' her eyes, or sit provocatively with legs apart. An exchange of sexual talk in a mixed group might have the same effect.

Many Australian Aboriginal societies provided in some way for pre- and extra-marital relations. At the same time, modesty, moderation in sexual activity and discretion were valued and emphasized in the training of both boys and girls. Through a variety of situations, they were introduced to local definitions of physical beauty and sexual attractiveness (see R. and C. Berndt 1951: 23–4; 1964: 161–2). And they were expected to reach puberty with a reasonably good understanding of the relevance of the sexual act and its associated responsibilities.

In a traditionally-oriented Aboriginal situation, privacy was at a minimum —or, rather, the contrast between 'private' and 'public' was geared to circumstances of open living, where most of what went on was audible or visible, or both, to everyone in the neighbourhood. There was little that passed unnoticed by people in such an environment—including children, who were normally all-pervasive. But in general the conventions of social etiquette allowed for a measure of 'as-if' privacy, charting a strategy of living-privately-in-public. People who had no reason to intervene or to show an interest in what was happening would appear to ignore it. Also, at the level of verbal behaviour, rules of varying strictness applied. In ordinary camp conversation, sexual topics were discussed freely and frankly before children, but restrictions were imposed in the presence of particular relatives who were tabu to the speakers, or stood to them in a relationship of constraint. The rules associated with specific kin, such as an actual or potential mother-in-law or a man's sister or a son's wife, were explicit about what should or should not be said in their presence. On the other hand, joking relationships were recognized between certain kin of the same or opposite sex. In their case, it was quite in order to bandy sexual references without restraint as the occasion demanded—references which, if used in relation to other persons might give offence, arouse anger or even precipitate a fight. However, camp swearing was common enough during times of emotional upheaval and quarrelling. Often, in that context, expressions and phrases of a sexual nature were used—as well as words with a secret-sacred connotation, which would not be uttered in normal circumstances.

Some subjects were talked about freely and without much reticence: a husband's preference for one wife at the expense of others, the adultery or excesses or promiscuity of a man or woman, the meeting of lovers, and so on. Where secrecy was especially important, for example in relation to pre- and extra-marital liaisons, the people concerned would meet well away from the main camp or in the dark of night. That such privacy was desirable at times, as on specifically sexual occasions, seems to have been recognized as a personal right, and not violated except by an irate spouse or an aggrieved lover. Privacy, generally, was framed in terms of exclusion—exclusion of some persons in relation to some particular activity: for example, women from the secret-sacred ground of fully initiated men; men from the secret rites of women, from childbirth scenes or from the menstrual camp; novices from certain areas of the ritual ground; and so on.

Small children were allowed much liberty in expressing themselves and indulging in erotic play when adults were present; and their actions often caused amusement, as they tried to replicate the actions and conversation of their elders (see R. and C. Berndt 1946: e.g. 69). In some areas, they had their own songs or adaptations of adult songs, some of which have an erotic content (see R. and C. Berndt 1943: 252–4; 1952: 364–76; 1953: 423–34; 1954: 501–8). In north-eastern Arnhem Land in the 1940s, probably the commonest exclamations used by children were '*Dagu wiin*!' (long vagina or vulva) and '*Gurga wiin*!' (long penis), repeated constantly in casual play, or in convulsive rage. Little boys and girls playing together liked to tease each other in this way, showing off their adult knowledge. As they grew older, particularly at the onset of puberty, they were obliged to be more restrained in this respect, and certainly less ostentatious.

Some Aboriginal societies, emphasizing obvious physical differences between men and women, referred to a male person as 'penis' and a female person as 'vulva' or 'vagina'. In north-eastern Arnhem Land, for instance, far more than on the western side, *gurga* (penis) was used in place of the ordinary word for a man, *diramu* (or *daramu*); and *dagu* (vulva or vagina) for the ordinary word for a woman, *daiga* or *mialg*: sometimes these alternative terms were used with the ending *-miri*, 'having' or 'with'. Here, too, the word for a child is *judu* (yudu), also meaning semen. *Judu* is the ordinary singular word for child; the plural, *djamarguli* or *djamawu*, was explained as meaning 'through work', 'working' a woman being to have coitus, and the child being a result of this. Thus, one word for penis was *nguru-djamawuru* ('nose for working', or for making children). The term *wagu* is used by a woman to refer to her own child, or by a man referring to his sister's child: this kinship term was said to be associated with *walg*, meaning uterus, navel cord, or very occasionally afterbirth blood (see R. Berndt 1952: 273–4). It was not unusual to hear someone calling, in effect, without any embarrassment, 'Here come a penis, a vulva and their semen!'—that is, parents and offspring.

This indirect sexual terminology—indirect because such terms were used without a sexual connotation and as a matter of common speech, the etymology of which was taken for granted—had a wide distribution in northern Arnhem Land. Physiographical features of the countryside were likened to male and female genitals, and some sacred and historic sites bear witness to the erotic activity of mythic and spirit beings who travelled through that country in the Dreaming era. The same is the case with natural species, where anthropomorphic significance may be implied. Imprints in rock, knee marks, tell a story of a mythic act of coitus; a sacred waterhole may symbolize a vagina; a shining white substance on a rock surface may represent semen; and so on. These signs humanize and validate the adventures of Dreaming characters. The same was the case in other areas of Aboriginal Australia, especially in reference to cave paintings and rock engravings. In everyday life, on the northern Arnhem Land coast, conical shells were symbolic penes, and vulvular cockles vaginas. The traditional pair of *dudji* firesticks, which in the late 1940s were still an essential piece of equipment in the bush, symbolized the union of male and female: the top drill is *judu* (child, signifying its 'making'), the man or *gurga* (penis, whose 'inside' or sacred name is *bugu*, forehead), while the bottom horizontal stick containing the oval or round depression is *jindi* (big), the woman or *dagu* (vulva, also called by the 'inside' name *mangudji*, eye). The twirling of the *judu* in the *jindi* is the act of coition: this, it is said, 'was the beginning of man and woman'.

Although these aspects imply a frank attitude towards sexual matters, modesty remained significant. Prudery, on the other hand, was irrelevant; but circumspection in sexual matters was a necessary feature of social existence. There were, of course, exceptions at the personal level and on particular occasions when, for example, sexual licence was part of a religious ritual; or in love-magic ritual where singing and dancing of a sexual nature was carried out by members of each sex separately or more rarely by both together. This was not a matter of immodesty. Although it undoubtedly had stimulatory or erotic undertones (in some cases, overtones), it also had implications of a symbolic kind over and above the acts themselves. Modesty was a quality generally considered especially important for young women, but also for young men. However, where sexual licence in a ritual or ceremonial context was called for, what actually took place was influenced considerably by those present and by the relationships existing between them.

Kinship in Aboriginal Australia was an overriding factor, in this setting as in others. The content of relationships had to do with behavioural patterns which should ideally exist, and often actually did exist, between particular persons. Some of these stipulated considerable constraint and avoidance. Others allowed more scope for flexibility and freedom in speech and action, indicating the degrees of intimacy and familiarity that were proper in the relationship concerned. One example with almost universal currency in

Aboriginal Australia was the extended use of terms that can be translated as 'spouse'. These general 'spouse' terms imply actual or potential sexual access. They are category-terms, pointing to possibilities that could become actualities under certain conditions: there was nothing automatic about the transition, whether the outcome was a marriage or merely a more transient liaison. In some areas the same terms were used between a husband and wife who formed a publicly recognized marital unit. In other areas there were specific terms for such actual, publicly acknowledged spouses. But this was not, in any way, a symptom of a permissive society. On the contrary, it defined spouse-surrogates who could be called upon for non-sexual as well as sexual responsibilities. Where sexual relations were concerned, this usually meant that permission had to be sought from an actual husband or an actual wife. (Because of the imbalance of rights, the consequences of *not* asking—or getting—permission could be more serious for a wife than for a husband.) Such a system, in general terms, served as a model and a basis for legitimizing both pre- and extra-marital associations.

There are two other issues that should be mentioned. Modesty was not usually a matter of covering one's body or genitals. In the case of a woman, it consisted of, for example, covering her head while in the presence of particular relatives, holding a sheet of bark before her, always sitting circumspectly, or purposely remaining undecorated for a dance in order not to draw attention to herself. Also, coitus was not usually carried out in public or in the presence of others (aside from co-wives, and babies), except during certain rituals and in a few rather rare circumstances. In fact, public demonstrations of physical affection between adults of opposite sex were infrequent. In contrast, affection between great friends of the same sex or between parents and children and some other relatives was shown openly and freely when the occasion warranted this. Many of the 'Gossip' songs of western Arnhem Land, already mentioned (page xiv), express longing for an absent spouse or lover. Public demonstrations of emotion were especially conspicuous, and lavish, during mourning: for example, after the death of a husband or wife, a child or a parent. Apart from the question of reasons for a public display at such a time (for instance, failure to show sorrow could be taken as a sign of responsibility for the death), the deep personal sorrow and sense of bereavement is clearly evident in the songs of grief that were a feature of mourning rites in north-eastern Arnhem Land and at Bathurst and Melville Islands (cf. C. Berndt 1950*a*).

Sex and Procreation

One of the most interesting controversies which have focused on Aboriginal belief hinges on whether or not sexual intercourse was recognized as a causal factor in bringing about pregnancy. Spencer and Gillen (1938; 1904: e.g.

330), among other earlier writers, held that it was not. Malinowski (1913: 128) cast doubt on this view. Ashley-Montagu in 1937 (in a volume which was revised and expanded in 1974) upheld it. I must emphasize that north-eastern Arnhem Land Aborigines did not doubt that there was a causal, sequential connection between sexual intercourse and childbirth, and for that matter saw the growth and renewal of nature generally in those terms.

Ashley-Montagu denied (in 1937) that any Australian Aborigines had such an understanding. To support his contention he set out a large amount of empirical material: some of it was unreliable and some had been bent to fit his theme. In his recent revised edition, new material is presented, some of it from the area that concerns us here. However, while Ashley-Montagu insists that his primary interest lies in discovering what the facts are, not in proving or disproving anything (1974: xxix), his orientation now does not differ appreciably from his earlier one. Evidence to the contrary has been forthcoming from Róheim (1933), Thomson (1936*a*) and Warner (1958), among others, including myself. One of the major difficulties which has dogged this argument from the beginning has been the lack of appreciation that spiritual elements and, specifically, the spiritual elements in conception, are of supreme importance in Aboriginal Australia: a physical organism is inconceivable without the spiritual aspect that gives it animation, that makes it 'live'. Because that aspect has most often been emphasized, it has been thought that physiological processes are not recognized. In fact, this is generally a superimposition of a spiritual ideology upon a basis of reasonably good knowledge of physiological implications. Or, alternatively, the physiological has been wrapped up in symbolic language (see R. Berndt 1974: fasc. 1: 4; fasc. 2: 11; fasc. 4: 24). In virtually all the areas in which I have carried out intensive field research, both aspects are regarded as significant. At an earlier period, I reported on this for the Western Desert (R. and C. Berndt 1943: 243–51; 1944: 227, 233–40). The evidence obtained there demonstrated the Aborigines' belief that (a) intercourse could or might result in pregnancy; (b) intercourse contributed to the formation and growth of the foetus; and (c) the foetus was animated by a spirit child who had mythic affiliations. It was this last, the spiritual possession of the foetus, which determined the child's future personality and social position. (As with the 'Central tribes' which Ashley-Montagu says 'had no idea of conception at all' [1974: 225], those of the Western Desert ['western tribes of South Australia'] appear to know 'the facts of physiological paternity' but 'there has been a great deal of contact with whites' [*ibid.*: 210, 229]. This ignores the fact that when my wife and I worked with these Western Desert people in 1941 they had little or no contact with Europeans. On the other hand, that point is not raised when the evidence appears to be congenial to him.)

But that aside, the situation in the Western Desert as noted by us was not dissimilar to the western Arnhem Land case, notwithstanding some variations (see R. and C. Berndt 1951: 80–6; 1970: 27). There, two basic ingredients were recognized as making up the psycho-physical identity of human beings —the material substance, plus something else. That something else is the animating spirit, who enters the foetus. That theme is much more pronounced in north-eastern Arnhem Land, especially in the Djanggawul mytho-ritual cycle (R. Berndt 1952: 6–7 *et seq.*), where direct statements are complemented by symbolic ones. It is also just as apparent in the Wawalag mythology and in its ritual expressions (R. Berndt 1951*a*), as we shall see.

Sex and Romance

Ashley-Montagu's attempt to separate the sexual act from probable pregnancy, denying (in the earlier edition of his book) any causal connection between them, led him to claim (1937: 188), quite dogmatically, that 'For the native "sexual desire", as far as we know, represents a merely propulsive power which enables him to satisfy his impulses, and to enjoy a certain amount of pleasure in doing so, it is nothing more, and perhaps a little less than this'. (In the recent edition [1974: 207] the same sentence stands, with 'power' altered to 'force', and the last part, after 'doing so' reading simply 'and nothing more'.) Or, again, according to Basedow (1935: 31–3), 'There is no real lovemaking among the Aborigines', and 'it is quite out of the question to observe demonstrative lovemaking . . .' I have already noted the widespread convention that public displays of this nature between adults of opposite sex were in bad taste. However, the evidence I have makes it quite plain that demonstrations of affection were not absent, but they took place in the setting that was considered appropriate to them—in private. Basedow (*ibid.*: 42) also says that 'the courtship and nuptials of an Aboriginal maiden are crude and unromantic'. Such views do not measure up to empirical facts. Given traditional conventions which dictate ways of approaching sexual situations, the whole concept of romantic love is of paramount significance. We (R. and C. Berndt 1964: 160–1) previously underestimated this aspect because (as we have noted elsewhere) 'so much is against it: the formal patterning of marriage preferences, infant and child betrothal, the narrow scope for individual initiative, the restraints written into the kinship system'. To some extent, this formal structure did tend to stereotype approaches of a sexual kind. Nevertheless, the crucial factor is that much of this was permeated with a tremendous amount of erotic material which enhanced and provided stimulation, excitement, desire and attachment to a love object—in terms of a particular person, or the pleasure of sexual association, or both. It is not simply a matter of such belief and action running contrary to established precedence, or that the focus was entirely on sexual partners who were not defined as potentially marriageable. Of course, much of it was both directly and indirectly concerned with sporadic and transitory sexual affairs—but much of it was not.

Further, while preferential marriage patterning might be the rule or convention, there existed simultaneously, in many Aboriginal societies, institutionalized modes of pre- and extra-marital sexual expression. Such structural provisions did not necessarily militate against formal marital patterning; and occasional elopements or the breaking of betrothal contracts did not necessarily invalidate traditional practice and formal marriage *per se*. If such a system satisfied sexual propensities, it did so within a frame of permitted relationships. In other words, such activity was normally confined, and not promiscuous in the accepted sense of that term. And there is also the question of 'wrong' marriages or 'wrong' sexual liaisons—wrong in varying degrees, provoking social sanctions or social action of some kind. But generally the institutionalization of sexual relations did no violence to kinship rules and provided a spread of affective and emotional ties, with the sexual act as a central component. Over and above the formal structure of marriage alignment and betrothal, it provided opportunities for individual attachment. This catered for needs that might not be satisfied in a particular marriage and might, in certain circumstances, lead to formal marriage or the discarding of one partner in favour of another. The question of rights over a sexual partner was always a significant factor which, if abused, could lead to dissension and fighting. Personal choice of a partner was something to be reckoned with, in spite of conventional measures to keep choice within bounds and to channel it in particular directions, especially in terms of approved kin categories. It is within this context that romantic love and all its trimmings were brought to the fore.

Such romanticism was expressed mostly through the medium of love songs, some having a magical significance, and many involving ritual action as well. These were usually colourful projections of what was desired, many of an imaginative and passionate nature. Some were virtually straightforward examples of fantasy or wish-fulfilment. Others were practical approaches to erotic needs, by both men and women. Many are of great beauty, reflective of the excitement of sexual pleasure, the vicissitudes of personal love, enduring affection and sentimental longing; others are blunt in their expression of direct and aggressive sexual desire. Such material, varying in emphasis, is and was abundantly available throughout traditional Aboriginal Australia. It appears obliquely in the older literature, but is treated in some detail by Róheim (1933), Kaberry (1939), R. and C. Berndt (1943: 135-49) and C. Berndt (1950*b*; 1965: 238-82). The 'Gossip' songs of western Arnhem Land (mentioned before) also have as their main theme romantic attachment and affection between men and women. Especially significant in the presentation of Aboriginal song-poetry are T. G. H. Strehlow's poetic translations

(1971: 462–541) of Central Australian songs. Outstandingly beautiful, these make clear the aesthetic sensitivity and also the romanticism of traditional Aranda culture—exemplified, for instance, in the song of the Kwalba Chief of Tera.

Most of the great love song cycles, whether or not they included any magical intent, were sponsored by mythic beings. Almost the only exceptions I know personally are the separate 'Gossip' songs, which are independently composed and have no mythic sponsorship. But even with these, the song-man or composer draws his inspiration from spirit (not necessarily mythic) beings. Most of these love song cycles were viewed as traditional; and some actually incorporated mythic characters, providing a guide to everyday behaviour. This means that many of them fall within the sphere of religion or are themselves linked to major religious rituals or themes. The Djarada is a case in point, although not especially so in its north-eastern Arnhem Land version. Moreover, although the romantic and erotic elements are dominant (in, for example, more widely known Djarada versions) and to some extent they serve personal ends, many were also interpreted as being concerned with sex in relation to fertility. In women's rituals in the Birrundudu region (C. Berndt 1950*b*: 71; 1965: 273), 'the strong emphasis . . . on sexual intercourse and reproduction is thus part of the general religious scheme'.

Sex and Ritual

I have already mentioned that religion in Aboriginal Australia was organized round primary themes, fertility of human and natural species and the life crises (see R. Berndt 1974). 'Fertility' implies seasonal and environmental renewal; and human beings are included in the overall scheme, through spiritual, or mythic, intervention. That natural sequence is mirrored in the life crises themselves—from birth to death, to re-birth. The achievement of birth demands both the material and the immaterial, the physical and the spiritual: the one attained through a sexual act, through human agency, the other through the agency of a mythic or spirit being. Both are equally important and both are recognized as being so—although one may be emphasized at the expense of the other. But one is not possible without the other. Aboriginal man projected his own belief system on to the environment in which he lived. He saw within it the same forces operating as he identified within his own process of living. The concept of the Dreaming and its totemistic expressions underlined that thesis. Procreation did not come about without some effort on his own part; sexual intercourse was therefore a necessary feature. In the ritual sphere, that physical process was transformed into symbolic representations and expanded to include the world of man and of nature conceived as a single entity.

This is not to say that every aspect of religious ritual concerned matters relevant to procreation in physical or symbolic terms. Much of it did not. The basic themes, however, were quite marked, and nowhere more obtrusive than in the rituals of north-eastern Arnhem Land (R. Berndt 1951*a*: 1952). This dominant theme of procreation in ritual terms has been briefly taken up by Hiatt (1971: 77–88), who proposes 'a division of secret pseudo-procreation rites into two types, phallic and uterine'. He notes, however, that his division is based on 'which form of sexuality (male or female) is being symbolically stressed'. I will not discuss this conceptual 'division' here, except to say that it is not possible to separate out one such 'type' from the other. Both are, or were, always present, though often with differing emphases. Where such rites do take place on the sacred or secret-sacred ritual ground, and where sexual motifs are involved, they are usually of two kinds. In one, postulants and actors perform acts of a sexual kind or assume postures of this kind relevant to mythic beings. As far as the last is concerned, various objects representing, for example, erect penes are attached to actors (see, for example, Róheim 1945: Plate 1; R. and C. Berndt 1946: Plate III; R. Berndt 1951*a*: Plate VI), and coitus is simulated by male actors representing male and female mythic beings. Basedow (1925: 282) speaks of 'sex worship' in relation to such rites. I exclude from this division the use of a wide range of ritual objects which could or do have sexual connotations. Many of these are manipulated by postulants.

The second kind of manifestation relates to coitus on or close to the ritual ground by male and female postulants. Excluded from this are examples of sexual licence which take place during or at the conclusion of a particular ritual and/or ceremony. A case in point is the *djamalag* of western Arnhem Land where the sexual act created goodwill and supplied a diversion for participants (R. and C. Berndt 1951: 142–6). There are many other examples of this kind in the literature. However, coitus as an integral part of ritual is a different matter. Spencer and Gillen (1904: 137–8) mention a Waramunga case. And there are the well-known *mindari* of the Dieri (Elkin 1934: 185) and the *kunapipi* (R. Berndt 1951*a*: 66–9, Plate XVII, plus extensive references). Further, ritual intercourse and defloration were often an important part of the initiation of girls (see R. and C. Berndt 1964: 150–5), and had fertility implications. The example noted by Cook (Hawkesworth 1773: vol. II, 128) was obviously of this kind.

One aspect must be re-emphasized in this context. When coitus is performed ritually, particular rules are adhered to, and sexual 'licence' is thereby regularized. Malinowski (1913: e.g. 123) made this point: 'Every form of licence must be subject to customary rules'. In other words, sexual 'licence' was in fact conformity. It took place within an agreed-upon framework where the kin relationship between sexual partners was significant. Moreover, in a religious situation, the ordinary rules relating to sexual access were reversed, so that those participating were often related to one another in terms of normal avoidance. In the *kunapipi* (R. Berndt 1951*a*: 47–53), for example, coitus took place between tabued persons, and because of that was considered to be especially efficacious in ensuring fertility.

Social Relations of Sex

Pre- and extra-marital liaisons, as I have said, usually brought together persons who were formally related to each other in acceptable ways—so that their union would not normally contravene the preferred patterns of betrothal and marriage. Such associations varied considerably in durability, from transient encounters to relationships of a more stable kind. The 'sweetheart relationship' is of the second variety. It could become formalized to such an extent that it disrupted the marriages of all the people immediately involved. Blatant behaviour on the part of one or both of such a sweetheart-pair, flaunting their relationship, would almost certainly arouse anger in a husband or wife who saw his or her rights in the other as being violated or his or her feelings slighted. The result could be quarrelling and fighting. However, much depended on what a husband or wife was prepared to regard as acceptable behaviour. In some areas there was what can be called 'secondary marriage'—the Dieri *pirauru*, or even the western Arnhem Land *mararaidj* (sweetheart) relationship are examples (see R. and C. Berndt 1964: 159–65).

A primary consideration in all such cases, except with those of an ephemeral kind, was the obligations and responsibilities that were set in train between the persons concerned. Any liaison undertaken either before or after betrothal and marriage was bound to have implications for others—not simply the respective spouses or the betrothed husband or wife. Rights over others were always relevant, especially a husband's rights over his wife. Except during sacred ritual, or occasionally at times of social effervescence, unless permission was forthcoming—unless the situation itself defined expected sexual behaviour—some risk was involved. Probably this element of risk served as an inducement. But it was in a social situation where little secrecy was possible.

It is remarkable that Spencer and Gillen (1938: 99–100) held that sexual jealousy among Aborigines was not very well developed; that where anger was aroused it was focused on the infringement of custom. Malinowski (1913: 124–9) also took this view. However, there is ample evidence to underline the significance of personal jealousy, in the case of sexual infidelity on the part of a spouse or betrothed. The question of infringement of rights is also of importance. In western Arnhem Land, for example, sexual jealousy could flare up between recognized sweethearts, as well as between legitimate spouses. Throughout Aboriginal Australia most quarrelling and serious fighting arose through difficulties over women, accusations centring on responsibility for a death, and infringements of rules relating to secret-sacred affairs—in that order, and overwhelmingly over women. The evidence therefore suggests that there were always persons willing to risk disruption and conflict in order to satisfy sexual desires and to pursue a passionate attachment outside the marriage bonds. Elopements were not uncommon, and in many areas were accepted as a more or less legitimate way of effecting marriage. Although I have emphasized the importance of sexual liaisons taking place within an accepted pattern of potentially preferred or potentially permissible partners in marriage, it is also true that elopement often took place where the pair concerned were related to each other in a socially unacceptable fashion or where their respective marital partners were notorious for their jealousy and for their ability and readiness to undertake aggressive action against the offending pair.

The basis of Aboriginal marriage (monogamous or polygynous), recognizing the economic issues involved, was the regularization of a sexual union for procreative purposes, providing legitimacy for the social descent (affiliation) of offspring. That primary reason was rarely if ever submerged by others. The (ideally) polygynous society of north-eastern Arnhem Land, while it emphasized the economic aspect of marriage and the prestige value of contracting unions which linked various families together in an intricate network of relationships that spread across a number of dialectal units, was quite firm in the emphasis it placed on procreation. The production of children was a dominant theme, expressed in song and in ritual. The love songs set out here demonstrate this point.

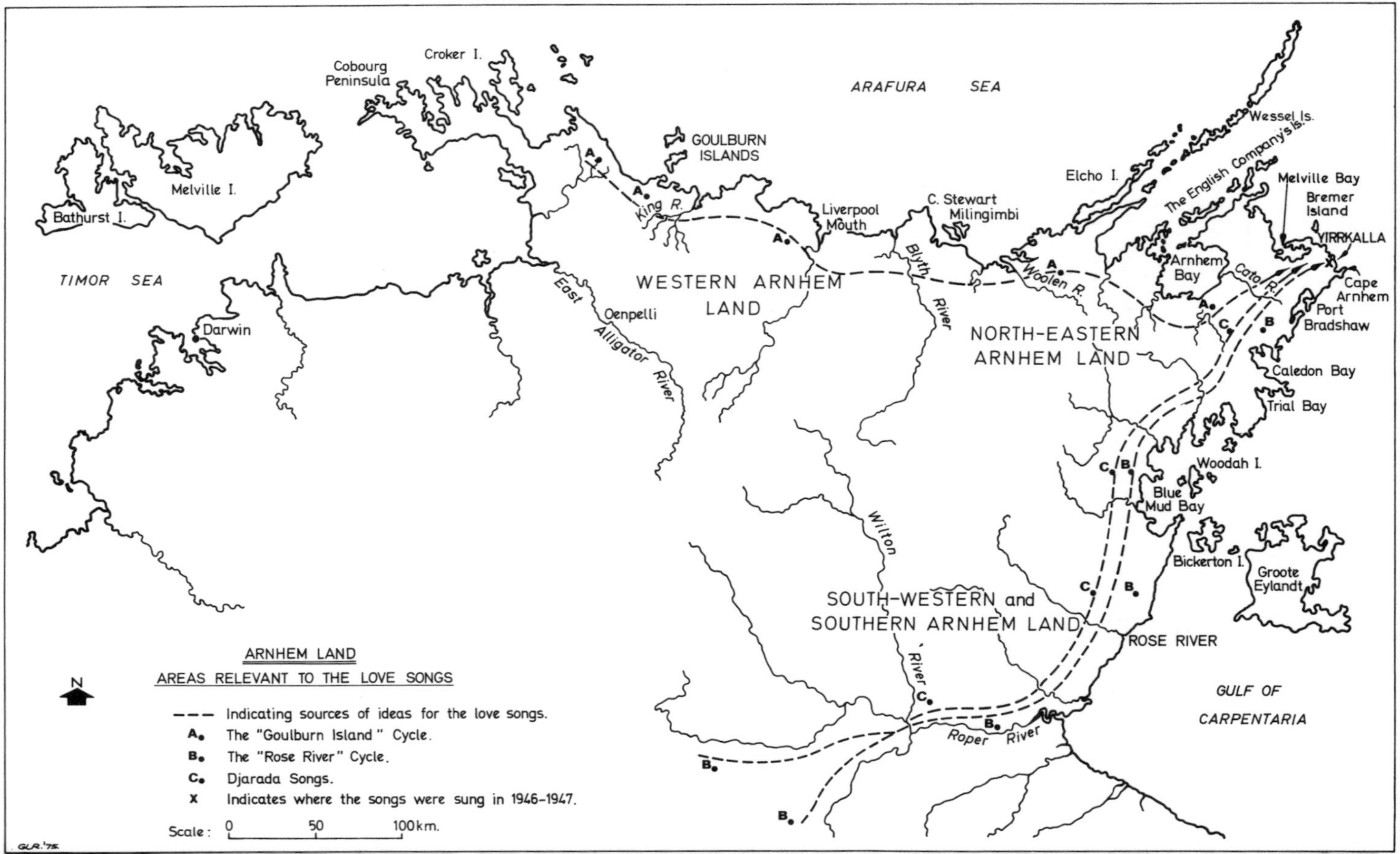

ARAFURA SEA
TIMOR SEA
Melville I.
Bathurst I.
Cobourg Peninsula
Croker I.
GOULBURN ISLANDS
King R.
Liverpool Mouth
C. Stewart
Milingimbi
Elcho I.
Wessel Is.
The English Company's Is.
Melville Bay
Bremer Island
YIRRKALLA
Cape Arnhem
Port Bradshaw
Arnhem Bay
Cato R.
Woolen R.
Blyth River
Darwin
East Alligator River
Oenpelli
WESTERN ARNHEM LAND
NORTH-EASTERN ARNHEM LAND
Caledon Bay
Trial Bay
Woodah I.
Blue Mud Bay
Bickerton I.
Groote Eylandt
Wilton River
SOUTH-WESTERN and SOUTHERN ARNHEM LAND
ROSE RIVER
Roper River
GULF OF CARPENTARIA
N
ARNHEM LAND
AREAS RELEVANT TO THE LOVE SONGS
Indicating sources of ideas for the love songs.
A. The "Goulburn Island" Cycle.
B. The "Rose River" Cycle.
C. Djarada Songs.
X Indicates where the songs were sung in 1946-1947.
Scale: 0 50 100km.
GLR.'75

2

THE AREA AND ITS THEMES

At Yirrkalla, on the north-eastern corner of the Arnhem Land Aboriginal Reserve, is a freshwater stream from which the place takes its name—Yirkalang, the Aborigines used to call it. There the Methodist Overseas Mission (now the United Church in North Australia) established a station in 1936. The scene in 1946 was of a mission house on a cliff above the stream, overlooking the sea, with a few Aboriginal huts clustered near the rough semi-open church and the dispensary. On the western side of the stream, other huts spread along the edge of a white curving beach. Mangroves grew thickly farther along the coast; and inland were scrub and swamps, wide grass flats easily inundated during the rainy season, and dense jungles. Like other parts of the Arnhem Land coast, the region was rich in indigenous foods, and fish were plentiful for the greater part of the year.

To this mission settlement, Aborigines came from many miles around. Their territories to the south and south-east were around Blue Mud, Trial and Caledon Bays and Port Bradshaw, with a few from Groote Eylandt, Woodah Island and Rose River. But the land-holdings of most of the people who were at Yirrkalla at that time were in the regions around Cape Arnhem, Bremer Island, Melville Bay and the English Company's Islands; some families were from Arnhem Bay and from the Wessel and Elcho Islands, others from as far west as Milingimbi in the Crocodile Islands and from the adjacent mainland. All of these people had and have, broadly, a common socio-cultural and language background, except those from Groote Eylandt, Woodah Island and Rose River.

In 1946 Yirrkalla was at the end of the run for the two mission boats based at Elcho, and their visits were less regular than they were to the other stations. Occasionally the government patrol vessel and other boats came by, usually anchoring in Melville Bay. Six kilometres from the mission station was a large airstrip called Gove, built by the RAAF, which had a base there during the last world war. Just before we arrived, the last of the air force personnel had departed, leaving behind them derelict huts and canteens and so forth, much of which had been dismantled but much of which was gradually being reclaimed by the natural environment. There was also a small wharf at Melville Bay, but little else. There was no regular air service, though the strip could be used for special flights, including Flying Doctor visits. Yirrkalla was virtually isolated, especially during the wet season. It is approximately 800 kilometres by sea from Darwin, 210 kilometres from the Church Missionary Society settlement on Groote Eylandt, and 140 kilometres from the nearest Methodist mission at Elcho Island. Goulburn Island is approximately 530 kilometres west of Yirrkalla and Rose River 240 kilometres south. The mission stations at Roper River, Oenpelli, Goulburn Islands, Milingimbi, Elcho Island, Yirrkalla and Groote Eylandt were all that fringed the great Arnhem Land Reserve, along with a small settlement at Ambu Kambu on Groote Eylandt subsidized by the Native Affairs Department (as it was then). At that time these were the only European settlements, the only channels through which consistent alien influences entered. Maningrida had not been established, and there were none of the outstations that have proliferated in recent years.

There had, of course, been other influences over the years—Indonesian ('Macassan') and Japanese as well as European (see, for example, R. and C. Berndt 1954). Essentially, however, in 1946, the population of the whole area was still traditionally-oriented. In spite of ten years or so of mission contact, their socio-cultural life remained almost unaltered. No more than about half a dozen men and women spoke English of any sort. That situation was soon to change. During the late 1950s the shadow of externally-based developments fell heavily upon that part of the reserve—developments which were being actively planned, unbeknown to the Aborigines. They were not kept long in ignorance, however.

By 1963 the Commonwealth government of the period had approved extensive leases of reserve land for mining bauxite. From that time onward, events gained momentum. In the same year the famous Aboriginal petition prepared by Yirrkalla people was presented to the Commonwealth House of Representatives. The local Aborigines had not been consulted before the excision of their land—land which they had always viewed as their own. The sequence of events culminated in 1968 in a full-scale legal action. Several Yirrkalla men sued the Nabalco Mining Company, which had begun operations, together with the Commonwealth government. The case was first heard in Darwin early in 1969, but their pleas were not accepted, although certain provisions enabled a further claim to be made in 1970. A long-drawn-out court case with hearings in Canberra resulted, in 1971, in the notorious judgment by Mr Justice Blackburn which, in essence, meant that the Aborigines had no legal rights to their own land. This, however, was mitigated by the setting up of an Aboriginal Land Rights Commission under Mr Justice Woodward which rendered its final report in April 1974. Land Councils are at present being set up in the Northern Territory. (See R. Berndt 1962; 1964; 1969 and 1971: 25–43.)

For the people of the Yirrkalla area, the damage had been done. It was no longer either a quiet backwater (from the viewpoint of Europeans), or an important centre of traditional culture (from the viewpoint of Aborigines). Hemmed in by mining leases, a stone's throw from what had become the third largest town in the Northern Territory, accessible to all sorts of aliens (even though the settlement itself was formally restricted to non-Aboriginal townsfolk), the Yirrkalla people found their mobility hindered, their rights in their own country questioned, and the whole tenor of living radically changed. Nhulunbuy, the township, is now the centre of the whole mining constellation, with increasing facilities for shipping and regular air services, linked directly with the southern cities. These features have impinged on all aspects of Aboriginal life to such an extent that by 1974 not much was left of the traditional society and culture we studied in 1946–47.

Social groups and social relations

North-eastern Arnhem Landers are probably as well-known in anthropological circles as the Aranda of Central Australia. Warner (1958) made the first substantial study of them. There were also others; for example, Webb, a missionary (1933: 406-11), Thomson (1936*b*: 31–4; 1949) and Elkin (e.g. 1933: 412-16; 1950: 1–20; his detailed publications on Arnhem Land religion and music refer to the southern sector of this region, although north-eastern influences are apparent).

Warner saw the whole north-eastern socio-cultural bloc from the vantage point of Milingimbi, while in this particular volume I take the perspective of the Yirrkalla people—although I have also worked at Milingimbi and, particularly, at Elcho Island. Warner applied the collective name 'Murngin' to this bloc, which he regarded as a group of clans forming a tribe. But it is simply one name for a small *dua* moiety clan, Murungun (red ochre), associated with two or more dialectal units (see R. Berndt 1976) and located mainly on Elcho Island. In other publications I used the name Wulamba as a collective label. This was a matter of convenience, in an attempt to find a more appropriate overall name. But it is probably better to call the north-eastern Arnhem Landers Malag, as their neighbours in western Arnhem Land do, because this points to a distinctive feature of their social organization, particularly the division into *mala* (clans), contrasting them with those people living outside this socio-cultural area. The name Miwoidj is also applied to them, but this refers to the different dialects (*mada*, 'tongue') that are linked with the *mala* (clan).

The mada-mala: The whole of the human, non-human and natural environment is divided into two exogamous patrilineal moieties, named *dua* and *jiridja* (yiridja). This categorization is important taxonomically for all aspects of social activity and for all things which come within the observation and experience of the north-eastern Arnhem Landers. Particularly, it has to do with the way *mada* and *mala* are distributed throughout the region. These are also exogamous and patrilineal in descent. Each *mada*, and each *mala*, belongs to one moiety or the other, never to both. Each has at least one name, usually more. And every person belongs to (is a member of) one linked *mada-mala* pair. Traditionally there is no choice in this affiliation: it must be the same as one's father's.

Mada is literally 'tongue'; but in its other and more general sense, in the context of social organization, it refers specifically to a dialect spoken by a particular group of people. In ordinary, non-specific reference *mala* means 'a crowd' or a 'lot' of things; in its specialized sense, in the context of social organization, it refers to a kind of social grouping, which I translate as 'clan'. So, membership in a *mada* and in a *mala*, and in a particular combination of these, is decided before a person's birth, the main clue being the membership ties of his (her) socially-acknowledged father. Members of any one *mada-mala* pair are assumed to speak a particular dialect of a common language and, simultaneously, hold in common particular mythic and ritual knowledge and belief. The *mala*, especially, points to the religious aspect and to territorial possession (see R. Berndt 1976). Any given *mada* may be associated from a membership point of view with several *mala*, and vice versa, but always within its own moiety.

Briefly, that is how it looks from the angle of personal membership. From the angle of the system as such, one of the most salient features is the patterning of *mada-mala* combinations, and the cross-linkages that help to give this its characteristic shape. For example, in one combination the *dua* moiety Djambarbingu *mada* is paired with the Durili *mala*, and in another with the Rawia *mala*; the Durili *mala* may be paired with the Gulamala *mada*, or with the Marangu *mada*. Similarly, the *jiridja* moiety Wonguri *mada* is paired with the Mandjigai *mala*; but the Mandjigai *mala* may also be paired with the Girgir *mada*, or the Gobubingu (Gobabingu) *mada*, or the Mandjeri *mada*, or the Manggalili *mada*. In both the Goulburn Island and Rose River cycles, but not in the Djarada, such clan and dialectal units are referred to quite frequently.

Any one pair, therefore, in the names it bears, provides clues, first to dialectal content, and secondly to its mythic heritage and through that to the territory it owns. Multi-affiliation provides a measure of common interest shared by some in contrast to others. This does not rest only on direct patrilineal ties; and links between *mada* and *mala* of opposite moieties take a variety of forms—or, rather, are based on various criteria and come to the fore in a variety of social circumstances. But part of the groundwork of the system consists of the interrelationship between *mada* and *mala* of the same moiety. For instance, Djambarbingu-Durili is closely aligned with Gulamala-Durili, especially in terms of mythic background, even though they possess different territories: and the Djambarbingu-Durili share with the Djambarbingu-Rawia a similar dialect but a slightly different mythic orientation.

Belonging to a particular *mada-mala* pair is of paramount significance then, since it defines not only a person's social position in the scheme of things but also his (her) particular religious perspective. Songs and rites are identified in those terms. *Mada-mala* territories do not contain only natural resources, which may be shared with various people whose paternal affiliations are different. They also contain secret-sacred, sacred, and other traditional sites and waterholes associated with or created by spirit and mythic beings (who may also be manifested at other localities). Adult male members are responsible for organizing the relevant rites and for performing them with the assistance of members of other *mada-mala* pairs of the opposite moiety. *Mada-mala* pairs are land-owning and land-tending units (see R. Berndt 1964: 264–9), and it is important to keep in mind that their members did not, traditionally, remain habitually within their own territories. For hunting and food-collecting purposes they would move over a fairly wide stretch of country. Traditionally, they probably did not move farther than a maximum radius of about 150 to 250 kilometres.

Mada-mala organization is to some extent complex, partly because of multi-affiliation, but partly because of the symbolic layers of mythic explanation which (as we will see) are reflected in the song cycles. Some name-labels for the various *mada* and *mala* are used in general conversation (a few have already been mentioned). In addition, there are 'inside' or sacred names which have mytho-ritual connotations. These are used on sacred ritual occasions. In one of the simplest, they are included in a special form of invocation known as *bugalili* (*jiridja*) or *bugali* (*dua*).

Traditionally, *mada-mala* affiliation is said to have been important in marriage arrangements: from the standpoint of any one *mada-mala* pair, certain *mada-mala* in the opposite moiety were preferred sources of marriage partners. Today, with enormously increased alien pressures, and with persons of many different units intermingling freely on the Arnhem Land settlements, the range of marriage choice is widened considerably. In the past the fact that marriages were, ideally, to be contracted only between members of specified groups does not seem to have prevented people from having sexual liaisons—provided they belonged to separate moieties. One primary concern among these Arnhem Landers at the time we first lived among them was the issue of a child's actual paternity. This was regarded as of vital importance, although the designation of a social father was significant too. Of course, these two were in many cases one and the same person, but it was recognized that they might not be. The social father was usually the husband of the child's mother at the time of the child's birth, and acknowledgement of the relationship meant protection and the shouldering of kin responsibilities. On the other hand, men claimed that identification of the actual father, the genitor, provided an assurance that the child's ritual life would be taken care of.

Ideally, a child should be able to trace his descent through the *mada-mala* pair of his *actual* father. While believing in spiritual animation of a child's foetus, the north-eastern Arnhem Landers recognized both physiological paternity and maternity. For that reason, pre- and extra-marital intercourse had to be to some extent formalized. Liaisons between members of traditionally intermarrying groups, or between persons who stood in the correct kin categories, even if not actually or potentially classified as husband and wife, did not provoke severe penalties, *provided* the other people immediately concerned (notably, a girl's actual or betrothed husband) raised no serious objections. For example, a Mandjigai-Gobubingu man might have relations with a Djambarbingu woman (of the correct intermarrying dialectal unit) whom he called classificatory spouse. Any child of such a union would automatically adopt the *mada-mala* grouping of his biological and socially recognized father. But supposing a woman became pregnant by a man of an alternative intermarrying group, and shortly afterward married (or was already married) in accordance with conventional *mada-mala* preferences, the child would belong to the *mada-mala* pair of its adoptive father: but it would also be affiliated to that of its actual father, especially if both men concerned belonged to the same *mala*, because that would define the child's ritual status—a consideration particularly important for a boy.

For instance, a Mandjigai-Gurlba man might be living with, or having regular relations with, a Miliwuru-Brangu woman (these being correct intermarrying groups), who was pregnant by him when she was abducted by a Mandjigai-Wonguri man (of an alternative intermarrying group, belonging to the same *mala* as the first man but to a different *mada*). The child would be regarded as a member of both the Gurlba and Wonguri *mada*, of the one *mala*. Or, in such circumstances, he might be designated as belonging to the *mada* of his actual father and not to that of his adoptive father.

If a woman had relations with a man who was not in the correct or alternative intermarrying *mada-mala* pair from her point of view, she had to be especially cautious and secretive about it. If pregnancy resulted, an 'actual' father had to be selected—and for purposes of public identification, that might be the social father. The men with whom I discussed the matter all said that the most likely candidate was the man with whom a woman had regular sexual relations, or the man with whom she had been associating shortly before her pregnancy was acknowledged. There was a general belief in this area that a woman could conceive only by accumulating a quantity of semen through regular coitus with one man. This emphasis on semen is treated indirectly in the Goulburn Island and the Rose River cycles and appears also in the Djarada.

The actual paternity of a child is significant too because its spirit (*djuwei*) is believed to come from the actual father's country, not from the country of its adoptive or social father. From the actual father, the child inherits *mada-mala* membership, together with sections of the mythic cycles and ritual *rangga* emblems. Warner (1958: 69) puts it like this: 'Sometimes a man steals another's wife while she is pregnant. The child when born is considered a member of the new man's clan; when he becomes older he usually returns to his own father's clan and identifies himself with it, although he may have strong attachments to his second father's group. All this indicates that patrilineal inheritance is from the actual father and his group, and not from a different clan, though of the same moiety; it also shows the importance of the actual father in Murngin thought'.

Connections with the actual father are indicated in the *babaru* ('of the father', or having to do with the father; see R. Berndt 1955; 1965: 79; 1975). The term is often used ambiguously, especially these days, but was formerly said to refer to a group smaller than the total span of a *mada-mala* pair, specifically pointing to a person's immediate forbears and descendants in the male line. It was in the rituals of the *babaru* that a man assumed full participation and responsibility towards his *rangga* emblems. It occasionally happened that the spirit-animator of a child (even where the actual father was also the social father) was believed to have come from a *mada* not of its own father's *babaru*. Such an association was called *malngud*. For example, to take another actual case: a particular man's *babaru* was Gumaidj *mada*, Raiung *mala*. However, his Spirit Dreaming (the animator or *djuwei*) made itself known to a classificatory father in the Waramiri *mada*, Bralbral *mala*, also of the *jiridja* moiety. Later, when he was born, his own father and mother were told about this spiritual visitation. When he became an adult and was admitted into the great ritual sequences, he was able to attend not only those of his own *babaru* but also those of his *malngud*. He was said to have 'two arms', and described himself as belonging to both the Waramiri and the Gumaidj *mada*.

The *malngud* relationship could also be derived in another way. A man, while visiting clan territory other than his own, might dream that his unborn child would come from a 'Spirit Landing' (a waterhole or any other sacred site) belonging to that particular local clan (*mala*). When that child was born, he would inherit not only the ritual segments and *rangga* of his own father's *babaru*, but also those associated with the other clan, his *malngud*. He would, however, be a full member only of his father's. It seems that the significance of the *malngud* stems from a desire to establish as far as possible, if any doubt is raised, the identity of a child's genitor. In the absence of definite information concerning a woman's partner at the time of conception, reliance is placed on the spiritual theory.

Every birth must be preceded, or traditionally had to be preceded, by a special dream about it. The *djuwei* appears in a dream to its potential father, father's sister or some other close relative. No matter who has the actual dream, the *djuwei*'s father is always stipulated. The dream is like a charter, establishing a child's credentials by demonstrating a clearcut pre-natal connection between father and child. The significance to the theme of this volume lies in the desirability of a child's legitimacy being established beyond reasonable doubt, and the implications this obviously has for regularizing sexual relations. It explains, to some extent, why the Djarada songs are not particularly popular in this region. It also underlines the point brought up in relation to both the Goulburn Island and Rose River songs: that is, every sexual relationship has, and is *expected* to have, social and ritual ramifications and repercussions.

Subsections and kinship: The subsection system is the name usually applied to a feature of social structure that was, and still is, quite widespread in Aboriginal Australia, especially in the centre and north (see R. and C. Berndt 1964: 50–3). In the Aboriginal societies where this system operated, everybody belonged to one of eight named divisions, or categories. Although patrilineal connections are important in this system, and recognized as being so, in allocating people to one category or another the main emphasis is always on matrilineal descent. The main reason for its popularity is that it provides a useful means of categorizing people: a blueprint which summarizes eight broad behavioural patterns or codes, so that a person in any one category can tell how he is expected to behave towards persons in every other category; and so on. Of course, it is more flexible than this. But because of its advantages, it has spread rapidly into regions where it was not traditionally available. North-eastern Arnhem Land was one of these. It first came to the Milingimbi area prior to Warner's (1958) fieldwork there in 1926–29, but had evidently reached Yirrkalla only a short time before our first period of fieldwork in 1946–47, having been brought up from the south and south-west, through Rose River and Blue Mud Bay. At that time it was not fully integrated into the local organization, and older people rarely referred to subsection labels. Some of them vigorously denied that subsections had any relevance to them. Subsections are not mentioned in the song cycles considered here, and so I shall not discuss them. (See R. Berndt 1971: 196–8; R. Berndt 1970*b*: especially 1056–62.) In adapting the system for local use, north-eastern Arnhem Landers have now correlated it with their patrilineal moiety labels, and this is made easy by the presence of alternating generation levels.

The song cycles also include no references to kin terms. However, the omission in this case does not mean that kinship is not important or has no relevance to the events depicted in the songs. On the contrary, independent evidence outside the actual songs shows clearly that it is, and does. What is implied is a general acceptance of a traditional social system based on specifically named social groups—the *mada-mala*—which are mentioned frequently in two of the cycles, and on kin relationships that are taken for granted as existing between members of such units. Or we could put it another way. The fact that members of specific groups interact within the broader frame of moiety exogamy implicitly suggests that particular kinds of relationships exist between participants. In the Goulburn Island cycle, it is men and women having contrasting moiety affiliation who interact on a sexual basis. Further, it is men and women who stand in particular kinds of relationship who may become sexual partners—and they are usually related to each other as potential or classificatory 'husbands' and 'wives', or in other ways which indicate that sexual access is traditionally permissible. With the Rose River cycle the situation is reversed, so that certain relatives not ordinarily considered to be eligible sexual partners become so only on the occasion of sacred ritual.

In these circumstances, a few words must be said about kinship. This kinship system, which has come to be known as the 'Murngin' system, has been the subject of some controversy. A great deal of that discussion has been irrelevant to the actuality of north-eastern Arnhem Land life. The most reliable statements, which incorporate or draw attention to basic data, are to be found in Warner (1958), Radcliffe-Brown (1951), R. Berndt (1971: 196–245) and C. Berndt (1970*a*: 29–50). So far, no detailed study of the total social structure and organization has been published.

At the core of the formal kinship system is the ideal or preferred marriage type: a man should marry someone he calls mother's brother's daughter (his matri-cross-cousin) and his sister should marry someone she calls father's sister's son (her patri-cross-cousin). The system can therefore be thought of as asymmetrical, being based on matrilateral cross-cousin marriage (patrilineal cross-cousin marriage from a woman's point of view); however, this really depends on whether the total system is seen through the eyes of only one sex, or of both. That aside, the formal pattern revolves round males marrying women of their own or senior alternate generation level, females marrying men of their own or junior alternate generation level. A man expects to marry either an actual mother's brother's daughter (his *galei*) or someone he calls by this term, which is used in a classificatory sense. For any one person there is a reservoir of eligible spouses—a range of women who are potential wives, as well as a range of men who are potential husbands (*duwei*). In these circumstances, there are several varieties of the *galei-duwei* relationship. It includes persons who are related genealogically in the way noted above, and those who use the relevant kin terms but have no recognized genealogical connection. The fundamental relationship serves as a model for all those of a similar order, emphasizing commitment and affection on the part of those involved and not simply a relationship of a sexual nature. Nevertheless, sexual access is one feature of this relationship, which is modified in certain conditions. It is formally curtailed if the girl or woman concerned is betrothed or married to a man's elder brother. In the Goulburn Island cycle, the ordinary *galei-duwei* relationship is implied.

Over and above this 'correct' or preferred form of marriage and/or sexual association, there are others classified as *ngurubilga*, or 'wrong'. In certain circumstances, a man may marry a 'long-way' (that is, distant in a classificatory sense) 'mother' (*ngandi*), *mumalgur* (mother's mother's mother's brother's daughter), *wogu* (sister's daughter and father's father's sister's daughter), *momo* (father's mother) and *gominjar* (daughter's daughter). Such far-distant relatives all belong to the opposite moiety, so that the question of incest (actual or implied) does not arise. Moreover, in the case of such a marriage taking place, the couple will call each other by the conventional terms for husband and wife (that is, *duwei-galei*).

Falling within the *ngurubilga* category are sexual associations which are normally discouraged. These refer mainly to tabued relatives—notably persons who stand to each other as *mugul-rumurung* (wife's mother) and *gurung* (daughter's husband). This is a pivotal relationship, involving constraint and avoidance, as well as indirect obligations, and carries with it a strict rule against sexual access (see R. Berndt 1971: 216–17). In the Rose River cycle, coitus may take place between persons who stand in this relationship—but only in a sacred context. If the same act had occurred outside the ritual ground it would be regarded as incestuous, since a *mugul-rumurung* and her *gurung* are of the same moiety, and it is specifically through her that he receives his actual wife. There are some interesting implications concerning this ritual act which we need not explore here (but see R. Berndt 1951*a*: 47–51). While the traditional picture seems to have been framed in those terms, more recent evidence suggests that it is 'distant brothers (classificatory) who exchange wives' (see Warner 1958: 306–7, and

R. Berndt 1951*a*: 48–9). Warner, incidentally, did not mention coitus with a *mugul-rumurung*.

Mytho-ritual substantiation of marriage and sexual activity

Ideas about the kinds of relationship which should ideally exist between men and women are set out in the great mytho-religious cycles of north-eastern Arnhem Land. Particularly, they are made explicit in the Djanggawul (Djanggau) and Wawalag cycles, which emphasize the complementary role of men and women in all their undertakings—in ordinary everyday living, as in sacred activities. Among these was physical satisfaction through their interaction and, as a corollary to this, their shared responsibility in the production of children. This last point had a much wider connotation, and was projected on to, or served as a model for, the fructification of the whole of nature.

These myth cycles, then, although they treat sexual intercourse, pregnancy and birth in a relatively direct way, do not usually spell out details of marital life (see R. Berndt 1965: 80–1). The reasons are not clear. Myth as a reflection of reality—traditional reality—was accepted by these people. Probably the explanation lies in the consequences or implications of male–female interaction rather than in the static relationship as such. It is held that certain relationships exist between men and women and that those which link a *galei* to a *duwei* are bound to be productive, seen as a natural sequence of events and also as resulting from that particular relationship. Mythic beings, too, are related to one another in particular ways, just as human beings are. The Djanggawul are a case in point (see R. Berndt 1952). They are perhaps the most important mythic characters of this area—important not merely to people of the *dua* moiety, with which the Djanggawul are identified. They are two Sisters who are more or less perpetually pregnant (symbolizing the 'true' function of women), and their Brother, whose desire for coitus expresses his role in this process of fertility. Their sexual act is incestuous, but it is never treated in that way. The Djanggawul are creative, and the availability of alternative sexual avenues is not referred to. They were, according to local belief, the first of all the mythic beings.

The imagery of the Djanggawul is projected on to the pattern of human procreation, seasonal changes, the growth and decay of vegetable and plant matter, and the regeneration of natural species. These aspects were of vital concern to the wellbeing and indeed to the physical survival of the population. Although this theme is most marked in Djanggawul mythology, it is also an underlying emphasis in other religious mythology—in the Wawalag, for instance, and to a lesser extent in the Laindjung and Banaidja. As we shall see, it is evident in the Goulburn Island and Rose River song cycles. While the

Djanggawul as a system of belief has influenced all sectors of local thought, especially about the nature of life, the Wawalag cycle has been just as pervasive in a different way. It is, therefore, difficult to evaluate the relative importance of these two great mytho-ritual constellations: they are in fact complementary. Certainly, the Wawalag has had a considerable bearing on both secular and sacred experience; but the Djanggawul has a far greater repertoire of symbolic allusion and deals more directly with fundamental issues. In contrast, the Wawalag is more obvious in its effects and probably has a socially wider spread of interest—particularly since youths are (were) exposed to it during early initiation procedures, which is not the case with the Djanggawul. It also includes 'outside' camp songs, which is not usually the case with the Djanggawul.

In the more general version (see R. Berndt 1951*a*), an elder and a younger Wawalag sister are the main characters; the elder sister gives birth to a child and her afterbirth blood attracts Yulunggul, a mythic python, who eventually swallows all of them. Other versions state that Yulunggul is attracted, not only by the afterbirth blood, but also by the menstruation of the younger sister. As we shall see in the Goulburn Island songs, the Wawalag are associated with generalized fertility. Blood is a constantly recurring theme in north-eastern Arnhem Land mythological thought; it triggers off a series of events, culminating in environmental transformation. Within that frame, it is implied, women are potential Wawalags; their activities from puberty up to the cessation of menstruation (including pregnancy) are based, so it was said, largely on those of the Two Sisters.

The Wawalag story is, or was, quite well known to both men and women. Menstruation and childbirth were considered to be sacred, although quite natural, phenomena, and in the relevant rituals (carried out separately by men or in conjunction with women) used to be treated in considerable detail. In everyday activity, a woman's sacred quality is enhanced at menstrual periods, and this aspect comes out in the Goulburn Island songs when young girls are described as being *mareiin* (that is, sacred). A further point which draws the Wawalag cycle close to the Djanggawul is emphasis on an incestuous union. Warner (1958: 250) refers to this, as does R. Berndt (1951*a*: 20). In some versions, the name of the mythic character responsible for the elder Wawalag's child is deliberately left vague; in others, it is Woial or Wudal (discussed by C. Berndt 1970*b*: 1311–15). It is this mythic incident which is re-enacted in *kunapipi* ritual and which is described in the Rose River cycle. However, while (as I have said) the sexual acts of the Djanggawul are not explicitly stated to be incestuous, in the case of the Wawalag they are.

Two further issues need to be mentioned at this juncture, since both are relevant to the interpretation of the cycles we shall discuss. First, the love songs are not simply erotic in content, nor are they designed solely to stimulate sexual desire. The images they provoke and the attitudes they reinforce relate intimately to north-eastern Arnhem Land religion. They express the principle that religion permeates all aspects of social living. Secondly, there is the positive value accorded to blood (whether menstrual or afterbirth, or from ritual defloration or penis incision). Not only is blood sacred, symbolizing as it does life-giving attributes; it also has a sexual connotation, which in turn emphasizes the social significance of coitus. Contrary to Warner's view (1958: 394–8), women's physiological functions were not regarded as being 'unclean' or as profaning sacred ritual (see C. Berndt 1965: 238–82). Also, while a menstruating woman was subject to certain tabus and ideally should not have intercourse at that time, there is evidence to suggest that this physical condition was seen as enhancing her sexual attractiveness. Again, this feature appears in the Goulburn Island and Rose River series.

While sacred mythology rarely considers the mundane problems of everyday marital and family life, it does not evade sexual issues which were believed to have a direct bearing on generalized (human and environmental) fertility. The same is the case in the non-sacred mythology, which mainly concerns subsidiary *wongar* (Dreaming) and *mogwoi* spirit beings. For the most part the state of marriage is taken for granted and treated quite casually. Infant betrothal, polygyny and socio-economic aspects of obtaining a spouse and of marriage generally are merely mentioned as matters of fact. This is true too of lovemaking and erotic behaviour, whether pre- or extramarital—they are not treated in any detail. However, one of the most popular of the non-sacred stories relating to this subject deals with a character named Bomaboma or Gwingul. There are many versions of these and Bomaboma has alternative names—for example, Ure or Namaranganin (see Warner 1958: 545–61, 564–5; R. and C. Berndt 1964: 345–6). Usually he is portrayed as a promiscuous person, motivated by abnormal sexual and incestuous desires, always attempting some asocial act or trick to satisfy his inordinate lust. He is described as a 'funny man', and such trickster stories are called *bialmag-dau* (funny story) or *wogal-dau* (play story). It is said that there were once special songs and dances associated with them; but these seem to be largely forgotten. (For an example of an ordinary tale of the *wogal-dau* variety, not relating to Bomaboma, see C. Berndt 1952: 216–39, 275–89.)

In some of these trickster stories, Bomaboma is called Wabalu (black eagle). In one he attempts to seduce a girl named Bunba (bat, or butterfly), who is his classificatory sister's daughter (*wogu*). In another, Wabalu again attempts to seduce Bunba, who is now said to be his actual sister's daughter. (In both cases, the girl is of the opposite moiety to Wabalu.) A further example tells how Bomaboma injures a girl named Yii (a small white duck), whom he calls *gurung* (father's sister's daughter's daughter, or sister's daughter's husband's sister); she is of the same moiety as himself and a tabued 'cousin' as it is sometimes called in English (the reciprocal kin term is *maralgur*, mother's mother's brother's son or wife's mother's brother). Persons standing in this relationship do not normally utter each other's names, and must partially avoid each other. Thus Bomaboma, in seducing his *gurung*, is doing the very thing he is supposed to avoid in everyday behaviour. His exploits were described as showing that a man who flouts convention is abnormal, he is like a trickster whose illdeeds bring social condemnation. One of the worse taunts a woman can offer a man who presses his unwelcome attentions is 'Are you Bomaboma?' In yet another such story, Bomaboma or Namaranganin is associated indirectly with sacred ritual. He removes from a woman's vagina a sacred emblematic stone called *dugaruru* (or *dagururu*) which has prevented her from having coitus and bearing children. This *dugaruru* became a *rangga* (secret-sacred emblem) of the Wonguri *mada*. There are several versions of this mythic incident. For instance, it is said that Wanabwingu (stone spear) actually 'opened' the woman and removed this stone. This is linked with vaginal introcision and defloration, not carried out in north-eastern Arnhem Land, although the latter is referred to in the Rose River cycle. (Incidentally, this myth was also said to substantiate a female operation practised in the past on Groote Eylandt, entailing the removal of one of the *labia majora*.)

The mythic significance of the *dugaruru* is worth noting briefly, since its counterpart is the armband said to be lodged within a female, mentioned in both the Goulburn Island and Rose River cycles. The *dugaruru* is a flat, oval, rather thick stone upon which cycad-palm nuts are pounded after special treatment. (Cycad-palm nut 'bread', wrapped in paperbark, was traditionally an important item in the local diet; its preparation when it was not declared tabu for ritual purposes, especially the crushing of the seeds or 'fruit', was primarily women's work.) In post-*wongar* (Dreaming) times, women were said to have carried such stones in their vaginas, removing them for use in pounding nuts. They were there at birth, and were not dislodged by first menstruation. This did not deter a man from having coitus with a young girl, although his penis could feel the stone within: nor did it prevent semen from entering her uterus. Eventually, however, the stone was dislodged at childbirth; it was carefully kept and later restored to what was regarded as a convenient place for carrying an article so frequently used. But having once been loosened, it could be forced out again at subsequent menstruation. Namaranganin, so it is said, did a service to womankind by removing this stone once and for all, making coitus much easier and decreasing the pains of childbirth. Since his time, no women have been born with such stones.

Other myths describe male spirit beings with elongated penes, the most notable being the Djanggawul Brother himself. But well known, too, is

Bodngu, the Thunder man, who lets down his long penis from his home in the clouds to urinate, making rain; and another is Burulu-burulu, whose long penis prevents him from marrying.

Marital relations

A few points regarding marital relations need mentioning, although they do not obtrude in the songs discussed here. A more detailed discussion will be found in R. Berndt (1965: 77–104). Within the formal system, polygyny is permitted. Basically it rested on the junior levirate where, through the redistribution of widows, a man could inherit the wife or wives of his deceased brother, providing he was the next in age and in genealogical closeness. Also, on his father's death, a man's own classificatory mothers (excluding those related to him in the same way as his actual mother) might pass to him. This custom, I have called the patriate (*ibid.:* 89–90). Apart from these ways of obtaining women (and men), there are others—for example, through normal betrothal or through elopement.

Polygyny, less popular today because of mission influence and socio-economic pressures, seems to have been no more frequent in the immediate past than monogamy. As far as we can judge, having more than one wife at the same time depended primarily on a man's temperament and whether or not he was interested in establishing a wide network of relationships—which had both disadvantages and advantages. It loaded a man with more responsibilities but it also provided him with more persons to support him in trouble. While moral pressures conventionally provided widows with an assurance that they would not be left without a male protector, actual examples demonstrate that personal choice was exercised both on their part and in the case of the man (or men) concerned. In this area, however, during our initial field work, there were a number of polygynous families, the heads of which were influential men. They were mainly entrepreneurial in orientation, in contrast to those men who had only one or two wives and who concentrated on religious matters. While it is difficult to generalize, it was common gossip at that time that men with a large collection of wives (more than a dozen or so: for example, seven men had between them, during their combined lifetimes, ninety-two women) could not keep them in order and that consequently such women had more opportunities to engage in surreptitious love affairs: it was physically impossible, so it was said, for a man to satisfy several wives at the one time and simultaneously keep an eye on all of them.

With some opportunity for choice in this matter, a man might settle down to voluntary monogamy or embark on the task of collecting around himself additional wives. In spite of custom, or his own wishes, there were cases when a man's first wife refused to allow him to take other wives; or he might be so much attached to her that he was reluctant to take other women who would have a formal right to his sexual attentions. In practice, women had a decisive say in such instances. In some cases, indeed, a wife controlled her husband's behaviour to such an extent that he was unable to make an important decision without her approval. Other wives, however, pressed their husbands to take additional women primarily for economic and sexual reasons. Reasons which might influence a man in this respect were not solely economic, but related to having more children, enhancing personal prestige, or even strengthening inter-*mada-mala* integration for ritual purposes. Additional wives did require an outlay and promise of goods, food (especially meat and fish), and the provision of services—and not just to the women who had joined or would eventually join the marital circle. It also concerned particular relatives who had a stake in the girls' future. All this involved increased work-energy on the prospective husband's part. Counterbalancing it, these women represented units which augmented a man's earning capacity. Extra wives meant more food-gathering and, these days, more goods of alien origin. Of great significance, however, was the value placed upon them as producers of children. Sexual associations and the production of children are dominant themes in the love songs discussed here. All marriages, monogamous or polygynous, underline these two features along with economic security, which in traditional terms meant the availability of natural food resources.

Polygynous unions helped to establish and preserve inter-*mada-mala* integration. Gifts were exchanged between a husband and those persons involved, and such affinal ties conventionally minimized conflict. Analysis of large polygynous-family genealogies reveals affinal relatives scattered over a great number of *mada-mala* (of both moieties) within that region. When this is extended to include their children's affinal relatives, it is evident that a complicated network extended through virtually all the *mada-mala* of north-eastern Arnhem Land.

The sexual element did, of course, have a significant bearing on the incidence of polygyny. It should not be regarded, however, as a primary reason and, to repeat, should be seen in conjunction with childbearing. Nevertheless, it was recognized as one way in which a man's sexual associations could be channelled and restricted to the conjugal circle, minimizing the risks and difficulties of extra-marital relations. Conversely, it is not true to say that a man possessing only one or two wives would more readily seek sexual satisfaction outside his marital group. No such limitations were imposed on men—although they were on women, at least formally. Much depended in either case on individual temperament and sexual appetite. Both men and women had available a number of persons who were potentially 'legal' wives or husbands; and, other things being equal, they could go to them without fear of social censure. However, it is true that younger and more sexually active men and women were expected to seek extra-marital partners more readily.

Men with several wives were not necessarily less jealous than men with one or two. Usually they seemed to be on the watch for incidents that might indicate adultery or plans for elopement on the part of their wives. A man might be prepared to allow another man access to a particular wife, in return for certain considerations (economic or ritual); but a wife could not openly and formally take the initiative in such matters without arousing her husband's anger and running the risk of being speared or otherwise punished. This possibility did not seem to deter a wife if she was set on having an extra-marital affair, although such arrangements had to be made under cover. There was what one can call an informal expectation in this respect. It does seem that women who paid lip-service to their husbands' formal authority and did not constantly reject their sexual attentions, might, if they felt so inclined, indulge their sexual whims without undue interference—as long as the rules of the game were adhered to.

At this point, we return to the question of betrothal and to the growth of sexual awareness on the part of the couple involved. After preliminary arrangements had been made by their parents and relatives, children were shown their prospective spouses (R. Berndt 1965: 83–4). This might happen shortly after the boy had been circumcised (at approximately eight years of age) and before a girl's first menstruation. In such a case, while formally they were not expected to play erotically together, informally they might do so, as well as with others who were related to them as classificatory *duwei* and *galei* (spouses). They would do this in relative secrecy, although adults often knew about it and found amusement in their immature experiments. Children of this age and even younger would often play 'husband and wife' together, making their own small camps, with wooden or paperbark dolls to represent children. But as puberty approached, their sexual play would become more meaningful and coitus might take place. It is this situation which is, to some extent, mirrored in the Goulburn Island cycle, although in that case the girls are pubescent and the men are presumably adult, or older than the girls. That, in fact, was the normal traditional picture—young girls and older men.

After her first menstruation (conventionally said to have been brought about through coitus: see the Goulburn Island cycle), a girl was normally ready for marriage and might be led to her husband's camp. Much depended on the respective ages of the pair, and on where they were living. It was not always possible for marriage to take place when *both* reached maturity, because of a disparity in age between them. Also, betrothal arrangements could be long-drawn-out if the parents-in-law lived some distance apart. If a boy happened to be younger than his betrothed, she might have to remain unmarried for several years. However, this was rarely the case. Much more usually, the husband was older than his wife—in some cases, much older. Whether or not he was already married, a man was more often than not obliged to wait some years for a promised wife (or wives) to come of age. During that period, he would keep an eye on her. When she was about six or seven years of age she might come to live in his camp, but not necessarily for sexual relations, since men with child-wives conventionally preferred to wait until they were almost adolescent. In some cases where parents preferred their daughters to remain with them for a little longer before marriage, the girls nevertheless insisted on going to live with their older husbands—mainly for the status of being a married woman and for the possibility of early sexual intercourse. Further, living in the camp of her betrothed husband prevented a girl from being betrothed to another man or from being abducted. By including her in his domestic circle, he was able not only to protect her but also (so men said) to restrain any tendency on her part to 'play around' with other men. Moreover, she represented an extra food-gatherer and helper, and his other wife or wives might welcome her in these terms.

Betrothal arrangements did not always run smoothly. A girl's father might make betrothal commitments with several different families, so that several men might claim her at or just before puberty. Or an irregular union on the part of a girl's parents might mean that she had more than one set of eligible betrothal partners, and this might lead to conflict and feuding which could delay her marriage. Under these circumstances, even if she did go to one man, others might continue to feel they had claims to her and go so far as to press these. Trouble was bound to ensue if a girl's parents behaved avariciously, trying to betroth one daughter to several different men. In such cases, the men to whom the girl had been promised had a right to claim her—especially since they had probably ratified the contract by making presents to her relatives. Or parents anxious to improve their economic position might give their marriageable daughter to a certain man but, if he failed to live up to their expectations, take her away and give her to someone else who would, they hoped, be more generous. But this juggling with a potential husband and wife's affections could be dangerous, particularly if a girl was pregnant or had borne a child from the first man. It was usually attempted only when she was young and had not conceived: but even then it could lead to fighting. Conventional betrothal arrangements might be upset, too, should the girl have a sweetheart to whom she was deeply attached, or if the betrothed husband already had one wife who strongly objected to his taking another. However, consistent jealousy on the part of a first wife was rare.

Apart from so-called 'wrong' marriages (not necessarily with tabued relatives or within the same moiety), which did occasionally take place, there were several acknowledged forms of sexual association which, while not officially desirable, were recognized as ways in which a wife could be obtained. Nevertheless, such cases caused a breach of the peace and could bring about a protracted feud. This often occurred with an elopement (as referred to in the Djarada) or an abduction. In the latter case, a man might steal a woman by force from her legitimate husband, spearing him in the course of fighting and taking over his wife or wives. Such occurrences are said to have been relatively frequent in the past in north-eastern Arnhem Land. In 1946–47 they took place only occasionally.

In this brief survey, the intention has been to cover the broad socio-cultural background of the song cycles, focusing on the subject of marital relations. Much, of course, has been omitted. Against the formalities which accompany betrothal and marriage arrangements, or the process of obtaining a sexual partner, there was sufficient room for manoeuvre on the part of the people concerned. There was also ample opportunity for differences of opinion and for conflict. On the one hand is the problem of betrothal and marriage. Each partner had a range of eligible spouses from which selection had to be made. The final choice was not necessarily, and in fact only rarely, made by the couple concerned. Where the junior levirate and patriate operated, younger men were placed at a disadvantage. Actual or classificatory brothers were rivals for virtually the same women, as a father and son might be on some occasions (see R. Berndt 1971: 202–4, 207–8). On the other hand, direct and oblique threats against marital stability came through pre- and extra-marital liaisons which, in the case of elopement, were more or less sanctioned.

Despite this situation, the Goulburn Island (particularly) and Rose River songs provide an ideal picture in which positive values are enunciated. The fulfilment of sexual relations is childbirth; and childbearing implies marriage, even if this is not spelt out. The symbolism of sex and resultant pregnancy is transformed or projected on to a wider environmental screen of natural fructification, underlined by the significance of human interaction. It is only with the Djarada that this pattern is changed through the infiltration of elements which reflect, in song, a closer approximation of actual male–female sexual associations.

two

THE DIFFERENT FACES OF LOVE

3

THE LOVE SONG CYCLES

These are not isolated songs, casually strung together. Mostly they are arranged in what I am calling cycles. In each, the overall progression is roughly linear. They proceed from a beginning to a recognized conclusion, in a fairly leisurely (*verbally* leisurely) sequence that allows for the development of stylized imagery, in a series of sketches that evoke specific situations. Along with human beings they include mythic personages, so that any one cycle is like an epic itself. Nearly always the characters are placed within a natural environment and their actions are stated, or implied, to have a bearing upon that environment. The view that is presented is one of nature and society as an integrated whole, not fragmented or segmental. The only exception is the Djarada. Nature is seen as a continuously changing and yet non-changing phenomenon, or constellation of phenomena: it is change within a setting of stability and fundamental order. In the two main cycles, referred to here by the names of the places they ostensibly deal with—the Goulburn Island and Rose River cycles—this basically immutable and nostalgic atmosphere is conveyed through such expressions as *niningoi*, *niningu*, *dawul'niningoi*, *baima*, or *buguweima*, translated as 'always there', or the 'people (or creatures)' who are 'always there', who *belong* there, implying a sense of permanency. This is a significant clue to the general appeal of such songs and to their social relevance.

The songs, or verses, in each of these two cycles vary in length and also in number. Each song is focused on a specific subject which is part of an overall theme, and uses a body of symbolism in order to carry that theme through in a consistent way. The symbolism also links any one cycle to others. In their

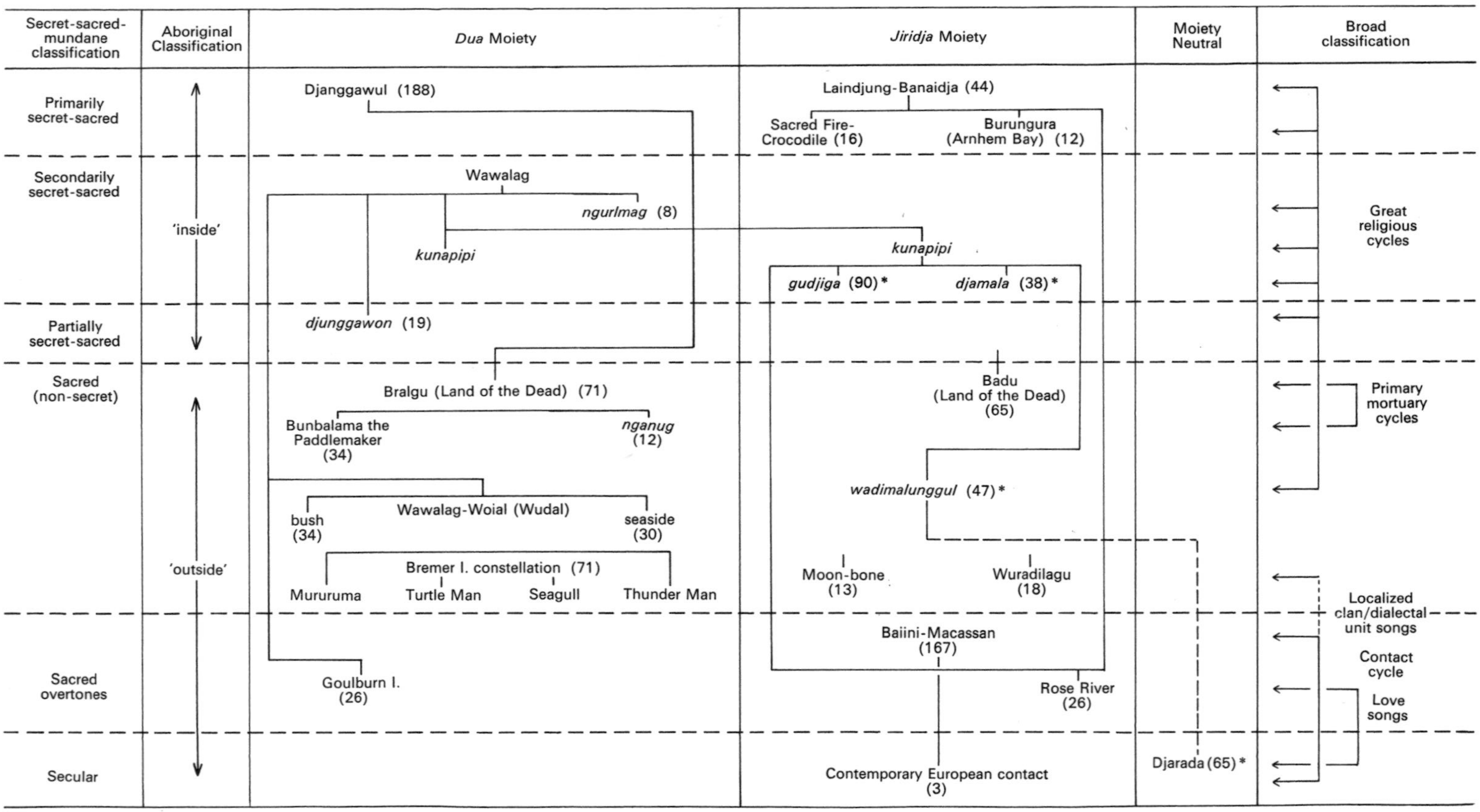

Diagram 1 Interrelationship of Song Cycles recorded at Yirrkalla in 1946–47 x = southern tradition: all others are in the traditional north-eastern Arnhem Land verse style

length, co-ordination and structure, such songs are uniquely of north-eastern Arnhem Land inspiration: there is nothing exactly comparable in any other part of Aboriginal Australia. They illustrate what can be assumed to be the traditional style of this culture, and they are in marked contrast to those associated with the *kunapipi* and Djarada. Before looking at this particular question in more detail, it is useful to consider the three song-sets in relation to others that are, or were, relevant to this region.

To help in doing this, I have compiled a diagram which shows the inter-relationship of various song cycles (Diagram 1). On the left-hand side of that diagram is my own categorization of the secret-sacred-mundane continuum, along with local Aboriginal classification into 'inside' and 'outside' songs. 'Inside' songs are most often associated with secret-sacred ritual, where restrictions are imposed on participation or access as well as on actual performance. The 'outside' cycles are normally subject to no such restrictions, except that limitations are more or less automatically imposed on the basis of their relevance to a particular *mada* and *mala* or a particular moiety. This implies differences in the ways people classify their *own* songs as against those of others, including other close relatives: differences between ownership, and ordinary participation or passive listening.

The cycles I have listed here are only those I collected at Yirrkalla in 1946–47. They do not include songs recorded by my wife, nor others that I have collected in other parts of north-eastern Arnhem Land—at Elcho Island and Milingimbi or, for that matter, on other occasions at Yirrkalla. They consist of representative cycles covering both moieties and the major religious constellations. It is unlikely that each cycle is 'complete'—but each was as complete as it could be at the time it was collected, given the conditions prevailing in the area. All such cycles would be recognized generally by the Yirrkalla people, even though rights to sing these songs are vested in specific persons through their *mada-mala* affiliations. All are acknowledged as part of the overall cultural heritage of these north-eastern Arnhem Landers, in mytho-ritual, symbolic and poetic terms. Against the name of each cycle I have noted the number of songs recorded in 1946–47. It is probable that a wider range of the localized *mada-mala* song sequences could have been obtained at that time, as they have been since then.

In the diagram I have indicated, by linking lines, inter-connectedness of theme and content. For instance, the great Djanggawul epic is closely associated with the cycle that deals with Bralgu, the *dua* moiety Land of the Dead. In some versions the Djanggawul originally came from Bralgu; in others they paused there on their way to the north-eastern Arnhem Land coast. The symbolic allusions in the Djanggawul sequence appear also in the Bralgu one where the well-known Morning Star songs are located. In turn, this cycle is connected with the series focused on Bunbalama the Paddlemaker and the *nganug* spirit of the dead (ghost). Paralleling the Djanggawul epic is the *jiridja* moiety Laindjung-Banaidja (barramundi) sequence, with interconnected themes: for example, the sacred fire, involving a crocodile, which destroyed a ritual ground and the emblems that were stored there; and the Burungura, with its theme of natural renewal. The connection between these and the song cycle about Badu, the *jiridja* moiety Land of the Dead, is not as clear as the Djanggawul-Bralgu association: but there is a connection between the Laindjung-Banaidja and the Rose River cycles.

The Wawalag-Yulunggul epic almost dominates the scene and is very pervasive. It is primarily of the *dua* moiety in content, but one of its three ritual expressions is of the *jiridja* moiety, although it should conventionally be *dua*. This is the *kunapipi* (*gunabibi*), which contains three song cycles, two 'inside' and one 'outside'. The fact that it is now classified as *jiridja* (see R. Berndt 1951*a*: 35) when its other two rituals are *dua* conforms with the western Arnhem Land *kunapipi* (R. and C. Berndt 1970: 122–4, 139). This probably underlines the importance of inter-moiety participation by 'owners' and 'helpers'. However, the more logical reason seems to be that the *kunapipi* is of southern origin. It is obviously so, since in its key-word short verse structure it differs markedly from indigenous north-eastern Arnhem Land songs—for instance, the *djunggawon* and *ngurlmag* ritual song cycles which are also linked directly with Wawalag mythology.

Its attachment to the *jiridja* moiety may also be explained by what appears to have been traditional procedure in the region, where all 'foreign' elements are relegated to that moiety: a case in point is the Baiini-Macassan cycle. However, this is not altogether straightforward because the Djanggawul, like the Laindjung, came from outside the north-eastern Arnhem Land cultural bloc, as did the Wawalag sisters. One contrast in the Bralgu and Badu cycles is that Bralgu is a single island while the image of Badu has two facets: it seems to be a mythic projection into the Torres Strait Islands of an unidentified island complex north of the Wessels, often called Mudilnga. In the world of everyday living, the Goulburn Islands are, or were, culturally and spatially farther away from north-eastern Arnhem Land society than Rose River was. However, non-Aboriginal events, objects and so on are centrally referred to only in *jiridja* moiety songs. The *kunapipi* seems to have inspired the Rose River cycle and, less consistently, the Djarada. The Wawalag, which includes the Yulunggul python(s), is manifested through the 'outside' Bush and Seaside epics which include Woial (or Wudal), a boomerang-legged mythic being whose special concentration is on honey and wild bees. The Goulburn Island cycle is more specifically linked with the primary symbolism of the Wawalag. The Wawalag, incidentally, are associated with the Djanggawul in Milingimbi versions, but not in the Yirrkalla versions.

A further comment should be made about my classifying these cycles as sacred. Over and above the way local Aborigines designate one cycle as 'inside' rather than 'outside', which offers a general clue to what is secret and what is public or publicly-available performance and knowledge, it is obvious that the concept of sacredness has much wider implications. My own criteria rest on two considerations. One is the range of vernacular terms and phrases that can be translated as sacred, set apart, and the like; in discussion and in the ways they were used in and about actual situations, these were not confined to 'secret' phenomena. The second is the extent to which the primary mytho-ritual symbolism infiltrates or is expressed in or through other cycles not specifically designated 'inside' by local Aboriginal opinion. It is content and not so much intention which appears to me to be significant here. At the same time, content and intention are closely correlated, and this is apparent when comparing the main Wawalag cycles with the Goulburn Island one, or the main *kunapipi* cycles with the Rose River one: both make use of primary religious symbolism—part of this, not its full range. Without knowledge of the basic mythology, implications would not be so easily identified in the love songs. Moreover, both draw on the *same* mythology: the Goulburn Island songs directly and selectively from the Wawalag myth; the Rose River songs directly and selectively from the *kunapipi* ritual, obliquely from the Wawalag myth, substituting a *jiridja* moiety mythic Lightning Snake for Yulunggul. It is this element, the *jiridja* mythic aspect, which in turn links the Rose River cycle to the Laindjung-Banaidja cycle.

So far, of the songs I recorded in written form in 1946–47, only the following have been published. The first (1948*a*) was the Moon-bone cycle; the second (1951*a*) *kunapipi* songs; and in 1952 the whole of the Yirrkalla Djanggawul cycle, in general translation (but without the vernacular text, owing to publication restrictions at the time; I hope it will eventually be available). The fourth, in 1966, was the Wuradilagu. A total of 1097 verses was recorded in 1946–47: 240 of these were in the southern short key-pattern style; 394 have already been published. This volume presents a further 117 songs (verses), leaving (except for some isolated single songs) 586 songs unpublished.

The question of style in north-eastern Arnhem Land songs is one of considerable interest. I have suggested elsewhere (R. Berndt 1958: 36–9) that contrasting art styles in western and north-eastern Arnhem Land could be related to the broader topic of socio-cultural patterning in the two regions. The songs are distinguished by their length, by the background material they provide, and the way they spell out details as 'pegs' for symbolic allusions. There is also repetition of words and phrases in a particular way. (In the general translations I have adopted the '. . .' convention to indicate that I have left out immediate repetition.) New ideas or scenes arise out of earlier ones, in order to achieve continuity and to create a kind of verisimilitude:

the use of alternative terms for ordinary words or names is part of this device. Some place names, for instance, have 'inside' or sacred versions. These 'inside' words are not restricted to the secret-sacred sphere but are used in, for example, the love song cycles discussed here. Nevertheless, in whatever context they are used, and even if their meanings are not understood generally, they indicate sacredness or imply some religious relevance. There are also 'singing' words—special terms for an ordinary name or word, used only in songs, and expressing various qualities of the subject that is referred to by the ordinary name. Invocations have this characteristic; so do place names, among others. The songs themselves are so constructed as to achieve maximum impact, through the use of these stylistic devices.

In this work, general renderings are given for all songs in the three cycles. However, in the appendixes interlinear translations are provided, with notes, to enable those who are interested to compare with my own translations. For instance, Song 1, line 1, of the Goulburn Island cycle appears in its Aboriginal rendering as:

> Because/ it/ make/ forked stick/ put/ rafter/ floor post/ make roof like sea-eagle nest

while my rendering is:

> Erecting forked sticks and rafters, posts for the floor, making the roof of the hut like a sea-eagle's nest:

Or again, Song 3, line 8:

> Beat/ fun/ feel/ invocation of western clouds/ invocation of western clouds/ invocation of western clouds/ invocation of western clouds/ invocation of western clouds

My rendering is:

> Sticks clapping, for we feel the urge for enjoyment: invoking the western rain clouds . . .

In order to achieve a general rendering, it was necessary to have an explanation of the context as well as discussion with Aborigines about meaning, over and above the direct form of translation. The songs were recorded in a group situation, in the company of a number of men. The main singer was usually the 'owner', or a man recognized as possessing rights to sing such a cycle. To put it another way, he was usually the person most competent to provide

1 Stilted stringybark wet-season or mosquito huts at Buckingham Bay, north-eastern Arnhem Land (1961).

Erecting forked sticks and rafters, posts for the floor, making the roof of the hut like a sea-eagle's nest:

They are always there, at the billabong of the goose eggs, at the wide expanse of water . . .

(Goulburn Island cycle, Song 1)

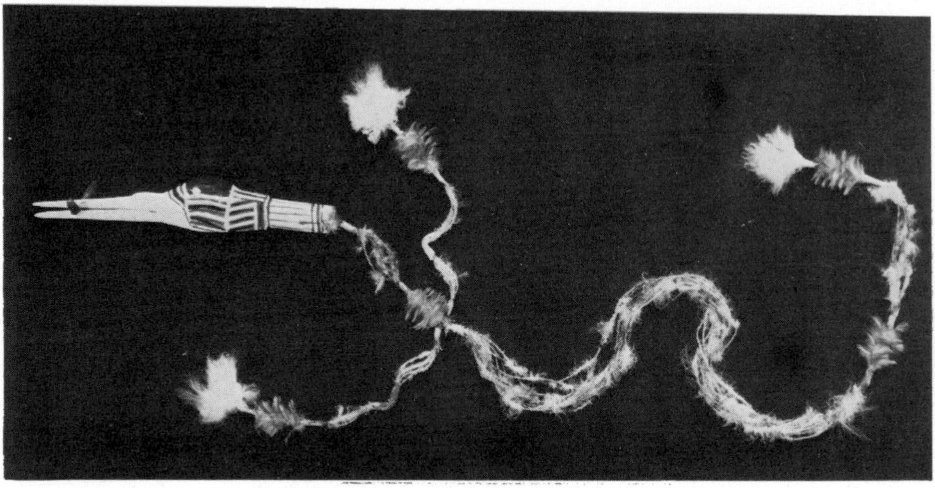

2 Love-magic. A wooden seagull head, the attached feathered string representing its body and wings. In its mouth it holds a beeswax worm.

The gull swoops low, skimming the water, at the wide expanse of billabong . . .
Keen beak probing, it searches for food, skimming the water . . .

(Goulburn Island cycle, Song 26)

3 Painted beeswax figure of Woial, or Wudal (linked with the Wawalag cycle). Surrounding him are two wooden seagull heads, with bodies of feathered string: one holds a moon fish in its beak, the other a mouse.

It is mine! [says the gull] I spear the mouse on its track, holding it in my beak . . .
The squeak of the mouse, and the cry of the gull, echoing up to the sky . . .

(Goulburn Island cycle, Song 27)

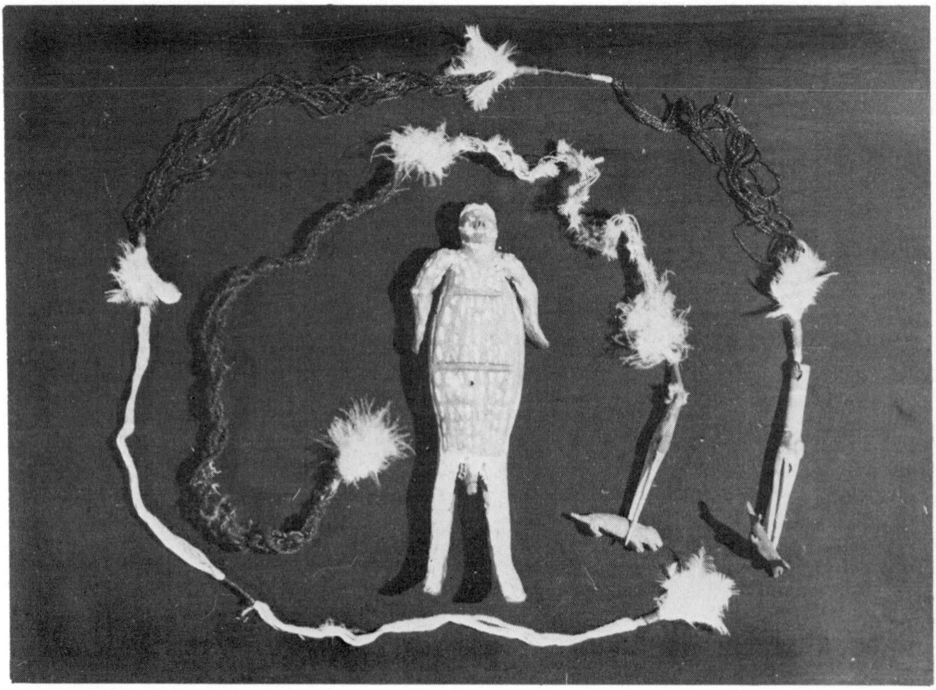

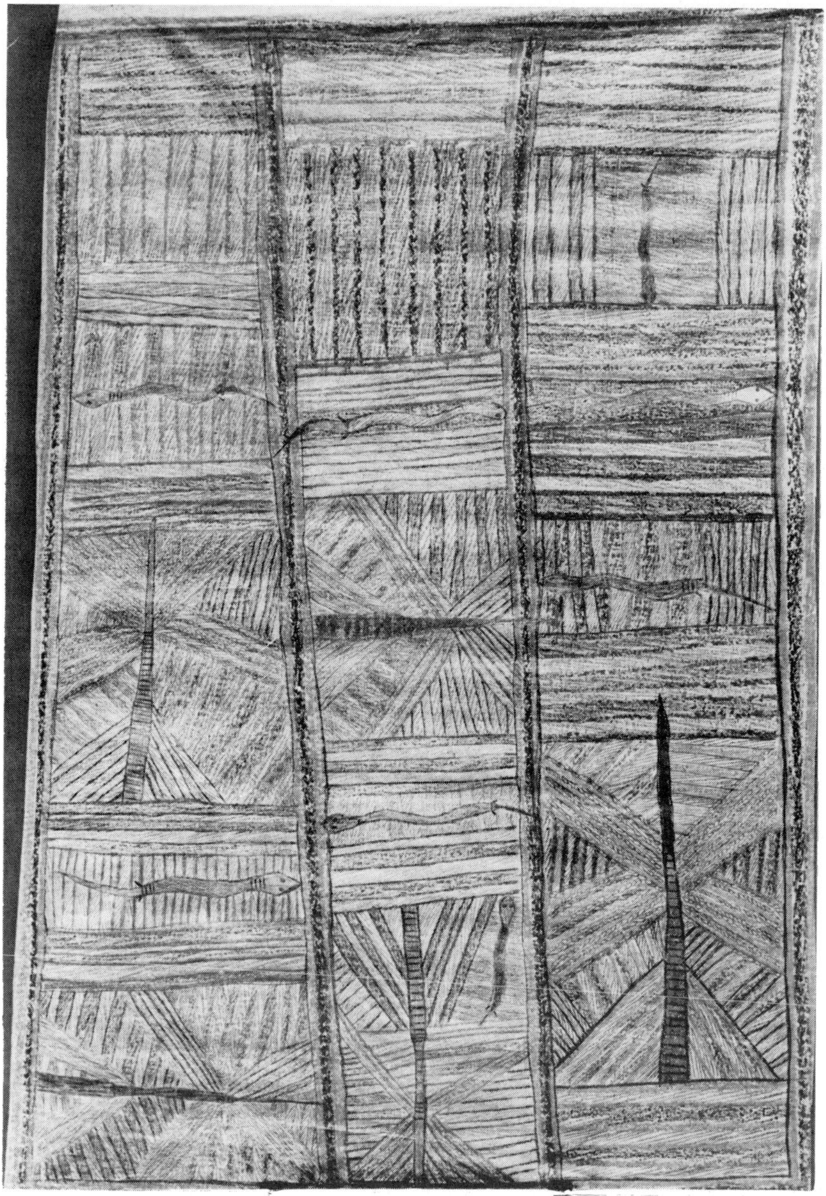

4 Goulburn Island cycle. Drawn by Mawulan and his son Wondjug, 11 April 1947 (No. 16, Series B, Book 29), at Yirrkalla. The drawing (in traditional style and closely resembling a bark painting) is on brown paper 88 cm by 56 cm (2′10½″ x 1′10″), in lumber crayon (red, green, blue and black) and pencil.

It shows a long low hill (*waringga*) on the mainland, near Goulburn Islands. The narrow vertical bands are sandbanks. Between them are cabbage palms (upright trunks with radiating branches), with branches dragging in the waters of the billabong. The left vertical panel includes two *gwoiii* fresh water snakes; the central panel, three *dugmundor* snakes with round 'noses'; the right-hand panel, two *gwoiii*, with one *dugmundor* at the top.

The tongues of the Lightning Snakes flicker and twist, one to the other . . .
They flash among the foliage of the cabbage palms . . .
. . .
It is always there, at the wide expanse of water, at the place of the snake . . .

(Goulburn Island cycle, Song 21)

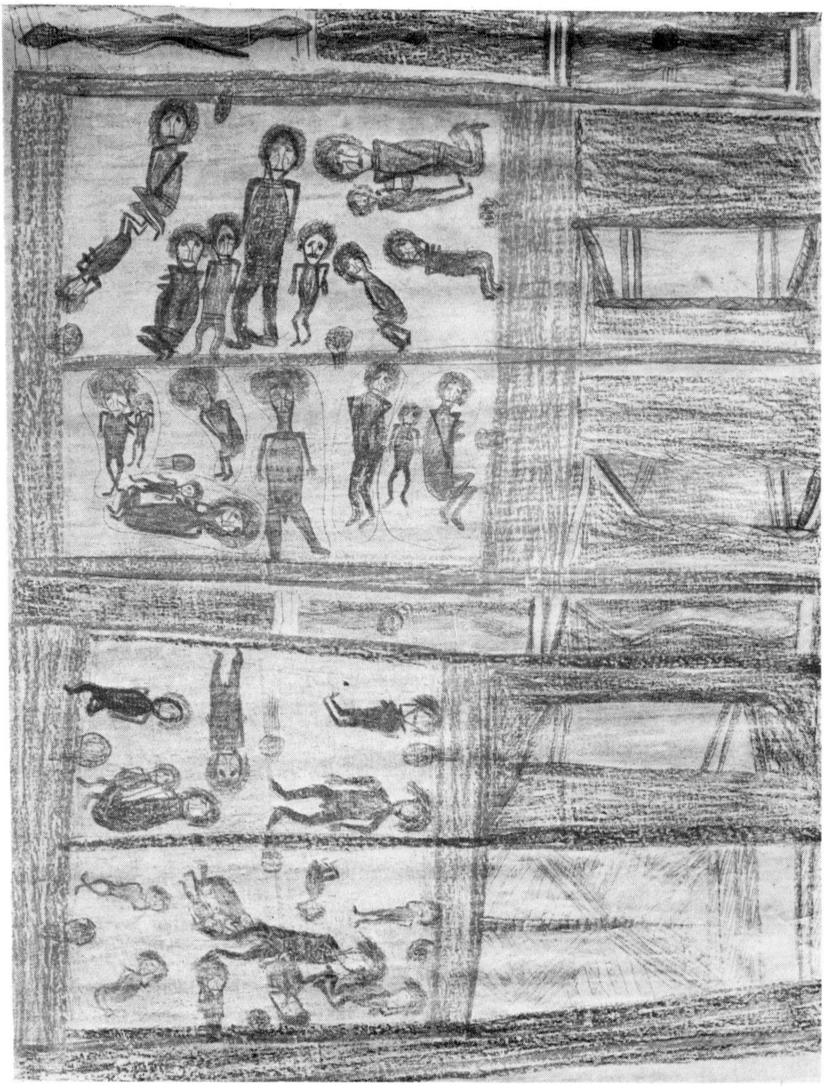

5 Goulburn Island cycle. Drawn by Mawulan on 28 June 1947 (No. A2, Book 41), at Yirrkalla: on brown paper 81 cm by 61 cm (2′8″ x 2′) in lumber crayon (red, green, blue and black) and pencil.

This drawing shows family life in the stilted houses at the billabong: there are four family groups. In the right-hand panel are three bark canoes (sewn with an edging of armband fibre) tied to house posts, and below them a cabbage palm with some of its leaves dragging in the water. The central horizontal band includes a *gwoiii* snake; the small circle is a well (*mangudji*, 'eye') associated with menstrual blood. In the top horizontal band are two *gwoiii* copulating; on the left, a single *gwoiii*, and a *mangudji* well with water bubbling up from the mud.

They talked together, we heard them speaking the western language:

. . .

They are always there, in the huts like sea-eagle nests: young girls leaning against the walls . . .

. . .

Heard them speaking, girls and men of the western tribes . . .

(Goulburn Island cycle, Song 15)

6 Detail of figures in Plate 5, upper panel.
Within the stilted house structures, the top left division shows a man, women and children. In the bottom left division there are a man, a woman with a child and young men and girls. Within each hut, domestic fires are burning.

7 Detail of figures in Plate 5, bottom panel.
Within the stilted house structures, the upper left division shows a woman and four men, one sitting on his folded left leg, and another holding a child. In the lower left division, there are children and young men and girls; a mother holds a child; and a man copulates with a woman from behind as they lie resting. Within each hut, domestic fires are burning.

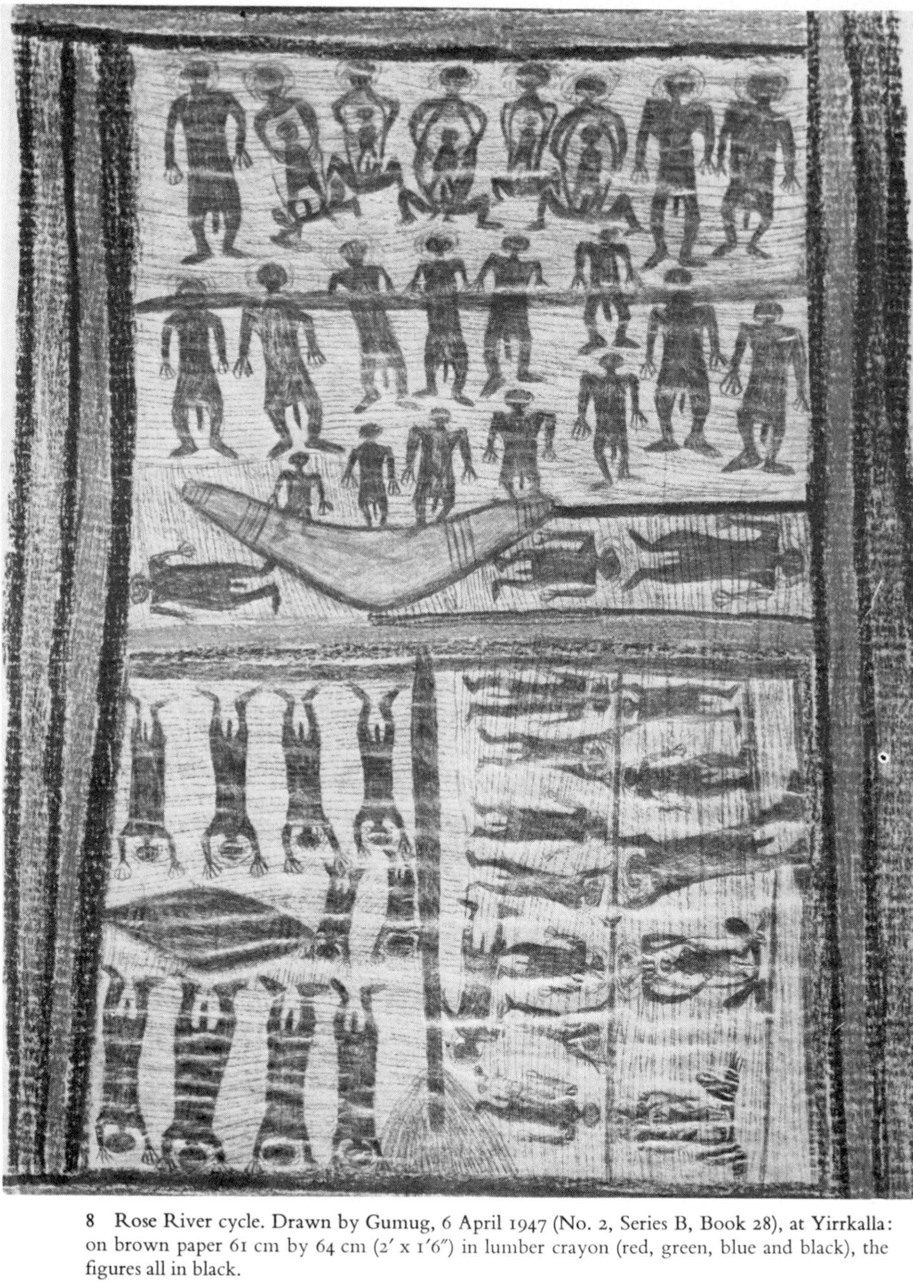

8 Rose River cycle. Drawn by Gumug, 6 April 1947 (No. 2, Series B, Book 28), at Yirrkalla: on brown paper 61 cm by 64 cm (2′ x 1′6″) in lumber crayon (red, green, blue and black), the figures all in black.

In the middle, at bottom of upper panel, is the defloration boomerang. In the upper row, the copulating partners (five pairs) are related to each other as *gurung-mugul*, normally a tabu relationship. Men at each side and below them await their turn. Around the boomerang are the girls' brothers, who do not look at them and do not participate in ritual coitus.

In the lower panel, middle, one man holds a *jelmalandji* emblem. At right, actual or classificatory husbands of the girls in the top panel await their turn with the two girls (and others not shown) similarly engaged in the lower right-hand corner; these are wives of the men in the top pairs. On the left is the *nanggaru*, with ritual possum-dancers ('fathers' of both lots of women).

They are copulating together, to the sound of singing, with penis erect . . .
Copulating together, to the sound of singing.

(Rose River cycle, Song 13)

9 Detail of Plate 8, depicting ritual coitus (upper row of figures). The drawing of the couples having coitus is stylized, giving the impression that the two figures merge. In the conventional position in this context the man bends forward, clasping his partner at the back so that his arms pass under hers while she grasps his back. She lies on the ground with legs apart, her thighs on his hips, and her feet are crossed at his back.

10 Detail of Plate 8, depicting coitus (lower figures), among other aspects of this ritual.

11 Family groups and coitus. Drawn by Wondjug on 6 July 1947 (Book 43) at Yirrkalla: on brown paper 74 cm by 61 cm (2′5″ x 2′) in lumber crayon (red, green, blue and black) and pencil.

12 Detail of Plate 11, upper left-hand side.
Sisters with their children. A man has coitus with one, while lying on his back: her right leg is on his thigh, her left leg across and above his right leg. They sit facing and holding each other, as in a canoe. The position is termed *durbuwaiun* (buttocks of woman down).

13 Detail of Plate 11, bottom left-hand side.
Three sisters with a child, and a woman sleeping with another child. A man lies on his back, with a woman astride him: she sits upright as in a canoe. The position is called *naagu-juwan* (like a canoe).

14 Detail of Plate 11, right-hand bottom section.
A man lies on his back; a woman sits on his penis, bending forward to clasp him at the chest and at the neck. The position is termed *baduwaduman* (legs clasping). They are surrounded by sleeping women and children.

15 Detail of Plate 11, right-hand upper section.
Surrounded by women and children, a woman sits on the penis of a reclining man; her right leg is across his thighs, her left leg bent so that her ankle rests against his ribs. The position is *naagu-juwan*.

16 The social aspect of sexual relations. Drawn by Wondjug on 28 June 1947 (No. A4, Book 41), at Yirrkalla: on brown paper 98 cm by 61 cm (3′2½″ x 2′) in lumber crayon (red, yellow, green, black and blue) and pencil.

This drawing depicts various ways of having coitus in its social setting, in relation to others. The horizontal and vertical bands represent the framework of huts.

17 Detail of Plate 16, bottom panel, left-hand section.
This shows an open-air camp, with domestic fires burning. Here there are women and girls, one with a child. A man and woman lie on their sides, in the position termed *durbujanggian* (from the back): her legs are flexed, one slightly above the other; the man puts one leg under both of hers, with the other leg across her hips.

18 Detail of Plate 16, bottom panel, right-hand section.
This shows another camp scene, with domestic fires. Here are four pairs of sisters, one pair sleeping (bottom right); also children and young girls. The central figure is a man copulating with a woman while her sister (to his left) waits for her turn. The man lies on his right side, while his partner is stretched full length with her right leg towards his legs, her other leg under his arm. This position is termed *bangduman* (open legs).

19 Detail of Plate 16, central panel, bottom left section.
Two girls rest, while a couple copulate. She has mounted him, her right leg resting on his knee, her left across his navel (again, *bangduman*).

20 Detail of Plate 16, central panel, bottom right section.
A woman lies on her back: the man mounts her, with legs flexed backward so that his feet are against her buttocks. He holds her around the shoulders, but she keeps her arms out-stretched. (Also, *bangduman* position). A girl lies resting nearby.

21 Detail of Plate 16, central panel, top left section.
Each partner lies on the side facing the other; the woman's left leg rests on the man's hips, the other on the ground. This position is also called *bangduman*. Their daughter sleeps beside them.

22 Detail of Plate 16, central panel, top right section.
Surrounded by women, a couple lie on their sides, the man entering her from the back (*durbujanggian* position).

23 Detail of Plate 16, top panel.
Top left: a woman, her daughter and a child. Below, a couple copulate: the man lies on his side, the girl on her back—her right leg is beneath his left, her left leg across his navel (*bangduman* position).
Top right: two sisters. Below, a man lies on his left side with a woman stretched out on her back: her right leg is put under and behind his hips, above his buttocks, the other rests across his left leg. The position is *banabum* or *bara-wadilman* (across).

24 Detail of Plate 16, top panel.
Women with daughters and small children. (At the top right-hand side are two sisters.) At bottom right, a man lies on his right side; the woman puts her right leg underneath his left knee, with her buttock on his right thigh (*bangduman* position).

both the original rendering and its explanations. In the case of the Goulburn Island cycle, it was Mawulan, a Riradjingu *mada* man (now dead), helped by his son Wondjug, who gave his rendering in that dialect. With the Rose River cycle, it was Munggeraui (Mungurawi), a Gumaidj *mada* man, who sang in his dialect. The third series, the Djarada, was provided by Gumug, of the Dalwongu *mada*, who used, he said, the original words that he had learned from southern people.

The procedure I adopted in recording a cycle was essentially within a traditional setting. The singer, accompanied by a didjeridu player, sang one song through several times in order to provide me with clues regarding content, along with ideas about its basic structure. I recorded it in a simplified phonetic script, all words being checked against the song. This was followed by the translation of each word, and discussion of the meaning of 'new' words as they were introduced. This was particularly the case with 'inside' and 'singing' names, the location of specific places and their significance, and so on, as well as the overall meaning of the song. I have already mentioned the presence of invocations in these songs. These are 'power names' chanted or called to invoke mythic beings relevant to the cycle, to ensure that their power or force is brought to bear on the songs themselves and on the intentions they express. With these invocations, the meanings often varied according to context.

Several men always joined in these discussions, so that no one song and its meaning or meanings depended on the singer alone, however knowledgeable he was considered to be. Then, and only then, was it possible to go on to the next song, when the process was repeated. Needless to say, this was a time-absorbing and long-drawn-out procedure. At the same time, it was the only way to check and re-check the songs and to obtain a deeper understanding of the theme as a whole. On other occasions there were further opportunities to hear the songs when they were sung in the main camp. The only exception to this was the Djarada. The Goulburn Island and Rose River songs were rarely sung straight through. Usually certain songs were repeated, so that the whole cycle would take several evenings to complete. No tape recorder was available to me in 1946–47. I had to rely on my written interlinear transcriptions.

The division into songs, or verses, conforms with local practice. The breaks in between, during performances, were quite clearly marked. The clapping sticks or boomerangs as well as the singing would stop, the didjeridu would be put down, and people would talk or clear their throats or perhaps move about for a little. After a varying interval, the action would start again with the next song.

One aspect which I considered necessary in presenting these translations was the imposition of a sentence structure. In the singing versions, subject matter was run together, being interspersed with breath-pauses and changes in didjeridu and singing rhythm. It was not always possible for me to indicate these. Instead, I have constructed the sentences on the basis of idea-sequences as they are manifested through the poetic song versions themselves. I have then broken these up accordingly and numbered them in the general rendering so that they can be correlated easily with the original texts. It was not possible at the time these songs were transcribed to correlate them with actual musical recordings. Nevertheless, it would seem that the way the words are arranged and placed and the forms that they take in the singing-versions, which do not always conform with what happens in ordinary conversational speech, are linguistically significant. In other words, the 'sounds' of particular words seem to have a bearing on the way they are sung, and vice versa. Again, the length of these verses exceeds those I have recorded elsewhere in north-eastern Arnhem Land. While I have been unable to tape-record these three cycles elsewhere, I have over the years been able to tape large numbers of songs of the Djanggawul, Laindjung-Banaidja, Wawalag-Yulunggul-Woial, Bralgu, Baiini-Macassan cycles, and so on. None of these has proved to be so extensive, or its verses so long, as any of those cycles noted in Diagram 1. The only explanation I can offer is that in 1946–47 Yirrkalla was the most conservative segment of the north-eastern Arnhem Land cultural bloc and had had, at that time, the least mission influence. Further, there were several outstanding songmen at Yirrkalla. Since then I have not met anyone who can be regarded as their equal. The telescoping of both song-verse and overall cycle length is becoming much more apparent these days, with the intrusion of other interests.

The actual composers of the Goulburn Island and Rose River songs, and the Djarada, are of course unknown. Although the content of each is supposedly projected, spatially, outside the north-eastern Arnhem Land area, to all intents and purposes they are 'traditional' in the sense of being indigenous to the Yirrkalla people. The peripheries of this socio-cultural and language bloc are relatively well-defined, and there is considerable evidence to suggest that in the west, as in the south-east, contact with the outside has been a continuing factor over a very long period of time: it is not just a result of increased mobility through alien contact. However, Yirrkalla people used to say that, for example, the Goulburn Island cycle was comparatively recent when compared with the Wawalag. On the other hand, the Rose River cycle is without question an earlier rendering of *kunapipi* content, 'composed' —one is led to believe—solely for (a) conveying what might be regarded as exotic material and (b) emphasizing its sexual aspects, or rather capitalizing on these for purposes of potential integration at the ritual level. The Djarada, as already mentioned, is of recent introduction. Although it came to Yirrkalla through Rose River, its recognized 'home' (from the point of view of Yirrkalla people) is really the Roper River.

Although I speak of these song cycles as being 'traditional', I do not want to imply that they have remained unaltered over the years. With the Djarada, for instance, the case may well be different. The songs are said to have remained virtually unaltered except for the inclusion of an occasional alien word. And this is more likely because of its special rhythm and its paucity of words: there is less opportunity for an individual songman to manoeuvre and to introduce his own version. The opposite is the case with 'traditional' north-eastern Arnhem Land song cycles. From my experience in recording different versions of any one cycle, it is apparent that changes in word structure with the insertion or deletion of material are quite common. It would not be going too far to say that all north-eastern Arnhem Land songs are constructed in such a way as to permit and indeed encourage personal innovation—but only within certain limits, since the 'flavour' of the theme and the relevant mythic-symbolic frame must remain more or less intact. The popularity of such songs—and I believe it is possible to speak, in this social context, of sacred songs as well—depends on the hearers' familiarity with the 'story' value of each. I mean by this that the ideas transmitted through a particular song need to be identified by those who listen to it, and fitted into a culturally congenial setting which they know, or assume they know, at least in part. And for this to take place effectively, change must be provided for as well as continuity.

Many songs, of any one cycle, are associated with some form of dance action, while some are related to specific objects (or emblems) which in turn explain or illustrate the song narrative. This is true for virtually all of those of a secret-sacred nature: some material representations are used in ceremony or ritual, although there is great variety in these. Both the Goulburn Island and Rose River songs were accompanied by dancing, openly, in the main camp. Led by a songman, clapping his sticks, with another blowing a didjeridu, a small group of men would move across the ground. Women would sometimes get up to dance, at one side. Dancing men would dramatize actions from the songs, to the evident amusement and pleasure of the circle or semicircle of onlookers. In the Rose River dancing, painted yam (digging) sticks or a replica of the defloration boomerang might be used, or men might dance with stone-bladed spears. In the Goulburn Island dancing, women might hold lengths of jungle twine, making string figures (appropriate to the songs) as they danced—just as the Goulburn Island girls did in the songs. And men would wear the 'ball' bag. Both these ceremonies were performed on several occasions during 1946–47 but only at night when I was unable to photograph them.

As far as the Djarada is concerned, I did not see an actual performance of this (these) at Yirrkalla, outside the place in which I recorded the songs. However, I have seen Djarada dancing in other areas. In this case, I am told that a group of men comes together to meet others in or away from the main camp. They sit round a fire, led by a Djarada songman who claps two boomerangs together to mark the beat: he would not normally be accompanied with a didjeridu. This form of singing resembles the *mandiela* mentioned in the Rose River cycle as being associated with the *kunapipi*. This is the *marndiella* of Warner (1958: 329–34), also called the *mandiwala* or *mandiwa*, which is circumcisional, and has come into Arnhem Land from the south: only the rhythm is similar to the Djarada. It is not, and was not traditionally, performed at Yirrkalla.

4

THE GOULBURN ISLAND CYCLE*

Song 1

Erecting forked sticks and rafters, posts for the floor, making the roof of the hut like a sea-eagle's nest:
They are always there, at the billabong of the goose eggs, at the wide expanse of water.
As they build, they think of the monsoon rains—rain and wind from the west, clouds spreading over the billabong . . .
They cover the sides of the hut, placing rails on the forked sticks.
We saw the heaving chests of the builders, calling invocations for the clouds rising in the west . . .
With heaving chests, calling the invocations . . .
Making the door of the hut, preparing it within . . .
They think of the coming rain, and the west wind . . . wind bringing the rain, spreading over this country.
Carefully, therefore, prepare the hut, with its roof, and its posts . . .
We saw the heaving chests of men of the Maiar'maiar clan, clans from the Woolen River . . .
They are always there at that place, that billabong edged with bamboo,
There by the wide expanse of water . . . carefully laying the rails.

The reference here is to the building of stilted houses in shallow billabongs and swamps, just before the wet monsoonal season. These are sometimes described as 'eagle-hawk [sea-eagle] nests floating on the surface of the water',

* This song cycle is associated with five *dua* moiety *mada*: Galbu, Djambarbingu, Djarwag, Maragulu and Riradjingu. The songs presented and discussed here are in Riradjingu.

and as being similar in construction to those made by 'Macassan' (or Indonesian) visitors to the north Australian coast. They are made before the rains begin and before the billabongs and swamps fill up. Holes are dug and posts raised, then rails are lashed to these to make a platform; living trees may be utilized in the same way. Sheets of stringybark form the floor of the hut, and upon them slabs of stone serve as a base for open fires. More posts and rails enclose the hut, with walls of brush, boughs and stringybark. The roof, of the same materials, is reinforced with specially treated 'ant-bed' (termite) mound spread over the roof and along the joins of the bark; on drying, this becomes hard and completely weatherproof.

In these huts live the so-called Goulburn Island people. To the north-eastern Arnhem Landers, 'Goulburn Island' was a broad term, covering the western language and cultural groups from Cape Stewart (just west of Milingimbi) to the Liverpool River and beyond, along the coastal swamps and plains. Occasionally included in this category were people from the mouth of the Woolen River, near the sacred site of Muruwul or Miraraminar, although these were really affiliated with the north-eastern groups and shared the same complex of language and culture. This site is particularly important, for there the two Wawalag sisters and their child were swallowed (and later revivified) by Yulunggul the Rock Python.

The large billabong specifically mentioned in this song has a number of other names. It was said to be situated in the bush on the mainland nearly opposite the Goulburn Islands, and noted for its abundance of goose eggs. Clouds come from the west, across the sea; they reach the mainland, spreading over the billabong where the houses are being built.

Stilted houses of the kind described here were fairly common along the north coast of Arnhem Land, especially about the Cato River, and in the low-lying Arafura country between and around the Blyth and Woolen Rivers (see Thomson 1939*a*: 8–9; 1939*b*: 121–6).

Song 2

There is the framework, the rafters and door of the hut.
We saw the heaving chests of Goulburn Island men and Burara men, as they made it,
Preparing the stilted hut, like a sea-eagle's nest in a tree.
We saw their heaving chests as they invoked the Yulunggul Snakes, their coiling, and crawling . . .
Invoking the coiling Snakes and their entrails . . . and building stilted huts all over the billabong,
At the place of the Rising Western Clouds . . . at the place of Standing Clouds: spreading all over the sky at the place of Coloured Reflections.

Huts all around, at the Sea-Eagle place, at Milingimbi Point, and over towards the Sandspit near Goulburn Islands . . .
My hut is nearing completion,
With forked sticks and roof like a sea-eagle's nest, with rails and door . . .
They are always there at that billabong, with the wide expanse of water . . .
It is almost ready. We make these huts all around, and north-east of Milingimbi.
Clouds banking along the horizon, passing north-eastward over the Crocodile Islands . . .
Thus they were making the huts. We saw their heaving chests and the rising clouds from the west, small clouds rising and spreading,
Saw their heaving chests, as black clouds came bringing a sheet of rain,
Sound of thunder, roaring of wind and rain . . .
I am making it for myself, with forked sticks and with rails . . .
Thunder leaving its noise for me, sound rolling along the bottom of the clouds,
Echoing on the billabong, across the wide expanse of water . . .
I am making my sea-eagle nest to float in the rising waters of the billabong.
I am making it, and later the lightning will play on its roof and on me inside,
For its tongue flickers along the horizon, and thunder rolls along the bottom of the clouds,
Clouds rising from the place of the Wawalag sisters, from where they were swallowed . . .
I am preparing for you, clouds massing along the horizon: using my posts, my forked sticks and my rails . . .
You, clouds, are banking along for me . . .
The wind brings clouds, of the *jiridja* moiety—clouds like penes.
A cool wind blows, easing the heat and bringing the small clouds . . .
Thunder rolling along the bottom of the clouds, as the lightning flashes . . .
I am making it ready for you, fixing the door and the inside:
Because I invoke the clouds rising from Goulburn Islands . . .
I am making it for myself, to float across the billabong,
Across the wide expanse of water, to float like a sea-eagle's nest . . .
We saw their heaving chests, as they invoked the clouds rising from Goulburn Islands . . .

These introductory songs create an effective setting for those which follow. As in other song cycles of north-eastern Arnhem Land, the principal theme is introduced and surrounded by much relevant and irrelevant material: for that, to local Aborigines, is the conventional and also the most desirable approach. Indeed, the true beauty of these songs frequently springs from the colourful atmosphere thus produced, the emotional appeal to listeners, and the intricate patterning of the theme with its subsidiary threads.

The 'floating huts' in this second song are like those mentioned in Song 1, but without stilts to raise them above the ground or water. Each is built on a raft; the framework is made of lashed poles, and the floor of posts and stringybark with a covering of treated ant-bed mound, thickly smeared to form a hard base. Both men and women help in such work. When the rains come and the low-lying country becomes inundated, the hut on its raft base either floats around or can be made fast by tying it to a tree.

Such huts were sometimes called 'watch houses', and two reasons were given for making them. The first was that people 'are too frightened of someone; that's why they make them in the water'. By being cut off from the land, the raft-dwellers were more or less protected and could be reached only by canoe or by swimming. To guard against possible attack, therefore, the huts were so placed that the people inside could have an uninterrupted view in all directions—hence the name 'watch house'. Secondly, the huts, with canoes tethered to them, were strategically placed for collecting food. Fish, wild fowl and eggs are plentiful and can be obtained from one's doorway with little effort. With leisure to spare, then, this is a time of song, relaxation and love-making.

In this second song, too, stress is placed on clouds that are passing from west to east, bringing the first rains that herald the coming wet season. Seeing them, people begin to construct their stilted and floating huts in readiness for the heavy falls that are to come.

Song 3

Get the clapping sticks and the didjeridu, for we feel the urge for enjoyment.
Hear the rhythmic beat, and the singing of Goulburn Island people, clans from the Woolen River . . .
Chests turned towards the cold west wind, and the sound of the didjeridu . . .
Rhythmically beating, within the huts like sea-eagle nests . . .
Sound from within the huts, spreading across the country . . .
Clapping-sticks at the Sandspit near Goulburn Islands, at the place of Western Clouds, and of Standing Clouds, and at Milingimbi Creek . . .
Opposite Milingimbi, at the place of Coloured Reflections . . . sticks clapping within the huts,
Sticks clapping, for we feel the urge for enjoyment: invoking the western rain clouds . . .
Sound rising like clouds, wafted across the waters to Milingimbi:

Like clouds banking up, the sound hovers over the Island of Clouds . . .
Cold wind from the west, striking their chests . . .
It is ours! With this singing the wind begins to blow, swaying the branches,
Cold stranger wind from somewhere, from Goulburn Islands!

The huts are completed, and singing begins. Men beat their sticks and blow the didjeridu, while women dance—for women's dancing does not involve the same vigorous movements as men's and should not damage the huts. Before the rains come, they dance on the cleared ground before the huts, but as the country becomes flooded they do this on the raised platforms or on attached rafts. While the dancing women are said to stimulate the men sexually, the main purpose of the singing is to bring the wind, the clouds and the rain.

Song 4

Take clay and coloured ochres, and put them on!
They paint chests and breasts with clay, in water-designs,
Hang round their necks the padded fighting-bags.
They paint themselves, those Goulburn Island people, and clans from the Woolen River . . .
They are always there, at the wide expanse of water . . .
They take more clay, for painting the fighting-sticks . . .
Paint on their chests designs of water-snakes . . .
And paint the boomerangs with coloured ochres . . .
Painting the small boomerangs . . .
Calling the invocations . . . all over the country, and at the place of the Wawalag sisters . . .
Painting themselves at Milingimbi Point, at the place of Standing Clouds.
At the place of the Western Clouds, at the place of Coloured Reflections . . .

The people decorate themselves for singing and dancing, painting on their chests designs of freshwater snakes. These creatures are found about the huts and are depicted as phallic symbols. The water designs (mentioned in line 2) symbolize the water that will fill the swamps and billabongs.

The bags noted in line 3 resemble small padded balls. Such a bag is woven from indigenous fibre (or, these days, from European wool), stuffed with wild cotton or native string and sewn up. It is worn as a necklet, hung by a length of fibre so that the ball itself rests on the chest. It was commonly used in dancing or held between the teeth during actual or ritualized fighting or peace-making ceremonies. The rationale put forward for biting on the ball was that it helped a man to concentrate on what he was doing; in fighting, for instance, he was able to contain as well as intensify his anger. In north-eastern Arnhem Land an ordinary stick, a sacred dilly bag, a spearthrower or the end of a man's own beard used to be held between the teeth for the same purpose. In the old days, most men in western Arnhem Land are said to have worn these ball bags. (The general term for all varieties is *badi*: 'bag', 'dilly bag' or 'basket'.)

Song 5

They grasp the padded fighting-bags, holding them in their mouths . . .
Come, let us dance, stepping along, biting the padded bags . . . !
Swaying branches from side to side:
They are always there, at those places near Goulburn Islands.
We dance, swaying branches from side to side, like the cold west wind . . .
We saw their chests, people short like new paperbark saplings:
Goulburn Island people, clans from the Woolen River, men with uncircumcised penes,
Clans of the long foreskins.
Thus they move their chests, swaying branches from side to side, around Milingimbi . . .
Thus the padded ball sways from side to side on their chests at Milingimbi Point, at the place of Standing Clouds, the place of the Western Clouds . . .
They dance, invoking the rising western clouds . . .
They dance, calling the invocations . . .
We saw their chests heave, as they called the invocations . . .
Because they are always there, at the stilted huts like sea-eagles' nests . . .

For the first time, the singers draw the listeners' direct attention to the long penes of the western Arnhem Landers, and the contrast with their own stimulates derision which has a certain erotic appeal. People from the east and south-east, however, coming in to the Goulburn Islands and Oenpelli, have now introduced circumcision in certain parts of that region. To the north-eastern Arnhem Landers, who customarily circumcise, absence of this trait was amusing: women, especially, liked to speculate on the differences it might involve. The term 'long penis' reflects the belief that an uncircumcised penis is longer than one from which the foreskin has been removed and the foreskin hangs loosely down over the apex.

The clan name, 'new paperbark saplings' (line 6), refers to the characteristically short stature of some groups in the Liverpool River region, on the mainland between Cape Stewart and Sandy Creek, opposite the Goulburn Islands.

Song 6

They have thrown aside their branches: the wind flings them into the cabbage palm foliage . . .
Leave the branches for me! [the wind says] The wind blows them along, calling the water,
At that billabong, at the wide expanse of water among the bamboos . . .
It blows them along, branches twisting and turning . . .
Branches tossed aside, and flung back.
The voice of the wind calls the open water, in Wawalag country.
Rain streams down their chests, and the wind flings it away:
Cold west wind, flinging away the branches.
It is our wind that we feel, the cold west wind! [the people say]
And another wind is ours, the north-west *jiridja* wind swaying the branches!
We feel the north-west winds, their coolness retracting our penes,
Flinging our branches away, blowing them down.
Blowing the branches, calling the names of the country . . .
Calling the names: the place of the Wawalag sisters, the place of the Python . . .

The song tells of wind and rain, gradually filling the billabong so that the 'watch huts' float and the stilted huts are surrounded by water. It suggests that people shelter inside, while the strong wind breaks down branches and tosses them across the billabong. The rains for which the people have prepared and sung have arrived.

In line 2 the wind is personalized, and speaks. So do the people themselves, claiming the wind as their own, remarking on its coolness. Branches are blown by the wind into the cabbage palm(s)—that is, in line 1; but later, after the rains, the rising water washes them away. There is a reference to 'something' (unidentified here, but later said to be menstrual blood or seminal fluid) which is hidden in the thick foliage of the palm and washed away by the flood waters. In line 6, the Wawalag country is said to be associated with the Wawalag sisters, for they were born there (at Djaningerngu, location unidentified), and made it their home before journeying to Muruwul and Miraraminar where they were eventually swallowed by Yulunggul (line 14). The birthplace of the Wawalag, however, is not noted in most versions of Wawalag mythology (see R. Berndt 1951*a*: Ch. III).

Song 7

Hang up the basket, the padded fighting-bag: put it on to the post,
On the forked stick of the hut, or on to the rail:
Men's bodies are tired from dancing, and swinging the branches. So put away the bag . . .

Take the possum fur headband, and hang it at the door of the hut . . .
That headband which has been worn; hang it up on the forked stick, or on the rafter rails.
We saw them wearing it: short people like paperbark saplings, from Goulburn Islands,
Men with uncircumcised penes.
We saw them, putting the padded fighting-bag on their chests,
The ball bag, hung at the door of the hut . . .
They hung it up on the forked sticks . . .
We saw their chests, heard them invoking the rising western clouds . . .
They are always there, at the wide expanse of water . . .

The ball bags are put away, along with the possum fur headbands, and people sit inside their huts listening to the driving storm from the west.

Song 8

Preparing strips of pandanus leaf, making the ball bags . . .
They are always there, at the wide expanse of water, those huts like sea-eagles' nests.
We saw the breasts of the young girls, girls of the Burara tribe and of clans from the Woolen River.
Girls from Goulburn Islands, from many clans: moving their hands, as they split the pandanus leaves to weave the baskets . . .
They are always there, at the place of Standing Clouds, near Milingimbi, where clouds spread all over the country . . .
We saw their moving breasts as they softened the strips of pandanus, weaving the padded fighting-bags . . .
Within those huts, at the wide expanse of water . . .
They are always there, at the billabong edged with bamboo . . .
Making them as they sit on the floor at the open doorwaas . . .
They are always there at the wide expanse of water, at the place of Standing Clouds, the place of the Sea-Eagle,
The place of Coloured Reflections, where the western clouds arise, towards Milingimbi.

Girls of various western Arnhem Land groups now make their appearance, and attention is drawn to the attractiveness of their breasts as they move while making baskets. They prepare pandanus leaves, splitting and softening them by heating over a fire, and then twining the strips into bags.

The first storms have passed, except for an occasional downpour, and the billabong has filled with water. The people move about outside. Women prepare the pandanus and men fish or go hunting.

Song 9

Girls take up their strings, to make 'cat's-cradles', girls from the Burara and Gunwinggu tribes . . .
They take their breast girdles, twisting the string. We saw their breasts, young girls of Goulburn Islands . . .
They are always there in that camp, at the wide expanse of water . . .
Making string figures, leaning back on the forked rails of the hut, the sea-eagle nest . . .
We saw their breasts, and their hands moving—Goulburn Island girls, clans from the Woolen River . . .
Their breasts in the cold west wind, as they flutter their eyes at the men:
Swaying their buttocks, speaking in Goulburn Island language.
This is our string, from our breast girdles [say the girls]: always there inside the huts, at the wide expanse of water.
They saw men of the Goulburn Island people . . . men with uncircumcised penes . . .
They flutter their eyelids, young girls of the Burara and Gunwinggu tribes.
They are always there at the billabong edged with bamboo, the wide expanse of water.
We saw their breasts, young girls of the western clans.
We twist the string in our hands, for we feel like playing [say the girls]: twisting our breast girdles, at the wide expanse of water.
They sway their buttocks, young Gunwinggu girls, girls from the western clans . . .
Thus they twist their string, watching the Goulburn Island men with their long penes . . .
We flutter our eyes at them as we twist the strings [say the girls].
Sitting among the cabbage palm foliage,
Leaning back on the forked rails of the hut, the sea-eagle nest . . .
They are always there at the place of Standing Clouds: clouds spreading all over the country, from near Milingimbi . . .
We saw their breasts . . . young girls from Goulburn Islands, girls from the western clans . . .
We saw their breasts . . . always there, at the billabong edged with bamboo . . .
Saw their breasts, as they moved the string in their fingers . . .
Twisting the string, leaning back on the forked rails of the hut . . .

The girls have turned aside from their basket-weaving to concentrate on attracting sweethearts. They play string games (as girls and young women often used to do before the birth of their first child), fluttering their eyes at men. The movement involved in making string figures causes their breasts to undulate seductively: this and the figure designs attract the interest of passing men. It was said that a man knows by the way a girl looks at him that she is willing to meet him later among the cabbage palms. (Women also stimulate men sexually by undulating their buttocks: this feature is mentioned as well in the Rose River songs.)

Song 10

The bird saw the young Burara girls, twisting their strings, making string figures.
Watching with head poised, the bird cries . . .
The pigeon saw the young Gunwinggu girls, twisting their strings . . .
With head poised, saw their hands moving, saw the blood as they moved their heels.
The pigeon watches them, flapping its wings and calling out as it sees the blood.
The cry goes out to Blue Mud Bay, among the new paperbark shoots . . .
The cry of the bird goes over to Goulburn Islands . . .
Perched on the topmost leaves of the cabbage palm . . .
Clasping the cabbage palm with its claws . . .
Crying out as it sees the blood.
It saw them twisting their strings, moving the string-patterns—young girls of the Gunwinggu tribe . . .

The girls who are making string figures have only just reached puberty and are menstruating. At this time, eastern Arnhem Landers used to say, the sexual urge is particularly intense, and it is just before and immediately after menstruation that they seek lovers.

The pigeon referred to in this song watches the girls as they sit modestly with one heel pressed against the vulva: it waits to see their menstrual blood. When they move their feet, the blood drips through the planks of the hut's floor into the water below and is washed away. Seeing this, the bird cries out, telling the whole camp that a particular girl has reached puberty: its cries drift across the countryside (see Appendix 1, page 174). Although this bird is said to be specially interested in the girls, it also watches older menstruating women. The bird perches on a cabbage palm 'because no one touches or has [that is, obtains food from] it'; it is a tabued tree because of its association, in this case, with menstruation. However, in Song 9, for instance, it is said that girls meet their lovers among the palm foliage: they hide there for the very reason that they *are* tabu and need not fear discovery during their lovemaking. Further, menstrual blood is believed to have an erotic appeal for men, and sacred Wawalag mythology deals with that theme. On the other hand, this palm tree is not normally tabu, except in certain places or for ritual purposes.

Song 11

They saw the young girls twisting their strings, Goulburn Island men and men from the Woolen River:
Young girls of the western clans, twisting their breast girdles among the cabbage palm foliage . . .
Stealthily creeping, the men grasp the cabbage tree leaves to search for their sweethearts.
Stealthily moving, they bend down to hide with their lovers among the foliage . . .
With penis erect, those Goulburn Island men, from the young girls' swaying buttocks . . .
They are always there, at the wide expanse of water . . .
Always there, at the billabong edged with bamboo.
Feeling the urge for play, as they saw the young girls of the western clans,
Saw the young girls hiding themselves, twisting the strings . . .
Girls twisting their breast girdles, making string figures: and men with erect penes,
Goulburn Island men, as the young girls sway their buttocks.

This song deals with the period immediately preceding menstruation. The girls have made assignations with their lovers, fluttering their eyes and constructing string figures. Here they sit or stand among the palms, pretending to attend to their own affairs, while the men stealthily approach them with erect penes. They seize the girls from behind and pull them back among the foliage.

Song 12

They seize the young girls of the western tribes, with their swaying buttocks—those Goulburn Island men . . .
Young girls squealing in pain, from the long penis . . .
Girls of the western clans, desiring pleasure, pushed on to their backs among the cabbage palm foliage . . .
Lying down, copulating—always there, moving their buttocks . . .
Men of Goulburn Islands, with long penes . . .
Seizing the beautiful young girls, of the western tribes . . .
They are always there at that billabong edged with bamboo . . .
Hear the sound of their buttocks, the men from Goulburn Islands moving their penes . . .
For these are beautiful girls, of the western tribes . . .
And the penis becomes erect, as their buttocks move . . .
They are always there at the place of Standing Clouds, of the rising western clouds,
Pushed on to their backs, lying down among the cabbage palm foliage . . .

This song is concerned with the erotic play of the lovers, and the enjoyment of intercourse is emphasized. In this context, it is important to note the use of the word *mareiin* (line 6: see Appendix 1, page 176), which is usually translateable as 'sacred': here it conveys an extra quality—of being extraordinarily attractive or beautiful.

The song notes (in line 2) that the girls squeal in pain: that is, 'the girls call out, frightened of the men'—they are hurt through having initial coitus since, so it is said, the men's penes are too large. Again, this could be interpreted as being squeals of pleasure. But in discussion it was pointed out that the men are not necessarily betrothed to the girls, 'they are different', and the girls are not used to their penes. In these circumstances, depending on their relationship to the men concerned, there could well be an element of risk involved, since this could be regarded as illicit coitus.

Song 13

Ejaculating into their vaginas—young girls of the western tribes.
Ejaculating semen, into the young Burara girls . . .
Those Goulburn Island men, with their long penes;
Semen flowing from them into the young girls . . .
For they are always there, moving their buttocks.
They are always there, at the wide expanse of water . . .
Ejaculating, among the cabbage palm foliage:
They cry out, those young girls of the Nagara tribe . . .
He ejaculates semen for her, among the cabbage palm foliage . . .
Ejaculating for the young girls of the western clans . . .
From the long penes of men from Goulburn Islands . . .
They are always there at the open expanse of water, at the sea-eagle nest . . .
Ejaculating semen, for the young girls . . .
Into the young girls of the western tribes . . .
For they are ours—it is for this that they make string figures . . . [the men say]
Thus we ejaculate for her—into the young girl's vagina.
Semen, among the cabbage palm foliage . . .
Thus we push her over, among the foliage;
We ejaculate semen into their vaginas—young girls of the western tribes . . .
Ejaculating semen, into the young Burara girls . . .
For they move their buttocks, those people from Goulburn Islands.

This song about coitus emphasizes semen, which is said to be equivalent to flowing water: and that theme is repeated. Here too the word *mareiin* is used, and in this case refers to vagina. The identification here is of some importance, and appears in both the Wawalag and Djanggawul mythology. In discussion, the meaning of line 15 was expanded as 'we ejaculate into these young girls because they are ours, and because they attracted us by playing at string figures and swaying their buttocks'.

Song 14

Blood is running down from the men's penes, men from Goulburn Islands . . .
Blood running down from the young girls, like blood from a speared kangaroo . . .
Running down among the cabbage palm foliage . . .
Blood that is sacred, running down from the young girl's uterus:
Flowing like water, from the young girls of the western tribes . . .
Blood running down, for the Goulburn Island men had seen their swaying buttocks . . .
Sacred blood running down . . .
Like blood from a speared kangaroo; sacred blood flows from the uterus . . .
They are always there, at the wide expanse of water, the sea-eagle nests . . .
They are sacred, those young girls of the western tribes, with their menstrual flow . . .
They are always there, moving their buttocks, those Goulburn Island people . . .
Sacred, with flowing blood—young girls of the western clans . . .
They are always there, sitting within their huts like sea-eagle nests, with blood flowing . . .
Flowing down from the sacred uterus of the young girl . . .
Sacred young girls from the western tribes, clans from the Woolen River:
Blood, flowing like water . . .
Always there, that blood, in the cabbage palm foliage . . .
Sacred blood flowing in all directions . . .
Like blood from a speared kangaroo, from the sacred uterus . . .

Several important references are made in this song. In the first place, blood flows from the girls as a result of coitus, the implication being that it is the sexual act which induces the onset of menstruation. This belief has it that the penis strikes a bone within the vagina at the entrance to the uterus: the force of coition breaks this, the blood stored in the uterus is released and on withdrawal of the penis, blood is seen to be smeared over it (lines 4, 8, 14 and 19: see Appendix 1, page 179). It is not clear, however, whether the blood results from the girl's hymen (*galnga*, skin) being pierced or from the normal menstrual flow. In the song it is apparent that coitus has taken place immediately before the first menses and it is to this blood that reference is made.

According to north-eastern Arnhem Land belief, blood released at menstruation is diverted, during pregnancy, to the building up of the foetus. Once the barrier between vagina and uterus has been 'cut' or broken, menstruation can occur at regular intervals; but intermittent or relatively promiscuous intercourse does not necessarily result in conception. Traditionally, a period of apparent immunity from becoming pregnant was recognized (compare with the more general idea that girls who have only recently reached puberty are infertile—see Ashley-Montagu 1937: 15–26; R. and C. Berndt 1951: 92). However, that position is not clear, and belief and fact cannot be separated empirically. In this region, men said, girls would attempt to eject semen by applying pressure to the lower abdomen and buttocks immediately after coitus, in the hope that semen would not enter the uterus by way of the broken barrier and so cause conception. But this was, so to speak, 'playing safe', because in the more consistently expressed and conventional view the only way to ensure conception was to have a number of ejaculations from one man: in that way, seminal fluid from repeated coitus would enter the uterus and mingle with the blood already there, closing the aperture between uterus and vagina and so causing the menstrual flow to cease. Together, the blood and semen would form a foetus, the semen going to make its bones and the blood its body.

The belief about the 'breaking of the bone' between vagina and uterus is traditional and is connected, on one hand, with myths dealing with the removal of the *dugaruru* stone (see Chapter 2) and, on the other, with the armband that was lodged within the Djanggawul sisters and broken only by repeated coitus (see R. Berndt 1952: Ch. 21–22, in reference to an internal armband possessed by the younger Djanggawul sister, Miralaidj, and broken by the Djanggawul brother during coitus). In many of the drawings or carvings of women from Yirrkalla, the genitals are shown as in Diagram 2.

The bone or armband, men said, could be broken only by the action of the penis; and from the drawings and other information available, it bears no relation to a girl's hymen. At the same time, the belief may well have its origin in the piercing of the hymen or in the custom of defloration mentioned in the Rose River songs. Normally, however, a girl's hymen would be broken well before puberty, for pre-adolescent intercourse seems to have been fairly general. Ordinarily, the expectation was that a girl would (should) be betrothed, at least, if not actually married and cohabiting with her husband, by the time she reached puberty.

One other aspect requires comment. The menstrual flow is itself sacred: men claimed that the blood was sacred and they were not supposed to see it: 'If we see it, women become angry and growl at us, just as we would growl at them if they were to see some of our *mareiin* [sacred, and in this case

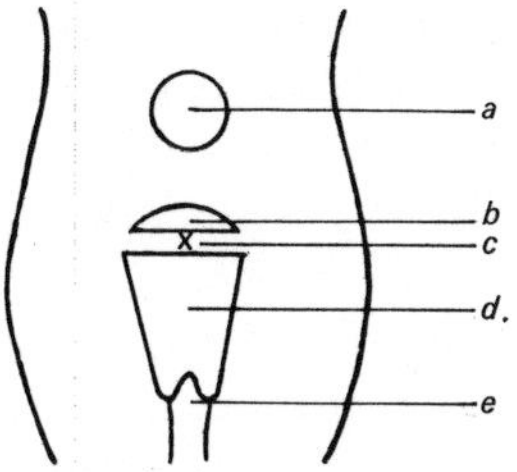

a upper uterus
b lower uterus containing menstrual blood, or large clot of blood
c the armband that all women are said to possess, dividing vaginal duct from uterus
d *mons veneris* or triangular pubic region
e vulva aperture, with *labia majora*
x the 'bone', or the armband by which it is symbolized, is broken at this juncture

Diagram 2 The 'Bone' or Armband

secret-sacred] rites or emblems'. However, in contrast to this view, in the song, men withdraw their penes after coitus and discover blood. This concept is in keeping with local religious ideology: since a girl's blood was sacred, she herself was especially so during her menstrual period. No reference is made to the traditional practice (in both western and north-eastern Arnhem Land) of secluding young girls outside the main camp at their first menstruation, a practice that was the norm when we first visited those areas. A possible explanation of its omission from this cycle is that it would not be practicable when the countryside is flooded. Nevertheless, some dry land would be available nearby, as the songs suggest, among the cabbage palms: and this place, visited by the men, might even be regarded as the girls' seclusion camp. Alternatively, because the menstrual blood drops into the billabong and is carried out of sight, that might constitute a sufficient reason for relaxing an otherwise firmly-observed custom. Not least, there is the mythical connection, as in the Wawalag myth: blood + fresh water → monsoon rains.

Song 15

They talked together, we heard them speaking the western language:
Heard their words—men from the western clans, and from Goulburn Islands.
They are always there, in the huts like sea-eagle nests: young girls leaning against the walls . . .
We heard the speech of the western clans, clans from the Woolen River . . .
Heard them speaking, girls and men of the western tribes . . .

Flinging their words into the cabbage palm foliage . . .
They are always talking there, at the billabong edged with bamboo: their words drift over the water . . .
There at the Sea-Eagle place, we heard them speaking the western language . . .
Heard their words at the Sea-Eagle place—clans from the Woolen River . . .
Talking there, Goulburn Island men of the long penes . . .
They are always there, at the wide expanse of water . . .
We heard their words, men from the western tribes, and clans from the Woolen River . . .

A period of relaxation follows sexual activity. Men and women sit in their huts talking: their words drift into the cabbage palms and across the water.

Song 16

Get the spears, for we feel like playing!
They are always there, at the billabong edged with bamboo . . .
They fling them one by one as they play, the bamboo-shafted spears . . .
Twirling the shaft, pretending to throw, then flinging them back and forth . . .
The wind catches the spear, and blows it point upwards into the cabbage palm . . .
Thin shaft twisting up like a snake, as they fling it in play . . .
Spears travelling to different places, and different tribes . . .
We saw the spear-throwers' chests and buttocks swinging—those Goulburn Island people . . .
They are always there, at the billabong edged with bamboo . . .
They feel like playing, and flinging spears—Goulburn Island men, clans from the Woolen River:
Twirling the shaft, pretending to throw: the point twists up like a snake . . .
They feel like play, leaning back on the forked sticks within the huts . . .

Men make bamboo-shafted spears and throw them. They are caught by the wind, and in their spirit form are carried to various places some distance away. The same feature of moving and drifting to a series of named places applies to wind, clouds and words, or the sound of talking: and so on.

Song 17

The pheasant cries out from the door of its nest . . .
Crying out from the door, at the sound of the coming rain . . .

Rain and wind from the west, spreading over the country . . .
It cries out, perched on the top rails of the huts.
It is always there, at the wide expanse of water, listening for the rising wind and rain:
Wind and rain from the west, as the pheasant cries out . . .
The pheasant, within its wet-season hut—for it has heard the coming rain . . .
Darkness, and heavy rain falling . . .
It is for me! [says the pheasant] My cry summons the wind and rain . . .
Noise of the rain, and of thunder rolling along the bottom of the clouds . . .
The pheasant cries out from its nest, from the door of its hut . . .
It is always there, at the billabong edged with bamboo.

The theme of the wet monsoonal season reappears, and is actually more obtrusive than that of erotic activities: the two are, however, complementary. The pheasant heralds the coming rains: when it hears the sound of the wind and rain, it cries, warning the people. Its nest, carefully constructed, is described in the same way as the stilted huts: and this bird, too, seeks refuge within from the heavy rains. Birds, animals and other characters are personalized: in this case, the pheasant speaks, taking credit for bringing the wet season.

Song 18

They take the fighting clubs, standing them upright . . .
We saw their chests, men of the western clans, of the rising clouds.
Carefully they stand them up in the ground, these groups of clubs . . .
Carefully, assembling them in rows, like a line of clouds in the west.
They are always there, at the wide expanse of water . . .
We saw their chests, men of the west, invoking the rising clouds . . .
Assembling the fighting clubs, like lines of clouds . . .
At the place of Standing Clouds, of the Rising Western Clouds, spreading all over the country.
They drift over the huts, the sea-eagle nests, at the billabong edged with bamboo:
Carefully they assemble the clubs in rows, like a line of clouds in the west . . .
From within these rows of clubs, from the lines of clouds, comes the western rain . . .
Thus we assemble the fighting clubs in rows, like lines of clouds . . .

In Song 17 the pheasant claimed to be responsible for bringing the wet season, not merely for heralding its approach. However, as the cycle reveals, this is only one of many causes that are (were) identified by the north-eastern Arnhem Landers. They saw this as a complicated network of associations, all of which had a bearing on the development of the monsoon. Without elaborating further, this song tells how clouds are attracted by fighting clubs which are placed in rows to symbolize rising clouds. As men brandish these, they call invocations to the clouds and to the coming wet season.

Song 19

From those fighting clubs, assembled in rows, come the western clouds . . .
Dark rain clouds and wind, rising up in the west . . .
They make them for us, clouds from within the rows of fighting clubs . . .
Clouds that spread all over the sky, drifting across . . .
Above Milingimbi, above the Island of Clouds . . .
Rising all over the country—at Goulburn Islands, and at the Sea-Eagle place,
Clouds building up, spreading across the country—at the place of the Rising Clouds, the place of Standing Clouds,
They spread all over the sky, clouds that they make in the camp at the billabong edged with bamboo . . .
At the open expanse of water—large rain clouds rising . . .
Dark rain clouds and wind, rising up in the west . . .
They come rising up, for thus we assemble the clubs,
Groups of fighting clubs, assembled in rows.

Dark rain clouds rise in the west, spreading across the countryside.

Song 20

Thunder rolls along the bottom of the clouds, at the wide expanse of water . . .
Thunder shaking the clouds, and the Lightning Snake flashing through them . . .
Large Snake, at the billabong edged with bamboo—its belly, its skin and its back!
Thunder and lightning over the camps, at the wide expanse of water . . .
Sound of thunder drifting to the place of the Wawalag Sisters, to the place of the Boomerang . . .
I make the thunder and lightning, pushing the clouds, at the billabong edged with bamboo [says the Lightning Snake] . . .
I make the crash of the thunder—I spit, and the lightning flashes!
Sound of thunder and storm—loud 'stranger' noise, coming from somewhere . . .
Coming to Caledon Bay, the storm from the west . . .

Thunder and rain spread across to Caledon Bay . . .
I make the thunder and lightning, at the billabong edged with bamboo!
[says the Lightning Snake]

With the spreading of the clouds, comes the storm, with thunder and lightning caused by the Lightning Snake who lives (or moves) among them. The snake—like other creatures before him—also claims credit for bringing the storm. This reinforces the main theme. In Song 2 Yulunggul is referred to, and in Song 4 freshwater snakes (the Yirawadbad snake: see Appendix 1, page 168). Both mythic snakes are associated with thunder and lightning.

There is also some erotic symbolism here. The Lightning Snake ejaculates from its 'tongue' a flash of lightning which impels the clouds to shed rain—just as in Song 14 the men's penes (= snakes) ejaculate semen (= flash of lightning) into the girls, breaking the bone and thus releasing their menstrual flow (= breaking of the cloud, with subsequent rain).

The storm, with the Lightning Snake, sweeps overland to Caledon Bay. In this way, the *dua* moiety concept becomes linked with its counterpart in the Rose River cycle, the Lightning Snake of the *jiridja* moiety. The reason for its going up among the clouds, so it is said, is that it has smelt the blood of the girls. Similarly, the Rose River snake is attracted by the blood shed by deflowered girls: it is this, in both cases, which brings about the lightning, thunder and rain.

Song 21

The tongues of the Lightning Snake flicker and twist, one to the other . . .
They flash among the foliage of the cabbage palms . . .
Lightning flashes through the clouds, with the flickering tongues of the Snake . . .
It is always there, at the wide expanse of water, at the place of the Sacred Tree . . .
Flashing above those people of the western clans . . .
All over the sky their tongues flicker: above the place of the Rising Clouds, the place of Standing Clouds . . .
All over the sky, tongues flickering and twisting . . .
They are always there, at the camp by the wide expanse of water . . .
All over the sky their tongues flicker: at the place of the Two Sisters, the place of the Wawalag . . .
Lightning flashes through the clouds, flash of the Lightning Snake . . .
Its blinding flash lights up the cabbage palm foliage . . .
Gleams on the cabbage palms, and on the shining semen among the leaves . . .

The Lightning flickers its tongue among the clouds; flashes of lightning play over the heads of the billabong people and over the countryside. The palms are illuminated, showing where the girls have been lying with their lovers. Thus, threads which have already appeared in the cycle are interwoven more closely into the main theme, while the cabbage palm itself is associated (and sometimes identified) with the Lightning Snake in ritual sequences. North-eastern Arnhem Landers saw this as an observable progression of inevitable events: coitus among the palms; the onset of the menstrual flow; the attraction of the clouds; the arrival of the Lightning Snake, drawn by the smell of the blood; and finally the coming of the monsoonal season.

Song 22

The 'swallow' approaches, flying through the west wind and the rain clouds.
The 'swallow' . . . its feathers blown by the wind . . .
It is always there, at the wide expanse of water . . .
Flying through the west wind, and the dark storm clouds,
Flying through the wind, close to the clouds . . .
It flies through the wind, close to the wide expanse of water . . .
All over the country, the bird flies low:
To the place of the Clouds, and the Sea-Eagle place, to Goulburn Islands, and Milingimbi Point,
All over the sky: to the place of Coloured Reflections, the place of the Western Clouds . . .
Bird, with its feathers blown by the wind . . .
The 'swallow', flying through the west wind and rain clouds . . .
Winds from the west calling, like sacred singing.
North-west winds of the *jiridja* moiety, clouds heavy with rain . . .

The lightning has gone, the thunder is stilled; out of the storm, the west wind continues to blow. A 'swallow', buffeted by the wind, brings further storm clouds: it skims the waters of the billabong on its way to the places mentioned in the song.

The sound of the west wind is like music to the ears of north-eastern Arnhem Landers. It is as if, men said, one hears the singing of many voices at a sacred ritual—compared, for example, with the exquisite *djamalara* singing (*djamalangani*; see Appendix 1, page 186, [line 12]) of the *kunapipi*, with the rise and fall of its delightful cadences.

Song 23

The strong wind comes close, tossing the branches . . .
Cold west wind, blowing across the country:

Small clouds running before the wind, tossed along:
Small clouds, like stranger children . . .
Wind blowing from somewhere—from the place of Standing Clouds, the place of the Western Clouds . . .
Cold west wind blowing, like sacred singing, and winds of the *jiridja* moiety, clouds heavy with rain . . .
Strong wind, tossing the branches, spreading over the sky . . .
West wind, from somewhere—from the wide expanse of water, the place of Coloured Reflections, the place of Standing Clouds . . .
From somewhere, tossing the branches—from the Goulburn Island Sandspit, from Milingimbi Point . . .
West wind blowing, like sacred singing, tossing the branches . . .
From the camp, the Sea-Eagle place, from the wide expanse of water, and the place of the Sacred Tree . . .

Storm after storm lashes the countryside, all heralded by the Lightning Snake, the fighting clubs, the birds, and by others. Line 1 refers to the boisterous winds from the west and north-west scattering the clouds far and wide so that they spread across the sky. Among the clouds being tossed along are small ones, said to be like children—'child' clouds, or immature clouds.

Song 24

Wind rustles the foliage of the cabbage palms, leaves stained with semen . . .
They are always there at the wide expanse of water, the billabong edged with bamboo . . .
The sound of the wind drifts to and fro through the cabbage palms, blown to different places . . .
Blowing through the cabbage palms; sound entering the waters . . .
At the wide expanse of water, the billabong edged with bamboo, the place of the Sacred Tree . . .
Hear its sound, at the place of Standing Clouds . . .
Sound all over the sky, at the place of the Western Clouds, the place of Standing Clouds . . .
Hear its sound, among the cabbage palm foliage . . .
Hear its sound—always there, at the Sea-Eagle place, at the place of Open Water,
At the billabong edged with bamboo, at the place of the Sacred Tree . . .
Sound drifts over the waters, around the billabong camp,
Voice of the wind, among the cabbage palm foliage . . .

The voice of the west wind is heard through the palms and skimming over the waters, spreading across the whole countryside.

Song 25

Water flows from among the cabbage palm foliage,
Rainwater flowing, foaming and white . . .
Flowing down from the roots of the cabbage palms . . .
Sacred water, foaming, spreading across the billabong.
Rainwater flowing down, banking up with foam,
Sound of running water among the cabbage palms—always there in those western camps,
At the wide expanse of water, the billabong edged with bamboo, the place of the Sacred Tree . . .
Always there, at the open stretch of water—for that flowing water is sacred . . .
Water, swirling with foam—flowing and banking up . . .
Water, running down from the cabbage palm roots . . .
Running down from among the cabbage palm foliage . . .
Sacred rainwater flowing, churned up and foaming . . .

Several figurative expressions are used in this as in other songs of this series, which can be appreciated only by examining the interlinear text (see Appendix 1, page 189). For example, certain words have a number of associated meanings that vary within a more or less limited range, according to context. The word *galwinbin* here refers to 'rainwater (flowing)'—see line 2 of the interlinear text. The same word also means semen and/or blood. These sustain the central theme of the songs: 'rainwater' symbolizes blood and/or semen; semen and/or blood attracts rain; a number of features finally lead to a desired result, impending fertility.

This symbolism is enhanced further by comparing the roots of the cabbage palms, washed by the flood waters, with penes flowing with semen (line 3, Appendix 1, page 189; also R. Berndt 1952 on the Djanggawul). And there is a parallel too with the girls' blood flowing after coitus. From its association with that blood (regarded as sacred), the water itself becomes sacred; and in its foaming 'cleanness' (see line 4, interlinear text) it is likened to semen.

Song 26

The seagull flaps its wings, flying along; it is always there, in the west, at the place of the Red Egg . . .
The voice of the seagull, its cry, drifts all over the country . . .
It circles low over the cabbage palm foliage . . .
Crying out, at the place of the fresh water,
The gull swoops low, skimming the water, at the wide expanse of billabong . . .
Keen beak probing, it searches for food, skimming the water . . .

Circling over the billabong grass and the water-lilies . . .
Circling around, in search of the freshwater leech . . .
Always there in the west, the sound of its cry: at the place of the Red Egg . . .
This string is mine [says the seagull], at the place of the billabong . . .
String, short string, and a bird's head . . .
The keen eyes of the gull search for food in the night, as a lover looks for his sweetheart . . .
Flapping its wings, and crying out as it flies . . .

It is not until this song that traditional north-eastern Arnhem Land love-magic is referred to, and implicitly sanctioned. Although the wood-and-feathered-string seagulls used in this magic are noted only incidentally, the song clearly substantiates or supports the rite: the gull speaks, saying it has a string (line 10). It is the living organic counterpart of the love-magic object, the bird's head attached to a length of feathered string; and it searches for food at night, 'as a lover looks for his sweetheart' (line 12; see also Appendix 1, page 191). The bird probes with its beak among the foliage which has grown in and about the billabong after the rains: it is looking for leeches. This is the symbolism of *dua* moiety love-magic. The wooden gull's head is carved with its beak open, holding a leech (or sometimes a worm, or a mouse, or a small fish) which represents a girl 'caught' by her lover.

Song 27

With its keen eyes, the gull saw the small tracks of the mice,
Mouse tracks, leading into the grass and the lily foliage . . .
The gull circles around, flapping its wings and crying . . .
It is always there, at the wide expanse of water, at the place of the Sacred Tree . . .
Diving down, probing about with its beak . . .
The sound of its flapping wings, as it swoops on a mouse . . .
It is always there, that bird, among the western people . . .
Its cry spreads over the country during the wet season, the time of the new grass . . .
And the squeaking cry of the mouse . . .
It is mine! [says the gull] I spear the mouse on its track, holding it in my beak . . .
The squeak of the mouse, and the cry of the gull, echoing up to the sky . . .

The cycle draws to a close, with a continuation of the love-magic symbolism referred to in the last song. The gull swoops, catching a small mouse in its beak: the 'victim' is a 'girl', the bird her lover. The gull speaks, saying it is 'spearing' the mouse, holding it in its beak: the squeaking of the mouse symbolizes the cries of girls during coitus (see Song 13).

Finally, it is suggested that the gull eats the mouse, which it has been hunting for that purpose. 'Eating' is (in this context) an indirect reference to coitus: to 'eat' a person is to have sexual relations with him or her. It is this act which is regarded as both the climax of the song cycle and an explanation of a sacred process having socio-environmental implications, all arising from a mundane, ordinary event.

5

THE SOCIAL FACE OF LOVE

In the course of presenting this cycle in the last chapter, I noted several features of its content as they appeared in the song-sequence. Now, at the risk of repetition, I shall sketch the overall patterning to point up basic and secondary themes. But first, a word of reminder. This is not western Arnhem Landers singing about local events in their home territory. It is traditional north-eastern Arnhem Land singing, in a blend of fantasy, poetry and mundane practical information, about this country from which (through which) came the vital west or north-west monsoon.

People in western Arnhem Land are building stilted huts around a large billabong, preparing for the monsoonal rain and floods. As they do so, they invoke the names of Yulunggul snakes, associated with rain and flood and with fecundity. Clouds appear from above various places in the west and come drifting eastward, heralding the approaching rains. The huts appear to be ready only just in time: scattered storms pass by and rain falls.

When this work is finished, people relax. They sing and dance, to the playing of the didjeridu and the rhythmic beating of clapping sticks. The sound echoes over the countryside. Although the singing and dancing are ostensibly for people's own enjoyment, they attract the heavy rain clouds and cooling west winds. Men and women paint their bodies, as well as their boomerangs and fighting sticks, with special designs representing rain. The men are uncircumcised. Around their necks hang ball bags, which they grip in their teeth when dancing, and they call invocations to the clouds.

The storm reaches the mainland, lashing the waters of the billabong, tossing branches and scattering leaves. The people, sheltering in their huts, enjoy the cool wind and rain, for the weather had been humid and hot. As the wind rushes through the trees, it calls out the names of places through which it must pass on its travels.

The singing and dancing are stilled now, and the bags are hung up, since they have served their purpose—the storm has become a reality.

Later, women prepare pandanus leaves to make more of these bags. Gracefully they move their hands and sway their breasts as they sit on the raised platforms facing the flooding billabong. Girls, leaning back against the walls of their huts, make string figures, moving their breasts and undulating their buttocks, glancing coyly at their prospective lovers.

While the girls play, a pigeon is watching them, calling out as it sees their menstrual blood: its sound drifts over towards various places.

The scene turns to events leading up to their menstruation. Young girls sit concealed among the thick foliage of the cabbage palms. Stealthily, men approach: they are sexually aroused, and coming up from behind pull the girls back into the foliage, where they 'play' together, the girls crying out in real or pretended pain. These girls belong to various 'clan' and 'tribal' groups of western Arnhem Land: they are described as *mareiin*, possessing a special sacred quality.

Coitus brings about the girls' first menses. Blood, sacred like the girls themselves, runs down among the foliage of the cabbage palms, and later drops through the floorboards of the huts into the waters of the billabong. It is like blood shed by a wounded kangaroo, since the girls have been 'speared'.

As men and women talk together, the sound drifts among the near-by palms and echoes across the billabong. They speak of their sweethearts, as men 'play' at flinging their spears. The points and shafts of the spears symbolize snakes: they too are caught by the wind, and carried towards the palms and to the various places mentioned in the songs.

A pheasant calls as it hears the approaching rains. It waits securely in its nest and, as the rain falls, boasts of its part in summoning the storm. Thunder crashes, and lowering clouds spread across the sky. Fighting clubs are placed in rows and invocations called to attract these rain clouds and hasten the monsoonal season. More clouds rise in the west and spread across the country: they seem to stand upright over certain places.

With the clouds comes the Lightning Snake, thundering and flashing, shaking the huts beside the billabong. The storm extends across the whole country as far as Caledon Bay. Snakes writhe in the sky, copulating, twisting and turning among the clouds. Lightning from their flickering tongues flashes among the palms, illuminating the people, spreading over all the countryside, and revealing where the lovers have been lying among the palm foliage.

A 'swallow' flies with the west wind, blown hither and thither. It skims the surface of the waters, passing various places on its way. The voice of the west wind is like sacred *kunapipi* singing. It blows boisterously, bringing small scattered clouds. With it comes another wind from the north-west, belonging to the *jiridja* moiety. This is the 'penis' wind, blowing from different places mentioned in the songs. These winds blow through the palms, rustling the leaves that are shining and stained with semen, and their sound drifts across the waters of the billabong and towards many important places. Flood waters flow among the roots and stems of the palms, churning and foaming. This is sacred water, roaring and splashing as it runs among the stilted huts, flooding the billabong, stretching across the immediate country.

A seagull flaps its wings, crying. It circles over the cabbage palms, skimming the surface of the waters, probing among the lily foliage and water grasses, in search of leeches. It symbolizes the *dua* moiety love-magic object which is made in its own image. This gull hunts at night, with its sharp eyes, as a lover searches for his beloved. It sees the tracks of mice among the grass and foliage, swooping to catch one in its beak. The cry of the bird and the squeaking of mice echo into the sky and across the countryside.

The dominant theme of this cycle is the coming of the wet monsoonal season, and its pattern is composed of features and incidents which lead up to this crisis. As a part of this basic concept, lovemaking assumes a dual function. The cycle has the underlying significance of setting in motion a train of events (more correctly, forces) which culminate in the season of fertility. It is also stimulatory, in an erotic sense. These two aspects, however, are closely linked and are not easily separated. The song cycle itself conforms, in ideology and in assumptions, with the great mytho-ritual cycles of north-eastern Arnhem Land—especially the Djanggawul and Wawalag (R. Berndt 1951*a*; 1952). In the cycle discussed here as well as in the Wawalag, Yulunggul (or Lightning Snake) is drawn to the blood of women, especially menstrual blood. This appears in the Rose River cycle too. In the sacred Wawalag, Yulunggul, attracted to the Two Sisters (and vice versa), swallows them, and this presages the onset of the monsoonal season (see R. Berndt 1951*a*: Ch. III; C. Berndt 1970*b*: 1321–5).

Warner (1958: 378), in his interpretation of 'Murngin' totemism based on an examination of the Wawalag and Djanggawul myths, reported that the Wawalag python is synonymous with seasonal change and that the climatic ideas which surround this mythic creature are not latent but are conscious and manifest in north-eastern Arnhem Land thinking. This is certainly true, except that there is intervening symbolic imagery, which is not immediately identifiable except within the frame of religious knowledge—not necessarily secret-sacred knowledge. Warner's python is the same Yulunggul which appears in this particular cycle. However, in Song 4, the Yirawadbad snake is mentioned, as well as the *dugmundur*, *djawalu* or *gawulgawul* snakes in Songs 20 and 21 (see Appendix 1, pages 184–6): these are identified with the Yulunggul and are known as Lightning Snakes. Yirawadbad is really the Gunwinggu (western Arnhem Land) name for a venomous snake who as a mythic being was responsible for instituting the secret-sacred ritual of the *ubar* (see R. and C. Berndt 1951: 114–26; 1970: 119–20, 128–32, 230–3). In that context Yirawadbad is only incidentally associated with seasonal and natural (including human) fertility, and not particularly with the monsoonal period. Nevertheless, there are ritual linkages between the Gunwinggu *ubar* and the north-eastern Arnhem Land *uwar*: both centre on a hollow-log drum, although the western *ubar* is not related to the Wawalag mythology. In general terms, the *ubar* is sponsored by Ngaljod, the Rainbow Snake, who is responsible for activating the wet season (see R. and C. Berndt 1951: 132–3).

In all this mythology and particularly in the Wawalag, male and female elements, either directly or symbolically represented, are complementary, interacting one with the other more or less in balance. In simple terms, Yulunggul symbolizes a penis, and rain, semen: female attributes are blood and clouds. Incidents in the cycle lead to a merging or convergence of these symbols, which represents sexual intercourse: this is extended to include other features, so that a specific statement is made about means and ends. Coitus, symbolic or actual, brings about the desired season of rain which, in turn, promotes fertility.

The sexual act is, therefore, a focal point in the cycle, and assumes an importance which is overridingly significant in the quest for food. Sexual intercourse among the natural species produces food, in so far as the Aborigines are concerned. Among human beings, it maintains the population and ensures 'tribal' continuity—but it also produces food, in that case indirectly. This is a basic assumption that is projected on to the universe as a whole. Only through the sexual act can the seasons rotate; only through it can the monsoonal season come to fertilize the earth; and only through it can trees, plants and vegetable matter grow. As we have emphasized, Aboriginal man in this region, as in others, saw himself as part of nature, for he lived close to it and was wholly dependent upon its resources. Consequently, he humanized that environment and identified cause and effect in natural sequences, as having an internal logic that was relevant to himself and could be applied to all around him. However, this materialism made up only part of the process he experienced himself and which he superimposed, through a complex mytho-ritual medium, on his environment. Other factors, too, had to be brought into action—otherwise this delicate psycho-physical scheme would not work.

Those other factors concern, primarily, the spiritual dimension—which was believed to give life and meaning to the material dimension. This was achieved by projecting mundane action into a mythic setting and clothing it with symbolic significance. Responsibility for activation ostensibly rested, in the last resort, with the spirit beings themselves, but human agents had to ensure that the necessary conditions were provided to enable all of this to take place. In one sense, the myths performed this function when they were ritually enacted by human beings. In the Goulburn Island songs, the situation is rather different. The cycle is not regarded as dealing with myth; it is supposed to be about living persons who themselves act out a series of events, in a ritualized fashion, in order to achieve a desired result. The explanation of those events must be sought in the overall patterning and in the symbolism, which, in turn, refer to primary religious mythic data.

Intention, therefore, assumes concrete expression, not only in the basic symbols already indicated, but also in various subsidiary ones. For example, the painted snake designs on men and women represent penes, as do boomerangs and fighting clubs, but they also refer to the Lightning Snakes responsible for rain. The ball bags are symbolic (female) clouds, but they also symbolize the fertile uterus, as in the Djanggawul: men hold these bags in their clenched teeth because they themselves and their forbears emerged from the uteri thus symbolized. This is an allusion to the Djanggawul Sisters, who were fertility mothers: from their wombs came the *rangga* (emblem) folk who were the progenitors of present-day people.

Turning to Songs 8 to 15, we reach the core of the cycle. From an oblique reference to sexual activity, coitus takes place in actuality, causing blood to flow. The scene is set for the coming monsoonal period, but the significance of the acts, viewed symbolically, must be sought in the Wawalag (and other) mythology. For example, spears = penes = snakes; fighting clubs = penes, placed to attract rain clouds = females = ball bags; clouds rise = females, joined by Lightning(s) = males; snakes writhe in the sky = copulation, resulting in rain = semen = blood, fertilizing the ground. These symbolic associations reaffirm the dual function of the cycle, underlining the relationship between the sexes and correlating human sexual intercourse with the intercourse of the elements.

The west winds are of the *dua* moiety and are sent by Yulunggul. They are the *gurga* (penis) winds and are accompanied by clouds = females, heavy with rain = pregnancy; rain falls = male urination = ejaculation of semen.

This is only a glimpse of the complex interplay of the moieties in relation to wind and clouds. At the beginning of the cycle, the north-west *jiridja* moiety wind blows up *jiridja* clouds: the *jiridja* wind copulates with *dua* clouds and *dua* wind with *jiridja* clouds; and there are also, in some contexts, male clouds. The *dua* west winds bring grass and floods and continue to blow until the trees begin to flower. Then the wind turns again to the north-west and north, signifying that it is now time to look for bush foods which have developed in the interim period. The north-east *jiridja* winds, although they may still bring rain, indicate that the season is changing. Again, the clouds from which thunder comes (containing Yulunggul and writhing smaller snakes = male + female elements = copulation) are followed or accompanied by female clouds = *jabeijaba* (yabeiyaba, 'two sisters') = Wawalag sisters. These meet or combine = copulation = Yulunggul swallowing the Wawalag, resulting in small clouds called, in Song 23, 'children'. When this happens, as Warner notes (1958: 382), all the snakes 'put their tails together and copulate'.

The ideology of the Goulburn Island cycle demonstrates reasonably well that the Aborigines themselves are aware of the symbolism through which they associate the rainy season with the Snake and its activities, and with copulation and menstruation of human beings. In this way, the measured order of the seasons is ensured, along with the fertilization and productivity of the earth, correlated with coitus, conception, pregnancy and childbirth. This has become virtually a basic 'given' in north-eastern Arnhem Land thinking.

It is a moot point as to how far we can speak of imitative or coercive magic in this respect. Love-magic is not directly referred to until the two final songs. However, it should be kept in mind that this cycle is about *one* of the many facets of love. It is not simply the love object, or the erotic elements surrounding these songs, or the reiteration of words, which has a sexual connotation. Rather, it is the whole atmosphere which is created: the interaction of men and women in a series of meaningful activities within the shadow of the coming monsoon: a kind of expanded aura which charges living with a heightened emotional and affective quality—which, *in toto*, has a bearing on the more narrowly defined aspect of the erotic. Love is not represented as an isolated act or attitude, although it can appear to be so at times; it has implications and must be seen in context. While the songs are regarded as stimulatory in an erotic sense, they are not concerned primarily with the satisfying of purely personal desire—although they may well do this incidentally. The frame is broadened, so that intercourse between the sexes has general as well as personal significance, with repercussions throughout the society. Gratification of the sexual appetite is not a transitory matter, of concern only to the two persons involved. Rather, it is a social activity which must be organized in accordance with traditional patterns. It should produce results which continue after erotic excitement on a person-to-person basis has passed. It is what I would call (and local Aborigines would probably concur) social love. Ideally, in north-eastern Arnhem Land thinking, sexual intercourse supplies a dominant theme in religious cycles and cults. In one perspective it may be regarded as sacred—if only because of its socio-religious consequences, and because it is sanctified by the mythic beings.

However, this is only part of the story. In the Goulburn Island songs, the face of sexual love is shown as social *and* sacred: but there are two other faces of love, as we shall see in the Rose River and Djarada cycles. There is also a further element which needs to be stressed. The act of sex is regarded as something entirely natural—as natural as the coming of the monsoonal rains. Men and women must, so it was said, behave in this way because they are an integral part of nature and must conform with a universal pattern. It is this natural view, with its linkage to the natural environment, which places it firmly within the sphere of the sacred.

Underlining this aspect is the use of the term *mareiin* (*maraiin*, or *madaiin*), 'sacred'. It has a specific connotation in regard to the secret-sacred, but is also used generally for sacred things. It is usually found in references to certain rituals, to emblems and postulants and to some mythic beings. In these songs, the concept has been extended to include a variety of elements, all more or less interrelated, and all significant to the overall theme as it is developed. As I have tried to make clear elsewhere, the idea of sacredness is not confined to religious cult life. On the contrary, it is reflected in basic everyday activities, of which coitus is but one aspect.

Although I have emphasized the inherently sacred quality of this cycle, I should add that it is not looked upon as being of ritual importance. It is not one of the 'big' religious song cycles like the *dua* and *jiridja* moiety *nara* (concerning the Djanggawul on one hand and Laindjung-Banaidja on the other) or even, for that matter, the Wawalag. But it does, as we have seen, have many similar attributes which have been developed into themes and which contain thereby a sacred essence. For example, the symbolism of the monsoonal season is essentially the same as in the Wawalag, and also in the Milingimbi versions of the Djanggawul. The only major difference in this respect lies in their degree of elaboration and more extensive use of symbolism. In the Goulburn Island cycle, as in the more significant mytho-ritual constellations, the basic needs and requirements of human beings are taken into account and are phrased in direct or symbolic terms. The Arnhem Lander's intimate relationship with the environment brings the concept of sacredness into perspective, as not limited and sectional in its application, but embracing the whole community and the fundamentals of everyday living.

Consistent with north-eastern Arnhem Land religious ideology is the extension of the concept of sacredness to include all persons—males and females—within specifically defined roles. Much has been written since the days of Durkheim (1954: 38 *et seq.*) and Warner (1958: 394–8) about Aboriginal women being 'profane', in contrast to the categorizing of men as 'sacred'. Kaberry (1939: e.g. 220–1, 276–8) was probably the first anthropologist to view this in different terms, recognizing that the quality of sacredness was attributed to women as it was to men. C. Berndt (e.g. 1965: 238–82) continued the discussion, emphasizing that there is no justification for trying to draw a bald distinction between males and females in this respect. There are various gradations of sacredness, which exclude women on some occasions but in others do not. Also, as Kaberry (*ibid.*: 277) put it, 'the male and female principles in some contexts are mutually dangerous and actually antagonistic' (see also R. Berndt 1974, fasc. 1: 12). None of this is enough to warrant the claim (made by Warner, for instance) that there was traditionally a dichotomy between sacred and profane in terms of men and women. The male and female principles as they appear in the Goulburn Island songs, and in their basic mytho-ritual models (for example, the Djanggawul and Wawalag) underline complementarity, not antagonism.

For example, while *mareiin* can be translated as 'sacred', it has other meanings too. The girls, as they play among the cabbage palms, are *sacred*—or, in an alternative meaning, they are 'out of the ordinary', which could also be a reference to their physical attractiveness. This usage of *mareiin* was quite deliberate on the part of the Aborigines concerned, and raises some interesting problems. In one sense, we may interpret it as having to do with sanctity, springing from the girls' direct association with basic elements of sacredness. In another sense, sacredness could well be said to imply (as I have noted before) aesthetic considerations of beauty, regularity, order and 'natural' behaviour. This latter view is supported by the fact that in north-eastern Arnhem Land there is no word specifically referring to sacred myth or ritual which can be translated as directly equivalent to 'set apart', although *mareiin* and similar terms could be used in that way; and this is in contrast to the western Arnhem Land situation, where the word *djamun* does, explicitly, convey that meaning (see R. and C. Berndt 1970).

One further point has to do with what Lévi-Strauss (1962: 53–4) called the complementarity of nature and society, the material and the spiritual, and man and woman (see also R. Berndt 1970*a*: 1063–4). The application of this frame to north-eastern Arnhem Land data brings us too close to the Durkheim-Warner hypothesis—even though it is phrased in different terms. The evidence submitted here in, for example, the Goulburn Island song cycle suggests that, while male-female complementarity is significant, contrasts between the material and the spiritual cannot be so easily sustained. They interact or intergrade too closely and too freely within the one frame, so that male elements are no less 'physical' than female ones, and vice versa. And if the 'spiritual' concerns the projection of symbolism (here, normally derived from a physical basis) on to a mytho-ritual plane, then again it would seem impracticable to separate out this symbolism into a series of correlations along these lines. The patterning of oppositions and mediators is much more complex than that. The only way it can be made to 'fit' into a simplistic schema is through misrepresentation of the empirical data.

Any interpretation of north-eastern Arnhem Land material of this kind must take into account the belief that woman is sacred—at least in religious thinking, not necessarily in ordinary everyday life. That quality is inborn, because she possesses physical attributes that are characteristically feminine, and is (ideologically) a living representation of the fertility mothers who produced the first ancestors of the present-day Arnhem Landers.

In the Creative Era, when the Dreaming (*wongar*) beings lived on earth in physical form, all the sacred rituals and emblems belonged to women, who alone wielded executive authority over them (see R. Berndt 1951*a*; 1952; 1972: 207; R. and C. Berndt 1951; 1964; 1970). This control was stolen from them, treacherously, by men. Much of what the men took had to do with women, especially in relation to fertility: and religious rituals in the contemporary era are, or were, principally concerned with this. The rituals are also vitally interested in the renewal of the natural species, the growth and decay of vegetation, and the rhythmic sequence of the seasons. The female aspect in all these is predominant. The rituals are *mareiin* and the participants themselves become *mareiin*; so do food, material objects and so on, as the occasion demands and within that particular context. But, although they too may be involved in ritual, women are now looked upon as the original instigators. They are in that sense naturally sacred, and remain so.

Men, therefore, maintain their executive role in sacred rituals: they manipulate the sacred symbolic emblems and declare this and that *mareiin*, and they can assume or divest themselves of the cloak of ritual sacredness almost at will. Women, in contrast, remain always in the state of being *mareiin*. They are born into this state, like their ancestresses, the Djanggawul and Wawalag. They can never be secularized or de-*mareiin*-ized or made profane—not in a generalized, intrinsically sex-linked way. What has developed is an ideology of partial exclusion, and in recent years this seems to have become in some respects more pronounced. Traditionally, however, this view of the special ('sacred') quality of femaleness was not at all obtrusive. Mostly it was more or less latent. And it did not, of course, obviate friction and physical violence in the ordinary give and take of camp life. But it was activated, or brought into prominence, in appropriate circumstances. At certain physiological crises in a woman's life her innate sacredness might be intensified, and during these periods the term *mareiin* might be more frequently used in ordinary everyday speech, in reference to her. For example, during menstruation (as indicated in the songs) she is, traditionally, *mareiin*, as is her menstrual blood: this is likened to the younger Wawalag sister's menstruation. Also, her vagina is sacred, because of its association with the blood; while her uterus is correspondingly sacred, for it is the repository of blood and semen and, after conception, of the foetus. This sequence is brought out clearly in the Djanggawul cycle. In the Djanggawul mythology, the vagina is really the source of sacredness, and is life-giving. It is associated with the vagina of the Sun Mother, from which the creative ancestresses, the Djanggawul, are originally said to have come: for from her vagina pour rays of light and heat. There is much symbolism in that cycle which does not appear in the Goulburn Island one.

Finally, it is useful in this context to present a diagrammatic profile of the Goulburn Island cycle (Diagram 3). This encapsulates the major ingredients (certainly not all) contained in the cycle itself, indicating their interconnectedness. The symbolism of equivalence or association has already been discussed and need not be repeated here. In any case, the song cycle itself spells out such aspects with a certain degree of obviousness. The in-built cross-references upon which the content of these songs rests, indicate expectations for the future which follow naturally from present and past events. I have selected, therefore, what can be regarded as repetitive signals or indicators. There are also many others—for instance, certain creatures which appear in the songs and by their actions emphasize or indicate the trend of events. Many of these appear in the relevant mythology, but they are in this context incidental to the primary patterning.

The crucial element is the correlation between mythic conjunction and human copulation in a non-ritual context. Although the Wawalag myth contains many incidents which occurred during the travels of the two Wawalag sisters from the south and south-east, the major focus from the perspective of north-eastern Arnhem Land is on their interaction with the mythic Yulunggul snake. At that juncture, the myth abounds in sexual symbolism, although it is not always made explicit (in direct mythic allusion or in discussion) that the Yulunggul and the Wawalag actually copulate. It is evident, however, from the material, that this is one interpretation which can be made, and the diagram indicates how it can be.

This diagram revolves round what can be called male-female discourse. The activities in the male sector of the left-hand circle refer to Yulunggul: the sound of the didjeridu, a male symbol, stimulates clouds (female symbols); fighting sticks (male symbols) are arranged to form or to induce clouds; ball bags are used by men but symbolize clouds—it is women who make the bags. In the female sector, references lead to the Wawalag. These symbolic actions, or actions of symbolic significance, are transformed into reality in the right-hand circle, which is a result of a combination of male-female elements (for

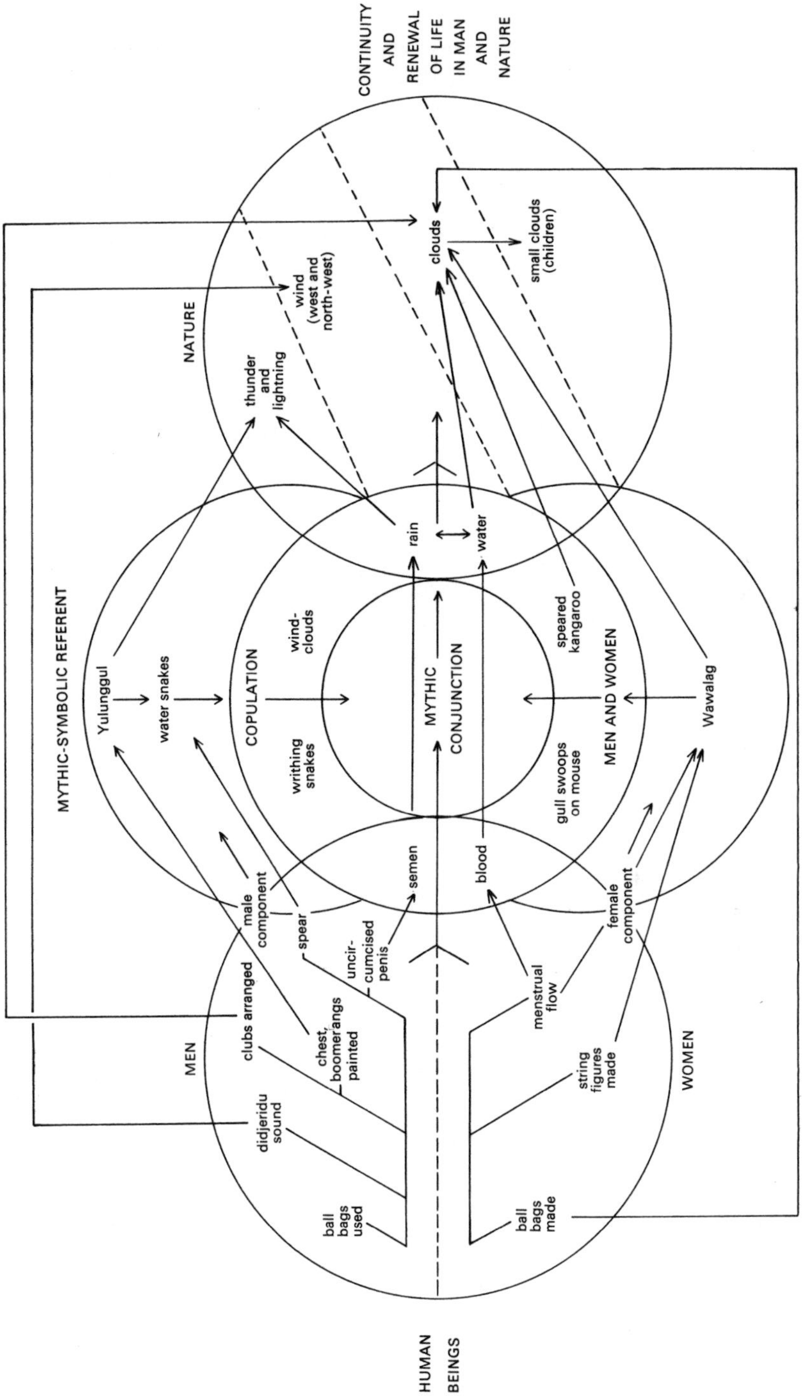

Diagram 3 Profile of the Goulburn Island Cycle

example, thunder and lightning *and* clouds brought together by wind). The central concentric circles represent human-mythic copulation, with two key elements—blood and semen, symbolizing rain. The wind is the logical prelude to clouds and rain, as is human-mythic copulation.

This cycle, then, is cast in a religious mould, using as its model certain major mytho-ritual constellations, applying some of their sequences but framing them within what purports to be a contemporary situation. The actions of ordinary human beings set in motion mythic actions, broadening the social and natural implications which could, in ordinary circumstances, have been quite narrowly confined.

One lesson the cycle has, for those who are in a position to learn it, is that ordinary events mirror transcendental events; that actions of individual persons cannot be evaluated only in their own terms; and that, while any individual action will inevitably have social repercussions, it must inevitably too have environmental repercussions, whether or not these are apparent. Because the total environment is categorized in human terms, it is quite logical to expect mutually sustaining influences of this kind. In the Goulburn Island cycle, then, one particular aspect or 'face' of love is manifested: but there are also others, for other times and for other contexts. The Rose River cycle presents one of these faces, and the Djarada yet another.

6

THE ROSE RIVER CYCLE[*]

Song 1

They are always there, men chipping at wooden boomerangs:
Men of the Rose River clans, of the barramundi and catfish . . .
Chips of wood fly out, from shaping the wooden boomerangs . . .
They are always there, women moving their buttocks . . .
Men chipping and shaping boomerangs, flattening their sides . . .
They think of the *nonggaru* place, of the sacred ground . . .
They are always there, men of the southern tribes:
Clans from the Rose River country, men with subincised penes . . .
Clans from the inland Bush . . .
They make the boomerangs, chipping and flattening the sides, and the defloration point . . .
Thinking about the dancing and rites of the *kunapipi*.
Men of the Rose River clans, and the Dalwongu tongue . . .
Thinking about the *mandiela*, the sacred dancing,
For now the boomerangs are nearing completion:
Spirits and people, subincised men from the Rose River clans . . .
Thinking, while they chip away at the boomerangs . . .
Flattening the sides, making the point for deflowering girls . . .
Clans from the Rose River country, all assembled together . . .
In that sacred place, in the middle of the *nonggaru*.

* This is associated with three *mada*, dialectal units, of the *jiridja* moiety—the Mararba, Gumaidj and Manggalili. The dialect used in the original of these songs is Gumaidj, and the subject matter was said to be of Rose River derivation.

These songs commence by referring to the sacred *kunapipi*: defloration boomerangs are prepared in anticipation of the forthcoming rites. The *nonggaru* hole is mentioned. This is dug on the ritual ground (for example, line 6), and it is there that coitus and defloration will take place. According to north-eastern Arnhem Land interpretation, the *nonggaru* is the billabong inhabited by Yulunggul, but traditionally it represents the uterus of the Kunapipi Mother who is its mythic sponsor.

Various Rose River clans are noted. Some, associated with the Dalwongu *mada*, participate in the *kunapipi*. However, they do not subincise, although this rite is especially significant in both the mythology and ritual of their southern neighbours. For this reason, north-eastern Arnhem Landers call the *kunapipi* by the term *wirii*, 'incisure', and also refer to part of this ritual as being the *mandiela* (see Chapter 3).

The theme of fertility is not yet apparent. However, the fact that the *kunapipi* and defloration are mentioned provides a clue to this.

Song 2

People of southern clans sit there, talking together . . .
Words flying into the air, as they speak, in those different dialects:
Words drift from in there, from that place in the middle of the *nonggaru*, from within the sacred shade . . .
Talking quickly together, like the voices of birds.
Talking to one another, twisting their tongues to make strange noises like birds . . .
Speech of different clans, mingling together . . .
Dua moiety clans, with their special distinct tongues.
People from Blue Mud Bay, clans of different tongues talking together . . .
Clans of the barramundi, and of the paperbark saplings:
Words flying over the country, like the voices of birds . . .
They talk, now quickly, now slowly: hear the sound of their words!
Clans from the Bush, from among the armband bushes, with *jiridja* moiety speech:
People of southern clans talking together, men of the subincised penes . . .
Talking quickly: words of the jungle people mingling with those from the inland Bush . . .
Talking quickly like birds, twisting their tongues.
Talking together quickly: hear the sound of their voices, those people of southern clans!
Twisting their tongues as they talk, speaking slowly in different dialects, all the clans together . . .
Talking along, talking quickly there in the camp . . .
In those places at Rose River, among the clumps of bamboo.

The sound drifts over towards the place of the Snake . . .
Always there, the speech of those people, talking slowly together: drifting towards the place of the Snake:
People talking together quickly, speech of the barramundi clans . . .
Barramundi people belonging to Laindjung, talking slowly; and others quickly.
Talking together slowly, moving their lips in speech. They are always there,
People of southern tribes: men of the subincised penes, clans of the young paperbark saplings . . .
Mingling their speech, their quick talk, twisting their tongues . . .
Different-moiety clans talking together as one, like mother and child.
Dua clans, with their special distinct tongues, talking together in the camps near Blue Mud Bay . . .
In the middle of the *nonggaru*, and among the bamboo clumps, in the Rose River country . . .
Talking in the middle of the *nonggaru*, within the shade of the branches . . .
Within the sacred *nonggaru*, towards the entrance, within the sacred shade.
Talking quickly to one another, like birds calling . . .
They are always there, those people with moving buttocks, with subincised penes:
People of southern clans talking quickly together, twisting their tongues like birds . . .
Southern clans, clans of the barramundi, all assembled together . . .
Talking with different tongues, there, in the sacred *nonggaru* . . .

This song refers to sounds made by people who speak different dialects and who come from southern areas as well as from north-eastern Arnhem Land. They are assembled for the *kunapipi* rituals and belong to the *jiridja* and *dua* moieties.

It is interesting to note that from the perspective of Yirrkalla in 1946–47 the *kunapipi* was regarded as of the *dua* moiety (see R. Berndt 1951*a*: 35, 86; and Chapter 3 of this volume), since it is concerned with *dua* Wawalag mythology. However, the *kunapipi* songs I recorded originally were *jiridja*. Further, it should be kept in mind that there is always a ritual division of labour between moieties, with all activity (whether the rites and associated verbal and other material are owned by members of one moiety or the other) being of a co-operative kind. The Rose River songs, although they also closely conform with certain features of the Wawalag and with *dua* ritual, are categorized as belonging to the *jiridja* moiety; their songs are in a *jiridja* dialect; and both *dua* and *jiridja* moiety persons participate.

Song 3

They are rubbing hard lumps of red ochre against the stones . . .
Chipping off fragments, pounding and grinding them into ochre-paint:
The sound of the scraping drifts across the country, into the place of the Snake . . .
They are sitting there, pounding red ochre,
Those spirits, people of southern clans with subincised penes . . .
Sound lifting into the air, from their pounding and scraping!
With chests moving, those red-ochre pounders, men of the southern clans . . .
For this is the hard red ochre . . .
They sit there, chipping off fragments, preparing paint.
We saw their chests moving, pounding the ochre, men of the southern clans . . .
The sound of their scraping rises into the air, at that place, among the clumps of bamboo . . .
Within the *nonggaru* place, in the Vagina, within the sacred shade . . .
They sit there, rubbing away at the red ochre . . . pounding the chips for paint . . .

Men prepare red ochre which they will eventually use to paint the defloration boomerangs and the young girls. In line 12, the *nonggaru* is referred to simply as 'Vagina'. It is, however, in this case, a small 'shade' or hut (sometimes a shallow windbreak) erected near the *nonggaru*: it is here, rather than in the *nonggaru* itself, that the women wait. It has an entrance which is known as the vagina (*dagu*) of the Kunapipi Mother.

Song 4

They spray red ochre and kangaroo fat on the boomerangs . . .
Paint from the red ochre chips, and kangaroo fat . . .
They cover the flat boomerang with pounded red ochre . . .
Thinking of ritual intercourse in the sacred shade, in the *nonggaru* place . . .
Spraying red ochre on to the small boomerangs . . .
Those people of southern clans, of the barramundi fish . . .
They think of the sacred ritual, as they prepare the boomerangs . . .
Smearing the defloration boomerang, making it ready . . .
We saw the moving chests of the spirit people, men of the southern clans,
Calling invocations to the hurricane, to the loud voice of the wind . . .
Smearing the boomerangs, with the pounded flakes of red ochre . . .
Spraying the red ochre, pounded for paint . . .
Smearing over them fat from the kangaroo . . .
Spraying the flat boomerangs, smeared with fat . . .
Men of the southern clans, in the sacred camp . . .

Men are preparing for the forthcoming rituals. Reference is now made to the coming monsoonal season: men paint their boomerangs with red ochre, invoking power names of the hurricane winds. And they decorate themselves in order to summon the Lightning Snake: for red ochre, symbolizing blood, can be a potent means of attraction. Thus, the men entice the Snake from its waterhole just as Yulunggul was attracted by the smell of the blood of the Wawalag.

Song 5

They stand ready in rows, men of the southern clans . . .
Leading into the sacred place of the *nonggaru*, into the Vagina . . .
Standing ready, poised on their toes: men of southern clans assembled together . . .
Leading into the place of the bamboo clumps, into the sacred *nonggaru*, into the branches of the sacred shade . . .
They stand ready, those men of southern clans, who are always there:
Clans of the subincised penes, grasping their boomerangs ready to throw.
Buttocks moving, into the branches of the *kunapipi* shade . . .
Standing ready in rows, leading into the branches of the sacred shade . . .
Thinking of ritual intercourse and defloration.
They are always there, people with moving buttocks:
Always there, clans with subincised penes, clans of the barramundi . . .
Standing there ready in rows, with feet poised, leading into the branches:
Standing there in the sacred place, in the *nonggaru* place . . .
This is the place of the southern clans . . . with fish scales scattered . . .
The place of the bamboo clumps, the sacred *nonggaru* place, the Vagina shade . . .

Assembled around the *nonggaru*, men throw their boomerangs, testing them before they are ritually used. There is a similarity between this song and Songs 18 and 19 of the Goulburn Island cycle: just as the clubs attracted clouds, so do the boomerangs (see next song).

Song 6

They are shaking their boomerangs, as they always do, with heaving chests . . .
Men of the southern clans, testing and throwing the new boomerangs . . .
New boomerangs, flat ones, small ones like children . . .
With heaving chests, those boomerang people, men of the southern clans . . .
Twirling the flying boomerangs, carefully made . . .
Shaking and throwing them, making them good . . .

Thus they twirled them, towards the place of the Snake, the place of the Crab . . .
Calling the place names, throwing the boomerangs:
Spirit people, men of the southern clans . . .
Thus they threw them, towards the place of the bamboo clumps, the place of the jungle . . .
Thus they threw them, towards the place of the Snake, the place of the Crab, the place of the Catfish . . .
Flying boomerangs, from the spirit people, clan of the paperbark saplings, with heaving chests . . .
Calling invocations to the hurricane, the loud voice of the wind . . .
Throwing the boomerangs towards Blue Mud Bay, to those inland places . . .
Towards Blue Mud Bay, the Vagina place, of the Mararba people . . .
Twirling the boomerangs, small ones and flat ones . . .
Special boomerangs, with flattened sides, and points made for defloration.
Thus they twirled them, throwing them towards those inland places, into the waters of the Dalwongu country . . .
Thus they threw them, into the depths of the water, skimming the sea's surface . . .
Through the rough seas, towards Groote Eylandt, the high peaks of the waves . . .
Spirit people, clans of the paperbark sapling . . .
Twirling the flying boomerangs, smeared with red ochre . . .

The theme of the previous song is continued. As men throw their boomerangs, more invocations are called to special sites in the Rose River area and to the heavy rain-bearing winds. In later songs, these boomerangs signify clouds and throwing them (in spirit form) towards these various places means, so it was said, that the clouds will come to them. It is not only the power of the invocations which attracts rain, but also the red ochre and fat with which the boomerangs have been painted.

Song 7

Putting the boomerangs along in a row, who are they? Men of the southern clans . . .
They put them along, leading into the camp: for our boomerangs have been well prepared!
They fly along through the air, our boomerangs! We put them here, leading into the camp:
Into the middle of the *nonggaru*, into the Vagina, into the branches of the sacred shade . . .

Southern clans, clans of the barramundi, all assembled together . . .
Well, our bodies are tired from throwing the boomerangs: we put them along in a row . . .
Leading into the place of the Snake, the place of the Crab, the place of the Catfish . . .

Symbolically, the boomerangs relate to the monsoonal season, their significance being enhanced because they are so arranged as to lead into the *nonggaru* and also to point towards various places mentioned in the songs.

Song 8

The sound of talking flies from among the branches, drifting like the cry of the Morning Pigeon . . .
Hear the sound of their speech, now fast, now slow—twisting their tongues, like birds . . .
Hear the sound of the southern clans as they talk together, sound drifting inland . . .
Drifting towards the clans of the armband bushes: *dua* people, with special distinct tongues . . .
Mothers belonging to *dua* moiety clans, with *jiridja* Dalwongu children . . .
Hear them talking like birds, quickly and slowly, *jiridja* clans . . .
Sound of their quick speech, from among the branches of the sacred shade . . .

The theme reverts to that of Song 2: the speech of persons belonging to several clans and dialectal units intermingles. *Dua* moiety women are speaking in dialects classified under that moiety, while their children speak in dialects of the other moiety, pointing up the strong emphasis on patrilineal descent—and, also, on the interdependence and interconnectedness of the two moieties.

Song 9

They arrange the branches about the *nonggaru* shade, and the sacred shade of the women . . .
Branches to screen the women's shade, at the *nonggaru* place, among the clumps of bamboo . . .
They are building the screen, arranging the branches . . .
Thinking of women's vaginas, and of coitus.
They are always there, people with moving buttocks:
Clans with subincised penes, clans of the barramundi . . .
All the southern clans, assembled together . . .

Towards the place of the Snake, the place of the Crab, the place of the Catfish . . .
Arranging the screen to hide the women within, with a wall of branches.
We saw the heaving chests of the southern clansmen, arranging the branches . . .
Building a screen of branches, beside the *nonggaru* . . .
They have made it well, covering the top of the shade with branches . . .
Shaking the branches, making the shade . . .
Men of the southern clans, in the spirit country, making the shade . . .
Thinking of play, of the *mandiela* dancing, and of the *kunapipi*.
They are always there, people with moving buttocks, men with subincised penes . . .
Men of the southern clans, men of the barramundi . . .
Making the screen to hide the women within, at the sacred shade, and arranging the branches . . .

The bush screen around the Vagina is constructed near the *nonggaru*, in readiness for ritual defloration and coitus. This screen, as we shall see, is intended to prevent husbands (potential or actual) from observing their betrothed or actual wives being deflowered or having coitus. Moreover, men who remain for various purposes in other parts of the sacred ground may not watch these proceedings. It was said: 'No one should see what they do to the women'.

Song 10

They arrange the branches with care at the *nonggaru* place, at the sacred Vagina shade.
Scales and bones of the barramundi, thrown aside . . .
Southern clans, clans of the barramundi, all assembled together . . .
In the sacred camp at the place of the bamboo clumps, the place of the Snake . . .
Carefully they arrange the screen of branches about the women's shade, and about the *nonggaru* . . .
Spirit people, men of southern clans, with subincised penes . . .
Carefully they arrange the branches about the shade, at the *nonggaru* place . . .

The screen around the women's shade is carefully made.

Song 11

There they stand close to the sacred shade, waiting for defloration . . .
Young girls, painted with red ochre, moving towards the branches screening the shade . . .

Arranging the girls, ready for defloration, for they are sacred . . .
Young girls from those inland places, the place of the jungle . . .
Bringing the boomerang close, into the branches . . .
Young girls of the barramundi clans, clans of the subincision . . .
They are always there, people with moving buttocks.
They stand, moving towards the shade, towards the sacred Vagina.

Young girls from the inland Bush country await defloration. They are *mareiin wirgul*, sacred girls. The word *mareiin*, as in the Goulburn Island songs, was said to indicate some outstanding or extraordinary quality: not simply pretty or beautiful but having an especially attractive quality of sacredness.

Conventionally, a man puts the defloration boomerang into someone to whom he stands in the formal relationship of *gurung* ('daughter's husband'; the reciprocal term is *mugul*, 'wife's mother'), and then has coitus with her. This is ordinarily a relationship of total, or almost-total avoidance. The *mugul* is potentially a mother-in-law of the *gurung*, and conversely he is her actual or classificatory 'son-in-law' (or her husband's sister's son), although there is usually a wide range of distant *mugul-gurung* available (see Chapter 2). She is ordinarily called in English a 'cousin' *mugul* (or a *mugul-rumurung*, which implies avoidance and tabu-ness) to distinguish her from a *baba mugul* (a father's sister). In the *kunapipi*, however, the sacredness of the occasion traditionally demands that coitus take place between these otherwise tabu relatives: it is considered to be far more potent from the point of view of fertility than between normally eligible partners (see R. Berndt 1951*a*: 48–53). This ritual act is sanctioned mythologically by both the Djanggawul and the Wawalag. Furthermore, defloration is associated with subincision.

Song 12

They bring close the pointed boomerang, raising her thighs on to the hips of a man . . .
Pushing her down, that young girl smeared with red ochre, raising her thighs . . .
They think of the boomerang, with its flattened point . . .
Pushing her down, that girl, on to a man's hips, into the branches . . .
Young girl, smeared with red ochre and kangaroo fat . . .
Pushing her down into the branches, into the shade, at the *nonggaru*.
They bring close the point of the boomerang, into her vulva . . .
Into the young girls smeared with red ochre, girls of the barramundi clans . . .
Girls crying out, pierced by the flattened point of the boomerang . . .
Their cries drift into the air at the place of the jungle, the place of the armband bushes . . .

Girls of the southern clans, from the place of the Snake, the place of the bamboo clumps . . .
Pierced by that point, the point of the flat boomerang.
Their cries drift into the air, at the place of the White Cockatoo . . .
The sound of the girls' cries, drifting out to the place of the Snake . . .
Drifting out to the place of the branches, the place of the spirit people, the place of the southern tribes . . .
The sound drifts, as they cry out from that boomerang . . .
The sound of their cries, groups of girls from the barramundi clans . . .
Crying out, raised on the men's thighs, among the branches within the sacred shade . . .
Sound of their cries, young girls painted with red ochre . . .
Sound in the sacred camp, in the *nonggaru* place, among the clumps of bamboos.

The young girls are deflowered by their *gurung*, and their cries drift across the country about Rose River, just as was the case in the Goulburn Island cycle, although in a different context.

Song 13

They are copulating together, to the sound of singing, with penis erect . . .
Copulating together, to the sound of singing.
The penis moves slowly, 'talking', as he ejaculates:
Erect penis copulating, moving forward.
Semen streams out into the young girl, within the screen of branches . . .
Copulating among the branches, to the sound of singing . . .
The penis moves slowly, 'talking', as he ejaculates.
Penis like a barramundi, with ridged apex . . .
Subincised penis growing erect, and copulating . . .
They are always there, with ridged penis and moving buttocks:
Semen ejaculating from the erect penis,
Large penis, entering the young girl.
Mouth of the penis, penis growing erect:
Its apex smells of the girl's vaginal juices . . .
Within the screen of branches, the sacred shade, the place of the ejaculating semen . . .
Copulating together, people of southern clans, clans of the barramundi . . .
All the southern clans, assembled together . . .
Girls moving, as the semen ejaculates . . .
Copulating with the young girls, to the sound of singing . . .
Girls from the Bush, from the Armband place, from the place of the Snake . . .

Subincised penis growing erect, and copulating.
People of southern clans, clans of the barramundi . . .
Returning to copulate, ejaculating . . .
At the place of the Snake, the place of the Rising Penis . . .
Men of the southern clans, clans of the subincision, with penes ridged and erect . . .

The importance of ritual coitus in broader terms has already been touched upon. Here, the scene portrayed is highly conventionalized and focuses on sexuality without noting also the sacred character of this act. Partly, that is because there was a customary emphasis on such material, and this is to be expected in a 'love song' cycle. Partly, according to the songman and others presenting and discussing it, the intention was to provide a reflection of reality—a picture of what actually took place in the past and takes place in the present at Rose River. It is not possible to assess the extent to which ritual copulation flourished in former times in that region. From all accounts, it was more popular in the past than it was at the time these songs were recorded, but there is no firm evidence on that. Yirrkalla people in the 1940s seem to have obtained a vicarious pleasure in supposing that what they sang about and heard was entirely true. But this aside, there is enough information available to suggest that this aspect of the *kunapipi*, wherever it was held, had an overwhelming appeal to participants—or at least to male participants. And that appeal included the songs and other such material connected with it.

One result of European contact, particularly in regions under mission influence, has been an official or unofficial ban on the carrying out of all *kunapipi* rites, whether or not they involved ritual coitus. Consequently, this particular feature vanished entirely in some areas. In others it was driven 'underground', with people leaving the immediate vicinity of a settlement in order to perform these traditional rites. Whereas previously Aborigines were quite frank in their approach to this aspect, some have become reticent and more self-conscious. In such circumstances, ritual coitus may be carried out surreptitiously, and the erotic element intensified.

Song 14

Weak from coitus, within the branches screening the shade, two young girls.
Semen flows from them as they strike their loins, flowing within the screen and among the branches . . .
Girls of the barramundi clans, smeared with red ochre, striking their bellies and dancing so that the semen flows . . .
Girls from the inland Bush, from the place of the Armband bushes, the place of the Snake . . .

Semen flows from them, as they strike their bellies . . .
Girls of the southern clans, clans of the barramundi: young 'subincised' girls . . .
Young girls within the screen of the shade, within the branches . . .
Semen flows from them as they strike their bellies, dancing the *mandiela* . . .
In that place, in the middle of the *nonggaru*, among the clumps of bamboo . . .
In the shade, in the *nonggaru* place, in the sacred Vagina shade . . .
Young girls, striking their bellies so that the semen flows . . .

The girls are weak after their experience, and through abdominal pressure and dancing they release semen from themselves. One Aboriginal remarked: 'Too many men did it to them, that's why those girls shake and hit themselves and the semen comes out'. The emitted semen symbolizes falling rain, presaging the wet season.

After defloration and coitus, a girl is referred to as being 'subincised' (line 6, *bala*)—as being equivalent in status, in this respect, to a subincised man. The symbolism here suggests a direct relationship between her vagina (which flows with semen and defloration blood) and a man's subincised penis. Conversely, this organ, when it is pierced at subsequent subincision rites, was said to be like a woman's vagina after ritual coitus and defloration.

Song 15

They smear red ochre and blood, with kangaroo fat, over the young girls . . .
Smearing the young girls, rubbing them all over with red ochre . . .
Their skin is shining, shining from ochre and fat . . .
Smearing them all over, young girls of the southern clans . . .

Before leaving the sacred ground, girls are smeared with kangaroo fat and red ochre as well as with their own defloration blood: see also Song 19. In later songs, it is this blood which attracts the Lightning Snake. Men, too, smear themselves with incisure blood. Moreover, when the blood-smeared (or red-ochred) men or women return to the main camp after this ritual, they were said to be emerging from the womb of the Kunapipi Mother. The blood upon them (or its equivalent, red ochre) was said to have been derived from their stay within her; and this part of the rite symbolizes their rebirth.

Song 16

Blood-red clouds, hanging above those inland places . . .
Red clouds shining, and yellow-tinged clouds: from blood and semen, spreading over the sky . . .

Red clouds from spraying and painting girls of the barramundi clans . . .
Red clouds from the 'subincised' girls, hanging above the place of the armband bushes.
Red clouds above the screen of branches, above the place of the Goose, the place of the running water . . .
Clouds shining over the sky, blood from the young girls of the barramundi clans . . .
Spreading over the sky, clouds red and tinged with yellow . . .
Shining above the bamboos, into the place of the Snake . . .
Shining all over the country, at the place of the Snake, the place of the Crab and the Catfish . . .
Always there, blood hanging above the clans of the barramundi:
Always there, people with moving buttocks:
Red clouds from that place, hanging over the barramundi clans:
In the sacred camp, among the clumps of bamboo: in the middle of the *nonggaru*, in the vagina shade . . .
They shine all over the sky.
Blood and ochre shining, from the young girls of the barramundi clans, from the place of the armband bushes.

This song treats an aspect which becomes more apparent later. Blood and semen, with red ochre, are manifested as red and yellow-tinged clouds, formed when the girls were sprayed with a liquid mixture made up of these substances. Spraying of this kind, usually with plain ochres, is done by mouth and is (or used to be) quite common throughout north-eastern Arnhem Land and other parts of Aboriginal Australia. The resulting red clouds shine in the sun, like the bodies of the girls after they have been sprayed or smeared; and they spread across the sky to hang lowering over various places at Rose River, their redness illuminating the surrounding country.

Song 17

They sit there together, men of the southern clans, clans of the barramundi . . .
Sitting down, leading into the camp, at the place of the bamboo clumps . . .
Sitting together, men of the southern clans, clans of the barramundi and of the frog . . .
Sitting down in a row, leading into the sacred camp, into the *nonggaru* place, into the Vagina shade . . .
Sitting down together, along in a row . . .
Sitting down in a row, men of the southern clans, clans of the barramundi . . .

Rows of men, stretching into the place of the bamboo clumps, the place of the armband bushes, the place of the shade . . .
Always there, people with moving buttocks, subincised people, clans of the barramundi . . .

The cycle now turns to subincision, regarded as complementary to the previous rites. This is part of the conventional southern *kunapipi* rituals, and in that area is (was) a 'men-only' affair, secret to men. At Yirrkalla these songs, like the others, were sung openly in the main camp.

Song 18

They are striking and flaking the stone blades, 'mother' blades of the *jiridja* clans . . .
Striking and flaking the stone blades, with moving chests . . .
Chests of the stone-spear makers, striking the stones . . .
Calling invocations to the hills above Blue Mud Bay, where the stone is quarried . . .
Chipping and shaping the blades, thinking of subincising.
Penis standing erect, with its apex ring: and the flaked blade . . .
They think of the rising penis, moving in coitus, ejaculating . . .
Thinking of copulating, and of the penis and apex ring, as they sit there flaking the stone . . .
Calling invocations to running spring water, to semen ejaculating . . .
They think of erect penes . . .

Stone blades are being prepared for subincision. As men do this, they think of copulation, since seminal fluid is said to flow more rapidly after subincision. (North-eastern Arnhem Landers said that ejaculation could then take place merely by thinking about coitus, or before a man was able to insert his penis. It will be recalled that subincision is not, and traditionally was not, practised in this area.)

The stone blade is of the *dua* moiety, and therefore referred to as a 'mother' of the *jiridja* people; it is prepared by *dua* moiety men. The stone itself comes from quarries at Blue Mud Bay (see Thomson 1949: Plates 1 and 4). Such a division of ritual work, between men of both moieties, is conventional in north-eastern Arnhem Land; and where it is not based on contrasting moieties, the subsections operate in more or less the same way. Men of one moiety prepare a ritual object, while those of the opposite moiety who own it use it in their dancing. This ensures that members of each moiety (or subsection) have a significant role to play in the rituals. In line 1 (see Appendix 2, page 216), the blade represents a penis, both being called by the same name. In line 9, ejaculating semen is associated with running water, underlining one of the main intents of this song cycle.

Song 19

They seize the erect penis, with open 'mouth' . . .
Lifting up the penis, holding it straight . . .
They hold the stone blade against the erect penis, ready to make the incision:
They are always there, men of the southern tribes, clans of the subincision . . .
Cutting along the incisure, cutting the erect penis, those southern clans . . .
They think of the young girls; smeared with blood and ochre and kangaroo fat . . .
In those inland camps, at the place of the bamboo clumps, in the *nonggaru* place . . .
Cutting along the incisure, below the ring at the apex . . .
They are always there, in that country, men of the Spring Water clans . . .

Subincision is carried out within the *nonggaru*. In the song, the penis is made erect to facilitate cutting: but what is meant, is that it is partially and not fully erect. Men discussing this, at the time these songs were recorded, added that an Arnhem Bay man named Dandaungu or Gunung of the Djarwag *mada* (*dua* moiety) had been subincised when he visited Rose River some years before to attend the *kunapipi* rituals. Later he returned to his own country and told of his experiences: the suggestion is that some of these were included in the cycle. There is, however, no further evidence for this, and I did not have the opportunity of meeting him.

Song 20

Clouds rise into the sky, bending down towards the place of the Snake . . .
Masses of yellow clouds with reaching hands, shaking and spreading high up over the sky . . .
Clouds bending down towards the place of the Snake, the place of the Crab, the place of the Catfish . . .
Bending over those southern places, about Rose River . . .
Clouds bending and shaking, crossed by black bands like young girls' breast girdles . . .
Like boomerangs flung up into the clouds, like breast girdles, merging together . . .
They rise high into the sky, spreading across, bending down over the place of the Snake . . .
They stand, indeed, stretching away inland, among the armband bushes, among the clumps of bamboo . . .
They rise, changing their shapes, with small clouds drifting upward . . .
They rise upward in columns, spreading all over the sky . . .
Above the tidal river, stretching above the sea and into the water . . .

Clouds bending down, reaching across like hands, and joining together . . .
Rising into the sky, spreading above the river, the shallows of low tide . . .
Bending down right on to the water, touching the surface . . .
Black bands across them, like breast girdles, like the mark of the crab . . .
Small pieces drift away, rising up like new clouds all over the sky.
Bending down above all those southern places, above Groote Eylandt . . .
Clouds stretching far away, yellow clouds bending down:
For it is the time of the monsoon . . .
The time of heavy rains, when the swamp grass grows, the time of the new shoots . . .
Clouds rise up, standing along in rows:
Shoots of the swamp grass appear, new shoots of grass coming up . . .
The clouds rise up, yellow clouds, reaching like hands into the far distance . . .
Above the barrier hills on Groote Eylandt, above the Sandspit at Ambu Kambu . . .
Clouds changing their shape, bending downward . . .
They stand high up above Groote Eylandt, black rain clouds spreading across them like breast girdles . . .
Dropping down into those southern places at Rose River and Groote Eylandt . . .
Standing above the Macassan Spirit Rocks near Ambu Kambu . . .
Clouds rising and bending down, striking those mainland places, stretching into the place of the Snake . . .
Yellow clouds rising, reaching across like hands, bending down above the Rose River country . . .
There they stand, above the Rose River country . . .
Rising indeed, stretching into the Snake's place, into the very camp of the Snake . . .
New faces appearing among the clouds, bending downward . . .
For here it is the time of the wet season, the time of the new rains . . .

The cycle moves towards its climax. Defloration, ritual coitus and subincision are symbolically manifested in the coming wet season. Clouds, having been formed from blood, ochre, semen and kangaroo fat, now spread over Rose River and Blue Mud Bay and as far as Groote Eylandt: their 'black' bands are likened to the breast girdles worn by young girls.

Much of the symbolism of the clouds, with the scattering of their 'young', is similar to that in the Goulburn Island cycle. Some of these clouds 'stand' or rise above the home of the Lightning Snake. Attracted by them, it emerges, smelling the blood: and with it come the lightning and thunder and the heavy rainstorms.

Song 21

The tongue of the Lightning flashes along the top of the clouds . . .
Making them shine like red ochre, flashing along the yellow clouds . . .
The Lightning Snake moving its tail, rearing its head quickly up from its hole . . .
Great Lightning Snake, flashing along on the clouds:
Coming out from its camp, striking the clouds . . .
The Snake, saltwater creature, making thin streaks of lightning.

Although the Lightning Snake is said to live 'at its home' on the mainland, in line 6 it is also described as living in the sea. Actually, several snakes are involved, and the last is probably a water snake which appears luminous as it slithers through the waters of a tidal creek.

Song 22

Snake crawling on its belly along the ground, leaving its hole . . .
With nose coming out from its hole, striking the ground . . .
Crawling along on its belly, smelling the blood of the girls, from far away . . .
Creature moving its tail, crawling along on its belly, leaving its camp.
Flashing along, with moving tail, as it swallows . . .
For here it is the time of the wet season, the time of the new rains.
It has smelt the young girls' blood, blood from the subincised penis, of the barramundi clansmen.
Swallowing blood as it travels along, flashing like red ochre, with tail moving . . .
Here I swallow the blood, and it goes into my belly . . . [says the Snake]
Flashing along, with its tongue and its tail moving . . .
Swallowing as it crawls along, flashing lightning . . .
Eating blood as it goes, into the place of the bamboo clumps, into the home of the southern clans . . .
Eating blood as it goes, flashing its tongue:
Drinking new rainwater, streaked with blood.
Great Snake, that lives in the salt water . . .
Great Snake, flashing along and making the lightning . . .
Snake, with its backbone, flashing the lightning . . .
Smelling the blood of the young girls, returning to eat:
It flashes its tongue into those inland places, the place of the jungle . . .
Blood from the young girls of the barramundi clans, of the southern tribes . . .
It returns to its home, eating, flashing lightning at the place of the Snake . . .
Flashing along as it moves its backbone . . .

Lightning flashing, thus it is eating blood at the Vagina place, the place of the Snake and the Growing Penis.
Swallowing blood, flashing lightning along like red ochre . . .
Moving its tail, smelling the blood of the young girls . . .
It has smelt the blood, and flashes along to eat . . .
Creature swimming along under the water, thin Snake eating the blood . . .
Crawling along, and swallowing: for here it is the time of the big rains . . .
The time when the swamp grass grows, the time of the new shoots . . .
Flashing along, flickering its tongue as it eats, moving its tail:
Snake in the salt water, moving the tip of its tail, protruding its nose . . .
It flashes along, with its tongue glowing:
Flashing along this way, into the waters, at the Vagina place, the place of the Snake . . .
Lightning flashing along, and vanishing.

The Snake hurries to lap up the blood spilt by the men and girls: as its tongue flickers, the lightning flashes. Rains have now fallen and washed the blood down into the creeks, streaking the water. (Comparison should be made with the Wawalag-Yulunggul mythology: see R. Berndt 1951*a*: Ch. III.) This song thus expresses the fulfilment of the rites.

In the next song the wet season has gone; the grasses are dry.

Song 23

They are lighting small fires, men of the barramundi clans . . .
Lighting small fires, burning along through the grass and foliage . . .
Fire burning low down among the grasses, burning the clumps so the new shoots may come . . .
Burning into the place of the Snake, among the bamboos . . .
Low fires burning, started by men of the southern clans, clans of the subincision . . .
Fire burning low through the place of the Snake . . . leaving long trails of smoke . . .
'How did the fire start?' people are asking.
Clouds of smoke rising like reaching hands, at the place of the Snake . . .
Fire burning the bamboo leaves at the place of the Snake, the place of the subincision, with long trails of smoke.

The wet season has come and gone: the grasses have grown but have now become dry. It is the 'burning grass' period. Fires are said to have been caused by people living in distant clan territories: the billowing 'hands' of smoke form a haze, or mist, across the country. This haze and smoke are likened to the clouds of the wet season, which are regarded as a logical ('natural') consequence of them.

Song 24

The spider goes round and round, spinning its new web, hiding behind its 'shield' . . .
Building its web among the bamboos, at the place of the Snake:
Moving its hands as it spins, among the bamboos at the place of the Snake, the place of the jungle . . .
Spider, twisting about, running along as it spins its thread . . .
In the armband bushes, among those inland places . . .
Building its web, making it large and round, moving its hands as it twists the thread . . .
It grows larger, stretching into the leaves, among the swamp grass and the new shoots . . .
Twisting the thread as it runs: spider, hanging there in its misty web, like haze from the smoke . . .
Twisting its thread among those people of southern clans, clans of the subincision, clans of the barramundi . . .
Spider, twisting its thread, so that its web grows large . . .

The spider's web is likened to the haze of smoke from the bush fires.

Song 25

Rats hopping along, shaking off the misty threads of the spider webs . . .
Grasping the foliage and leaves of the new shoots and the swamp grass . . .
Rats running to and fro, squealing and gossiping among the grasses . . .
Rats running through spider webs, their bodies covered with mist and haze . . .
Rats hopping along, leaving messages on their little tracks.
Hopping along, grasping the foliage at the place of the Snake . . .
Hopping through the bamboos, through the mist of the spider threads.
Rats leaving pawmark messages along their tracks . . .
Among the swamp grasses, and among the new shoots . . .

Among the foliage and spider webs are rats. This small creature is called a 'mouse' by Aborigines. However, it is probably the small marsupial rat; the female of the species is pouched. The rats, so men said, run to and fro like women gossiping, causing trouble (see R. Berndt 1948*a*: 29–32, Song 12). Their squealing resembles the cry of young girls (see Song 12, pages 93–4): compare with Song 27 of the Goulburn Island cycle where a bird catches this rat ('mouse') as it runs along its tracks among the grass.

Song 26

The Morning Pigeon is calling . . .
Bird, with its voice like the speech of those clans, people who talk like birds.
Its cries sound through the haze, through the mist of smoke and of spider threads . . .
Bird, ruffling its feathers and crying . . .
In that sacred camp, in the place of the *nonggaru.*
It flies low, touching the branches of the *nonggaru* shade, of the armband bushes.
Its cry sounds through the mist, like the speech of the southern clans, clans of the subincision . . .
Its cry sounds through the mist, like the speech of the southern clans, clans of the barramundi . . .
In the sacred camp, within the Vagina shade, among the branches at the *nonggaru* place . . .
Bird, with its cry through the mist like the speech of the spirit people, clans of the barramundi . . .
Its cry echoing out, as it enters its nest . . .

The cycle is brought to a close, demonstrating that the rhythm of the seasons is closely co-ordinated with the ways of man. As a dramatic finale, the *jiridja* moiety Morning Star pigeon is heard crying through the smoke haze, its cries resembling the speech heard on the sacred ground at the beginning (for example, in Song 2).

7

THE RITUAL FACE OF LOVE

The theme of the Rose River cycle bears a close resemblance to the Goulburn Island one, although it has a number of important differences. The subject matter of the songs is built up in the following way and is presented for the same reasons as mentioned in Chapter 5.

Men are making defloration boomerangs for the *kunapipi* rites: as they do so, they think about these and about the *nonggaru*. People from various places assemble, some from coastal regions, others from the inland, speaking different dialects and languages. Their voices intermingle, and the sound drifts across the country.

Then men prepare red ochre. Again, the sound drifts across to various places around Rose River. It is heard at the *nonggaru* and at the sacred shade which will later be occupied by women. The boomerangs are smeared with fat and ochre. Thinking of the forthcoming rituals, men invoke the hurricane wind, smearing their own bodies with the same substance.

Men range themselves in rows within the precincts of the sacred ground, talking, standing among the branches of the *nonggaru* and the women's shade. They twirl their boomerangs, throwing them in various directions, calling out the place names and again invoking the hurricane. The boomerangs in their spirit form skim the surface of the sea. Afterwards, they are set out in rows leading into the *nonggaru* and the Vagina shade.

The sound of talking, drifting like the cry of the Morning Pigeon, comes from the sacred shade. Speech of coastal people mingles with inland speech, and *dua* moiety dialects with *jiridja* dialects. A screen is set up to ensure privacy during defloration and ritual coitus. As they build it, men think of the women and of dancing.

The rites begin. Girls are placed ready for defloration. Most come from inland, from the Bush country and belong to subincising groups. Near the screen, girls and women await their turn. Female novices are smeared with fat and red ochre and then deflowered: they squeal, and this sound also drifts over the country around Rose River.

Ritual coitus takes place, between each girl and a series of men. The men's penes are likened to barramundi fish. Two girls rise from the shade and pummel their bellies to release semen: they shake themselves, and dance. Now they are said to have been 'subincised'. They are again smeared with fat and ochre, and with defloration blood, until their bodies shine. Red clouds derived from this blood rise and hover over places near Rose River: they are joined by others, tinged with yellow, representing semen; they merge and spread across the sky, shining like the girls.

The scene changes. Men prepare for subincision. Again, they sit in rows around the *nonggaru* and about the Vagina shade. *Dua* moiety men prepare stone blades for subincising, for the *dua* blade is 'mother' to *jiridja* people. They call invocations to the hills from which the stone is quarried; and they think of copulation and invoke running water.

The subincising begins. The penis is held in position and the incision made with the stone blade. As this takes place, postulants and initiators think of the girls who will be smeared with blood, ochre and fat. One section of the *kunapipi* rites is completed.

In consequence of these rituals, clouds continue to spread across the sky, bending towards Rose River. With them, like young girls' breast girdles, come bands of dark lowering rain clouds. They hover above various places in the Bush and then move towards the coast, skimming the surface of the sea. When the sunlight catches them, they shine like the red-ochred bodies of the girls. Wind scatters them, so that smaller clouds appear, but the main mass bends towards sites on Groote Eylandt; other clouds hover above the home of the Lightning Snake. It is the time of the wet season, when new grass grows.

The Lightning Snake emerges, moving along the bank of clouds, flashing lightning as it goes. As it crawls on its belly along the ground (in its physical, material form), it smells the blood shed by the girls and men. It finds fragments of congealed blood and swallows them, flicking its tongue and flashing lightning, and drinks water streaked with this blood as it crawls through various places. The flashing lightning goes in all directions, around Rose River and Blue Mud Bay, and on to the Vagina shade at the *kunapipi* ground.

The wet season has come and gone. The grasses have dried and fires sweep across the country, lit by people far away. Large masses of clouds rise from them, and haze spreads across the whole country. A spider spins its web among the foliage, and the 'misty' web is likened to the haze of smoke. Rats hop through the foliage and grass, becoming entangled in the spider's threads.

Finally, the Morning Star Pigeon cries. Its sound, like the speech of people of various dialects, 'breaks through' the haze; and it ruffles its feathers, freeing them of webs through which it has flown. It flies over the sacred *kunapipi* ground, over the Bush country, and its cries echo through all those places before it returns to its nest.

From this summary, we are able to glimpse the overall pattern of the cycle. Through the performance of particular parts of the *kunapipi*, the monsoonal season can be induced to come about. The cycle conforms with the accepted local pattern, as expressed through the great religious myths. On the other hand, the actual subject matter is, or was in 1946, to some extent foreign to the north-eastern Arnhem Landers and presumably to the original composers. However, they seem to have found that if the content were to have local appeal it needed to be linked to the traditional north-eastern approach and put within the local framework of assumptions.

Interestingly enough, this was not done in the case of the Djarada (see Chapter 8) which, perhaps for that reason, has never really captured the imagination of people in north-eastern Arnhem Land. Instead, it has remained an alien and intrusive element, in the possession (in 1946–47) of only a few individuals scattered through the various *mada*. Further, the Djarada was not in the local idiom, especially in so far as erotic appeal was concerned. The attitudes of north-eastern Arnhem Landers towards lovemaking are not only conventional and traditionally framed, but have also a certain religious flavour. I have already suggested that for such songs to have an erotic appeal they need to be wrapped up with something else, and to have implications in social, environmental and/or ritual terms. The Djarada, from their point of view, is lacking in these qualities.

The Goulburn Island and Rose River cycles have maintained their popularity because their appeal is not restricted to only a few members of the community. While erotic stimulation may be one of their main aims, or one of their main functions, they have been so thoroughly integrated with established local themes that they are something more than mere vehicles for expressing or releasing sexual emotions. The point needs re-emphasizing, at this juncture, that sexual activity and enjoyment are not isolated or isolable phenomena, confined to the human or even to the animal world. They are an integral part of the general scheme of existence and must therefore be viewed in context, for the principle which underlies them is manifested in a number of different ways. The sexual act itself sets in motion a series of repercussions, affecting not only the persons most intimately concerned but the whole society. In the Goulburn Island sequence, love has this other face—which looks towards the social implications.

The Rose River cycle, while making use of common mythic and symbolic themes, presents a different face. Basically, it finds its inspiration in the *kunapipi* rituals, or in some parts of them. Kunapipi is herself a fertility mother, an unseen but ever-present and all-important figure behind these rituals. She symbolizes the eternal replenishment of natural resources. From her uterus all human and 'totemic' creatures emerged: and their spiritual manifestations continue to receive her stimulation and, in effect, her sponsorship. In her role as Mother, she is linked with a Rainbow Snake (Yulunggul, a rock python or a Lightning Snake), regarded as a symbolic penis. This completes the dual concept of Kunapipi.

In the Rose River cycle, while the significance of the *nonggaru* is apparent, and the ritual acts of defloration, subincision and coitus are aligned mytho-ritually to Kunapipi, Yulunggul is replaced by a *jiridja* moiety Lightning Snake: but the symbolism involved is similar. Copulation, fertilization and procreation are its basic themes, viewed as being interdependent. These themes, as far as the Rose River cycle is concerned, are expressed through defloration, sexual intercourse and subincision.

In other words, the cycle is selective in its content, because many other aspects are covered in the total performance of the *kunapipi*. Defloration, for example, was merely an adjunct to the main ritual sequence and was not always present. When it did take place, it usually preceded ritual coitus. Nevertheless, it does make sense within this particular context. Further, hymen-piercing was seen as complementary to subincision, although these rites were not practised in north-eastern Arnhem Land. The symbolism, however, with the subsequent smearing of participants' bodies with red ochre, grease and defloration or incisure blood, emphasizes ritual commonalty between men and women; both are designated *bala* (subincised = deflowered), while the incised penis = vagina. Symbolically, this refers directly to the fertility Mother's vagina (= uterus).

The matter of smearing blood over the girls and subincised men is ritually significant because, as noted, some of that blood is from the girls themselves. The mytho-ritual cycle of the *kunapipi* is structured on the thematic basis of what can be called a 'return to the Mother's womb', with potential rebirth at emergence. Blood serves as a symbolic focus in this context, and is not simply defloration or incisure blood but is equivalent to afterbirth blood. Arm blood could serve the same purpose, since blood was considered a source of life, containing the essence or 'power' of a spiritual element derived from the Dreaming. Male and female participants in the *kunapipi*, as they entered the ritual ground, symbolically entered the Mother's womb. (The Mother, in this case, is Kunapipi; or, from a north-eastern Arnhem Land perspective, the two Wawalag sisters, or by extension the creative Djanggawul sisters.) The grease, blood and ochre were said to be derived from their stay in the 'womb'. When they were 'reborn', and when they entered the main camp after conclusion of these rites, this blood was living proof of their direct spiritual association with the Mother.

Ritual coitus receives more attention than defloration and subincision. This is because of its direct connection with fecundity. Normally, it served as a climax to a long series of *kunapipi* rituals, the culminating point of many weeks of religious activity. Over and above its stated function, it served to release pent-up emotion, ostensibly to re-establish goodwill between participants. But more importantly, as with ritual defloration, it served to draw the women into the ritual sphere, enabling them to participate in a more than usually direct and positive way. While possessing already an innate essence of sacredness, they were thus brought into the centre of this scheme of ritualization which was (is) more particularly the responsibility of men. At the beginning of things, it will be recalled, women were said to have been both owners and instigators of sacred ritual, with men having a subordinate role in this respect. By sharing in this intimate association between men and women, outside the marital bond but sanctioned in a special way, women assume again their rightful ritual position and, in the process, enhance their procreative ability. It is this aspect which permeates (permeated) the whole of the cycle and the *kunapipi* ritual itself. Thus ritual coitus was extended and elaborated so that it corresponded symbolically to similar phenomena among the natural species and in fact the whole of nature. Within such a setting, a symbolic but dynamic vision of seasonal fluctuation was established.

Ritual intercourse especially (with its subsidiary elements), as expressed through the Rose River cycle, substantiated indigenous religious values. In addition, however, it constituted a vehicle for the erotic. North-eastern Arnhem Landers, being in the position of 'outsiders', viewed such material as sexually exciting, but since they were not too far removed from it spatially they recognized its sacred character. Further, the mythic and ideological structure was dovetailed into their own traditional frame of reference. Nevertheless, the *kunapipi* as such, in 1946–47, still had a glamorous or exotic quality which, while emphasizing eroticism, did not detract from its religious significance. The *kunapipi* in its original form is most sacred.

The similarities between the Goulburn Island cycle and the Rose River cycle are quite marked. In the former, the focus is on the Wawalag-Yulunggul myth (with the Djanggawul in the background). In the Rose River cycle, the intrusive *kunapipi* is also substantiated by Wawalag mythology, but in a different way. That difference lies in two directions.

Firstly, the 'original' mythology (in so far as source mythology is concerned) of the *kunapipi* was not that of the Wawalag (see R. Berndt 1951*a*: 85–7, 144–54). As already mentioned, it was cast within the idiom of the Wawalag and so made more acceptable for local consumption. Referring, for the moment, to the Djarada: it will be recalled that stylistically the songs depended on a compressed key-word patterning which is essentially of southern derivation. That pattern was also adhered to in secret-sacred and 'outside' (sacred, non-secret) *kunapipi* singing in north-eastern Arnhem Land (R. Berndt 1951*a*: Ch. VII and VIII). In that case, the style or verse structure was not altered, although some adjustment took place in relation to content. On the other hand, the Rose River cycle has gone more than a step further. Its original and, no doubt, subsequent composers selected certain elements within the original *kunapipi* and transformed both style *and* content.

Secondly, the mythic basis of *both* love song cycles is the Wawalag (plus accretions), in its secret-sacred and 'outside' expressions. However, the Goulburn Island cycle makes use of only one aspect of Wawalag mythology—namely, the events which occurred in the vicinity of the sacred waterhole in which Yulunggul resided, and subsequent happenings which led to the swallowing of the two sisters. Its ritual equivalent is the *djunggawon* rituals, relating to circumcision, and a clue to this is a transposition of the ritual situation suggested by the uncircumcised condition of Goulburn Island men. On the other hand, the Rose River cycle uses a different sector of the Wawalag mythology, and one which more closely approximates original *kunapipi* source-mythology. It focuses on the initial incestuous relations of the elder Wawalag sister with a clansman, before the two sisters commenced their journey to Yulunggul's waterhole. Attached to this is the theme of birth and rebirth, and of fertility in general terms. It therefore corresponds quite directly with the north-eastern Arnhem Land Wawalag-sponsored *kunapipi*. However, that essential *kunapipi* theme is altered (at least to some extent) by the inclusion of a *jiridja* moiety mythic Lightning Snake.

Wawalag mythology is manifested through three ritual sequences: the *djunggawon*, *kunapipi* and *ngurlmag*. The first re-enacts the swallowing of the two sisters, and of the various creatures which they had caught for food but which escaped into the sacred waterhole when put into the ashes for cooking. The second concerns the swallowing of young men, the presence of Yulunggul after the Wawalag-swallowing, and various dances relating to copulation and procreation. And the third and final sequence relates to a special shade or shelter (*murlg*) and to other snakes associated with Yulunggul (see R. Berndt 1951*a*: 37). However, although such divisions as these are made, each sequence draws to some degree on the total myth. The love song cycles are therefore constructed so as to conform with recognized themes, or sections of these, which are worked out in much more detail in the main religious rituals. In contrast to the Goulburn Island cycle, the emphasis in the Rose River songs is on ritual *per se*.

The songs mention the *nonggaru* and the sacred shade. The *nonggaru* (or *nanggaru*) in north-eastern Arnhem Land represents the sacred waterhole or billabong, Muruwul or Miraraminar, from which the Yulunggul emerged. On the sacred ground where the ritual reenactment takes place, it is symbolized by a large hole. Complementing this, although no reference is made to it here, is the *ganala* (*kanala*), a crescent-shaped trench. Nearby is the *murlg* (the shade or shelter representing the actual hut used by the Wawalag at Muruwul: this is equivalent to the sacred shade mentioned in the songs). Other temporary constructions are the Vagina shade in which coitus takes place, and the dividing screen. The *nonggaru* was also symbolically interpreted (in the original *kunapipi* versions) as the uterus of the Mother, the *ganala* as the channel ('river') or passage of the vagina (or in some cases, directly as the uterus). Also, both the *murlg* and the special Vagina shade were interpreted as being symbolic of the uterus.

Further, coitus was ritualized. While dancing was in progress, *kunapipi* partners would retire to the Vagina shade or *murlg*; or, since there are variations to this theme, they might already be there if they had been or were to be deflowered. The women concerned either stayed in the hut to receive other men, or returned to the dancing. Should more men than women be present at the ritual, the women would most likely (according to reports of such events) be expected to remain in the hut for the entire evening. In that case, there might be several huts or windbreaks, with screens, on or near the sacred ground, one for each woman. And, additionally, there is the ritual importance of subincision.

A major difference between the two cycles lies in their varying focus on ritual. In the Goulburn Island songs, erotic manifestations are primarily social. The implications relate to other persons, as persons. Further, sexual actions have implications which concern the environment and result in bringing about the monsoonal season. The emphasis, therefore, is on *social* action in the form of social relationships and not on specifically ritual action (although, of course, ritual can still be spoken of as being social), and it is this which brings about the desired result. Or, to put it another way, it is the symbolism of the sacred myth which is used to achieve these ends, not its transformation in ritual—even though some aspects of ritual are implied. As I have noted, that particular face of love is social *and* sacred.

The Rose River cycle presents a different face of love. It is one which is highly formalized and ritually circumscribed. There is no doubt that this can be just as exciting (to quote Aboriginal opinion) as can the other, although it permits little room for choice. Further, participants, both male and female, are regarded as intermediaries—not as direct agents in achieving their goals. They are subordinated to ritual supplication through the Mother and her mythic companion, the *jiridja* moiety Lightning Snake, who are *jointly* responsible for universal fertility—although the instrument through which this is achieved is human action. The sexual act itself is sanctified; and the partners concerned are *ritual partners* rather than sexual partners, since they should necessarily in ordinary mundane life be tabu to each other. I am not saying that this involves a diminution of eroticism, because where the *kunapipi* is known and performed Aborigines generally identify (or used to identify) sexuality in these terms. Also, it is quite obvious that the Rose River cycle has capitalized on that particular aspect and has attempted to enhance it. The *idea* of it is sufficient to stimulate erotic feelings. After all, presumably, this is part of the intent of the songs. Nevertheless, responses are stimulated by a particular kind of symbolism, and the context itself—the ritual context—and its implications vis-à-vis *kunapipi* ideology are significant elements.

It is useful, then, to compare the respective profiles of the Rose River and Goulburn Island cycles. Both draw on the same mythology, but the Rose River cycle concentrates on some aspects of *kunapipi* ritual and indirectly on the Wawalag myth itself. The central focus is the *nonggaru*, as a primary ritual representation or symbol within which or near which human ritual takes place in defloration, subincision and coitus. The Wawalag and *dua* moiety *nonggaru* is balanced by the *jiridja* moiety Lightning Snake (replacing the *dua* Yulunggul usually seen in relation to the Wawalag). Mytho-ritual conjunction is symbolically implied. An interesting symbolic reversal is thus presented. In the Goulburn Island cycle, mythic conjunction takes place between the Wawalag and Yulunggul, who are of the same moiety, while human copulation is inter-moiety. In the Rose River cycle, mythic conjunction is inter-moiety while, traditionally, human ritual copulation on the *kunapipi* ground is intra-moiety.

Diagram 4 depicts four elements of its symbolic character: preparation, ritual expression, fulfilment of aims, and aftermath. In the first (left-hand circle), actions relate to the preparation of a symbolic frame which enables (lower right-hand circle) natural growth to take place. For instance, boomerangs (= penes) are placed in rows, upright, leading into the *sanctum sanctorum* (the *nonggaru*); their throwing = coitus: but their placement in that particular way simulates or engenders clouds which presage the wet season. Together, with the attributes of kangaroo fat (= semen) and red ochre (= blood), they represent a life-giving force which is released through the holy power of the Kunapipi (= *nonggaru*).

The significant diagrammatic interpretation of the left-hand circle concerns

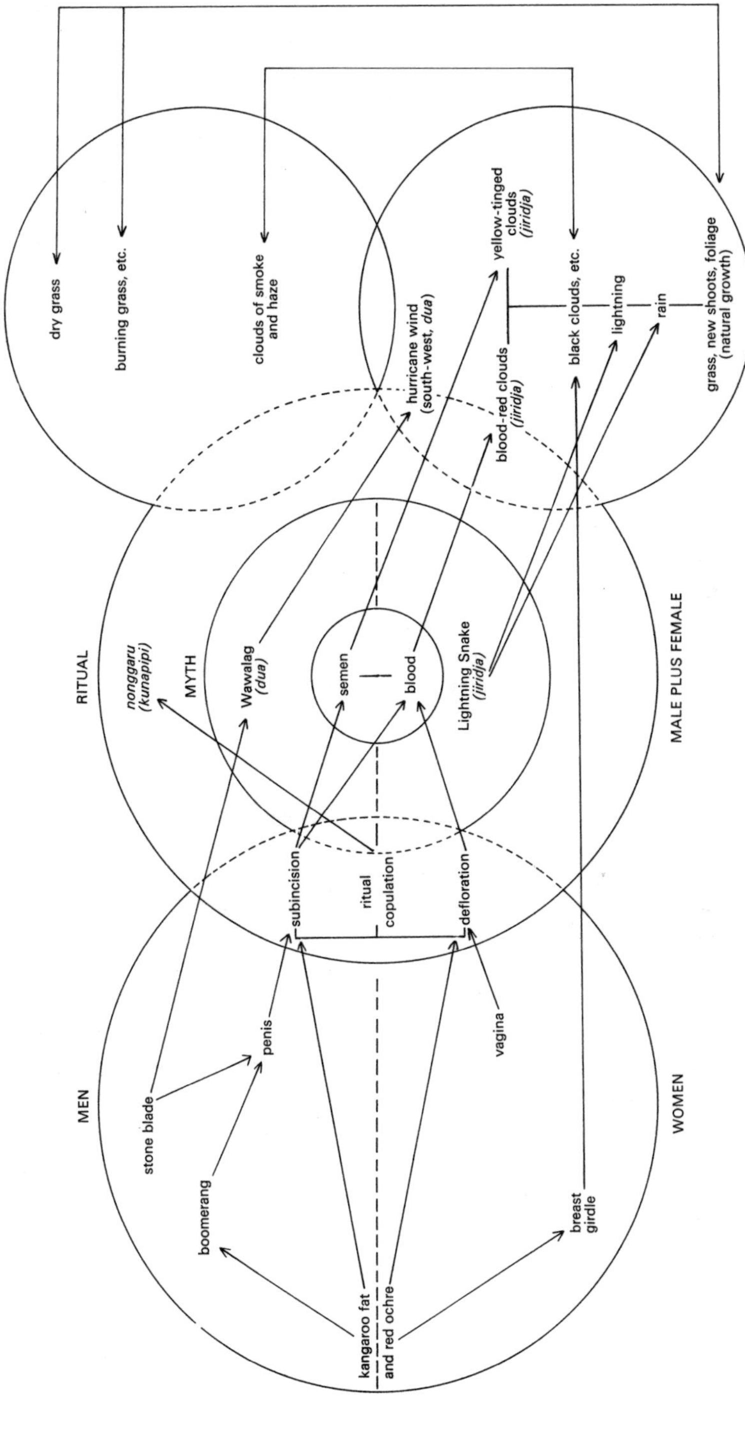

Diagram 4 Profile of the Rose River Cycle

the equivalence of males and females. Their essential ingredients may be separated out: for instance, subincised penis—vagina; semen—blood; stone blade—breast girdle; etc. They are brought together in the defloration-subincision equation. A girl on being deflowered is equivalent to a man having been incised; a man on being subincised is equivalent to a menstruating female. Ritually, they are made equal, and this is emphasized in two ways—through ritual coitus as an act in itself; and through (traditionally) intra-moiety coitus in terms of specific persons. That is, inter-moiety sexual relations are the ordinary rule, in which each of the partners involved belongs (must belong) to a different moiety. Here, they have the *same* moiety affiliation, which is said to obliterate sexual distinctions. However, although sexual equality at the ritual level is recognized, it is not sustained in the mytho-ritual sphere, nor in the focus on the two life-giving elements, semen and blood.

In the lower right-hand circle, male and female aspects are apparent. It is the Wawalag myth that brings about the south-west *dua* moiety hurricane wind which disperses the clouds symbolically derived from blood and semen, and from which emerge the black, rain-laden clouds. The *jiridja* moiety Lightning Snake is responsible for the rain which falls and, in conjunction with female elements, for natural growth.

The upper right-hand circle continues the theme further, providing it with a more direct *jiridja* moiety slant. The Lightning Snake and the burning of the grass provide a link with the Laindjung-Banaidja mytho-ritual constellation. The sequence from one season to another, from wet to dry, has in this particular song cycle no transition period. For that one must refer to the 'honey wind' and rain for which the *dua* moiety mythic being Woial, or Wudal, is responsible (see C. Berndt 1970*b*: 1311–5, especially 1321).

The Rose River cycle, then, is concerned—among other things—with life-renewal (as is the Goulburn Island cycle), but also, in one sense, with decay or death. While this aspect of the cycle does have undertones of the *jiridja* moiety Land of the Dead (Badu) cycle, they are muted, and it is perhaps irrelevant to refer to them here. Further, the dry season is not markedly a period of decay or food scarcity, since (as Songs 24 and 25 make clear) it is a period of harvesting what the wet season has caused to grow. But the last four songs do present a vision of the future—emphasizing the recycling of events, signalled by the cry of the *jiridja* moiety Morning Star pigeon which returns to its nest in the sacred *nonggaru*, 'like a *jiridja* child returning to its *dua* mother'.

8

THE DJARADA

The third cycle is the north-eastern Arnhem Land version of the Djarada (or Djarara), which has been brought into this region by way of Rose River. I have used the term 'cycle' for it merely as a matter of convenience. It is not really a 'cycle' in the same way as the Goulburn Island and Rose River series are. Rather, it consists of a range or collection of songs which are not necessarily connected one with another in the sense of forming a sequence. What they share is a theme, a set of assumptions and beliefs about the magical power of such songs to shape people's behaviour and attitudes. But they deal with similar, not common, aims.

The name Djarada was explained locally to mean: 'If you sing these songs you get something out of them—that is, a girl. This way, we can get sweethearts'. Djarada are also sung by women, but not in this area. As far as the Yirrkalla area is concerned, my wife recorded none from women, although Songs 19 and 20 were said to be sung by them. All were sung for me by men, as part of the men's Djarada. Since I recorded these in 1946–47, I have not been able to collect further examples at Yirrkalla or, for that matter, elsewhere in north-eastern Arnhem Land. Reference should be made to R. Berndt (1951*a*: 17, 59, 174), where this series is linked to the *kunapipi*. In western Arnhem Land too, the Djarada was not generally known. However, my wife recorded some there in 1949–50 from an earlier friend of hers, a Wadaman woman visiting Oenpelli with her Maiali husband (see C. Berndt 1965: 248, 251–4; also, for the central-west of the Northern Territory, C. Berndt 1950*b*: Ch. V). And I have collected others from different areas over the years.

This particular cycle is associated with Gargan, or Gargain (Chicken Hawk Dreaming man), and conforms to some extent with the Roper River Djarada as well as the west-central Northern Territory versions. All of the comments, except when references are made to other areas, are based on Aboriginal explanations. It was usual, when I recorded these songs, for the men concerned to interpret these succinct renderings in their own terms: to say what they understood the words to mean, and then to elaborate on that meaning.

Song 1

Swelling breasts, protuberant nipples . . .

A man sings of his sweetheart's breasts.

Song 2

The fly I send attracts her notice . . .

Through the agency of the song, a small fly flickers persistently round a girl's eyes as she walks or sits in the camp. She blinks, and realizes that someone is trying to attract her attention. She looks round, and sees a man. Once he has her attention, he touches his shoulder, intimating by a sign what direction he will take. This 'hitting the shoulder' is said to 'send her out to the bush' where they meet and copulate: the power of the Djarada is strong enough to make her comply with his wishes.

Song 3

Singing, I see her blood flowing . . .

A man sings of his sweetheart's menstruation and of her desirability. As noted in the Goulburn Island cycle, menstruation was said to trigger off an emotional state in both sexes: sexual excitement was intensified and a girl's attractiveness enhanced. There are two reasons why this might be so. At such periods, a woman was normally subject to certain tabus, including a ban on sexual relations. The assumption is that men are stimulated by this inaccessibility. A man might, therefore, sing about his sweetheart, persuading her to meet him as soon as she was able to do so. (This belief has some parallels in other areas, for example, in the central-west of the Northern Territory and in north-western South Australia.) Also, much emphasis is placed on this aspect in the Wawalag and Djanggawul songs, and on the mixture of attraction and danger which contributes to the quality of sacredness.

Song 4

Hail and rain stream down her body,
Spreading out into pools around her.
The chicken hawk cries as it sees her . . .

A man sings of the girl he hopes to attract. As he sings, he makes the cry of a chicken hawk (he 'takes sound for this bird'; 'he sends the cry to get her'), which is heard by the girl. He envisages her as standing naked, with rain streaming down her body to form pools of spreading water, which symbolically refers to semen. This image of her is said to enhance her attractiveness.

Song 5

She is soaping her hair and washing her body,
And her vulva is stinging.
The cry of the chicken hawk as it sees her!

Soap (see Appendix 3, page 228) stings a girl's vulva as she washes herself: but this is because a particular man is singing Djarada for her. As she rubs herself, she turns and sees him hiding behind a tree. He beckons, and she goes to him.

Song 6

Our handkerchiefs, blown by the wind, are
flapping about our necks.

Handkerchiefs (see Appendix 3, page 228) have been exchanged between lovers, who wear them knotted around their necks. This implies mutual attachment and sexual intimacy. Usually, such an exchange (which could refer to a variety of articles) would take place away from the camp when the lovers were playing together.

Song 7

Throat feathers from the emu, blown in the wind . . .
Throat feathers from the emu, tell her to go out into the bush . . .

A man prepares a small bunch of emu throat feathers. He sings over them, so that they are magically blown towards a girl, enter her vagina, and tickle her. She immediately goes out into the bush to join him.

Song 8

Smoke spreads out from the quickly twirling firestick,
Singeing the chicken hawk's feathers.

The force of the Djarada singing wafts the smell of singeing chicken hawk feathers towards a man's sweetheart: when it reaches her, she runs to meet him.

The song is symbolic. In practice, the feathers would not be singed. This is a mythological reference inseparable from conventional Djarada. The smell is from smoke made by twirling a firestick (see Chapter 1, page 7 and Appendix 3, page 229).

Song 9

A flock of chicken hawks, crying out as they fly:
Crying as they skim over a girl's head . . .

Chicken hawks fly over a girl, plucking some of her hair. Immediately she knows that her sweetheart wants her and that the magic of the Djarada has entered her. The man sees the chicken hawks, too. He seizes his spear and 'thrower' and runs into the bush, following the circling birds. The girl leaves what she is doing and goes after him, hiding behind a large paperbark tree. The persistent hawks encircle her, guiding him to her, and as they do so they cry: 'She is there! She is there!' (see Appendix 3, page 229).

By the time the man reaches her, she is asleep. Bending down, he moves her head from side to side to awaken her, saying, 'You can get up now. What's wrong with you? Why are you asleep?' She awakens and looking up at him says, 'I want you'.

If she already has a husband, she says: 'I don't want my own husband, I'll leave him. I want you!' He replies, 'Why is that? If I take you, there'll be trouble from him'. 'No', she insists, 'I don't want him. You are the man I want. You have been singing for me, you sent the chicken hawks. You sent them skimming over me'. He admits this. They copulate, then they elope to another territory or stay in hiding in almost inaccessible country for an extended period.

In actual examples of elopement, a couple might stay away from their home camp or home area until the first child was born, then return to face the girl's husband. Usually fighting of some kind would be involved. If a rapprochement was reached, the aggrieved husband would demand some kind of settlement, and some kind of compensation. If no child were born, the girl might return to her original husband or to her parents' camp. Many elopements seem to have been love matches, and then the couple would go to a great deal of trouble to stay together. But other elopements were short-lived—some (apparently) because they were prompted simply by a desire for excitement and adventure, or because the idea, the person and the opportunity happened to coincide. In such cases, when the guilty pair returned, it was the man more often than the woman who bore the full brunt of punishment.

There are also reported examples where a woman tried to seduce a man more or less against his will: she would persuade him to elope and then, after staying with him for a short period, leave to return to her own home camp and husband, accusing the interloper of having seduced her. For this reason, men asserted, a man needed to be clear about what a woman wanted to do before taking the serious step of eloping—because, however mild the consequences, he would be answerable sooner or later to the girl's family and to her husband, as well as to his own kin. It was not usually something one could embark on casually. Hence the exchange between the Djarada singer and the girl; the intention, said the men discussing this, was to convey to those who heard the song that clarity of purpose was necessary, along with some awareness of the likely outcome. The matter could be far more serious in the case of a married woman. But even if it were a girl who was still unmarried and living with her parents, she would almost certainly be betrothed, and then the repercussions might be virtually the same. If she was not betrothed, for example if a prearranged betrothal had fallen through, the elopement might be regarded as a form of marriage and little argument might follow—provided compensatory payments were made to those concerned, *and* provided the two were in a correct intermarrying relationship.

In any case, the singing of such a Djarada song as this was said to be dangerous, because it was (and is) generally recognized that even a harmless pre- or extra-marital liaison could potentially implicate a relatively large number of persons. However, such a song might involve no more than a transitory, more or less illicit interlude.

Song 10

Giving her tea for drinking . . .

A man gives a cup of tea (see Appendix 3, page 229) to a woman he desires. This tea has been 'sung over', and contains within it the Djarada's power. After drinking it, she becomes anxious to be with him.

The commentators described what they said was an actual incident associated with such love-magic. Having drunk the tea, a woman sought out the singer and found him lying down on his back. She squatted over him, and had coitus in that position.

This form of intercourse was said to be favoured by a woman who wanted to take the initiative—even though a man might claim responsibility for stimulating her in the first place, for instance through the Djarada. In one example, at Yirrkalla, a middle-aged man told me of such an experience. He was lying asleep beside a bush track, he said, having an erotic dream, and his penis was erect. Several women came along the track and saw him lying beside it. Quietly, they crept towards him: one squatted over him and inserted his penis and moved up and down a little; then another took her place and did likewise. She was followed by two or three others, until he ejaculated. At that point, he awoke and was surprised to find a woman over him: he had thought he was dreaming. The women walked off thinking it a great joke.

Song 11

Flaking a fragment of dark tobacco . . .

This situation referred to is similar to that noted in Song 12.

Song 12

Rolling flaked tobacco in paper . . .

A man rolls a cigarette, giving it to his sweetheart: she smokes this and becomes 'drunk' (giddy) and 'dies' (faints), falling asleep. The man goes out into the bush and she follows him when she has recovered. When they meet, she says, 'You gave me a different smoke by singing Djarada. I want you now, you can take me'.

Song 13

Kneading and shaping the damper, ready for cooking.

After a man has prepared damper, he gives some to his sweetheart to eat. Later that same night, she comes to him. He has 'sung Djarada' into the damper and this proves irresistible to her. (Compare with Song 16.)

Song 14

Holding his penis during coitus . . .

The group of north-eastern Arnhem Landers discussing this song explained it as follows. A frustrated man whose advances a woman has consistently resisted sings this Djarada in petty revenge. He sneaks around the camp until he finds a couple copulating, or surreptitiously follows someone he thinks may be hurrying to keep a secret assignation. It is not necessary that the woman should be the one who has refused him. Coming upon them unseen, he sings this song: its magic causes interlocation, the man's penis being held by the girl's vagina. The lovers go to sleep in this position. A little later, the other pretends to stumble upon them. They awaken, and the man attempts to withdraw his penis but is unable to do so. He asks the other to help him: 'Can you pull me? I have been copulating with this girl [who may or may not be his wife], and I've tried to pull out my penis but it won't come. Would you help me?' The other seizes him by the hips and tries to pull him away from her, but his penis remains firmly within her. It all depends, the commentators said, on the singer. If he 'sings back' the Djarada, the victim's penis retracts and all is well. If he refuses, the period of interlocation could be prolonged—but the time limit was not specified, and the possible endings were left to the imagination.

Song 15

Sending to you the native companion bird . . .

A man sees two women leaving the camp for food-collecting: he then sings this Djarada. The women 'feel its magic'. They take their digging sticks and stand them upright in the ground, symbolizing a native companion's beak, which in turn symbolizes a man's penis: putting it into the ground suggests coitus. After performing this rite, they look round for the singer. They see him nearby and run towards him: they finger his penis, and he copulates with each in turn.

Song 16

Hurting herself with her yam stick . . .

A man sings the power of this song towards a particular woman. Feeling it, she takes up her digging stick and leaves the main camp with a group of women. They go out among the paperbark trees, and there she begins to strip off the bark, using her stick as a wedge. As she inserts the stick and levers it, it slips and falls, striking her heel. She turns to the others and says, 'I've hurt myself badly. You go back and leave me here till I feel better, then I'll follow you'. The others leave her to rest. When they are out of sight, she goes to meet the singer, who is waiting nearby. Later she rejoins her companions and they all return to the camp together. (Compare with Song 13.)

Song 17

Oh, the girl's urine and faeces!

Again, the commentators elaborated on the meaning of the song. A man leaves the camp in search of the place where the girl he desires has defecated. Finding it, he sings this Djarada song while putting a stick into the middle of it and moving it up and down to signify coition. (This love-magic technique was said to be sometimes practised in the Western Desert: see R. and C. Berndt 1943: 134–5.) Then he partially defaces her footmarks, rubbing out the imprint of toe and sole and leaving only the heel. Facing in the direction opposite the way her original tracks were leading, he superimposes his own footprint, leaving her heel so that it appears to be joined to his.

Later, when the Djarada power has had time to work, the girl may go out to collect bush food. On the way, she feels a sexual urge: her vagina itches and she scratches her pubic hair. Returning to the camp, she thinks about this, and decides that some one has 'sung' her. That day she sees the man responsible for this, and makes a sign that she will talk to him in the seclusion of the nearby bushes. When they meet she asks: 'What's wrong with you?' He feigns ignorance: 'What do you mean?' 'You know very well', she answers. 'You have been singing Djarada for me. You put that stick into the middle of that urine I left: you have made my vagina itch.' 'No, I didn't do it', he replies. 'Ah, you're trying to trick me', she continues, 'but I know you've been singing for me!' She takes hold of him and laughingly they struggle together and have coitus.

Song 18

See her pubic hairs, under her skirt. . . !

A man projects the power of the Djarada towards a girl. This causes the wind to blow aside her skirt (see Appendix 3, page 230), revealing her pubes. The wind blows her pubic hairs, and she feels the Djarada: she knows some one has been 'singing' her. She looks round, and seeing the man says, 'I want you, I don't want my own husband. You have to take me!' (See Song 9.)

Song 19

Cutting himself as he shaves . . .

Although this song is incorporated in the male Djarada, men said that women may sing it too.

Seeing a man shaving, a woman sings this, making him cut himself slightly. As the blood oozes from the cut he realizes that the Djarada has caused it: looking round, he sees the girl. He watches the direction she takes and soon afterwards follows her.

Song 20

Lifting his hat to scratch his hair . . .

A woman desiring a man may sing this Djarada song, although (as with the last) it belongs to the men's series. The singing causes a man's hat to blow off. It is carried towards a woman who seizes it and runs off with it into the bush. He chases her and finds her waiting: they have coitus and she returns his hat. (Hats of this kind, with wide upturned brims, were commonly used by Aboriginal stockmen on cattle stations near the Roper River and also by mission workers in that area. In 1946–47, they were only infrequently worn on the northern Arnhem Land coast.)

Song 21

There she is, opening oysters and eating them . . .

Singing, a man watches his sweetheart opening oysters and eating them. She feels the song enter her, and walks round in search of the singer. They go out into the bush to 'play'. (Such a song may also be associated with elopement. The song implies that the woman will become a food-collector for her lover and not for her own husband.)

Song 22

The blue-tongue lizard there, with its tail . . .

A man sings this Djarada for a girl who lies resting in her camp. It causes a blue-tongue lizard to crawl towards her, awakening her with its tail (= penis). Rising, she goes to her lover, who is waiting in the bush. There she unties his naga (cotton loin covering, commonly worn at that time). Pulling at his penis (saying, 'Blue-tongue lizard tail, awaken me!'), she moves quickly away, still holding it. He pushes her on to the ground and, before having coitus, drags his penis over her body, like the tail of the lizard.

Song 23

Tail of the scorpion, standing upright . . .

A man's sweetheart may be sick, or not feel like erotic play: she lies in her camp with clay marks across her breasts (indicating sickness). He is sorry for her and would like to see her well and happy. So, he sings this Djarada, which symbolically refers to his penis (= scorpion's upright tail), which 'bites' (= is inserted into her) and arouses her.

Soon she feels better, gets up and flutters her eyes at him. She desires sexual attention, and will probably take the initiative in lovemaking. She comes over and sits with him, or sneaks up to his camp at night; or she may seize his arm, dragging him into the seclusion of some bushes.

Song 24

Ah, the blanket lizard with upright frill . . .

After singing this song, a man kills a blanket lizard and cooks it over the coals. He hangs it up for his sweetheart, and then sings the song again. After a while she comes to him, and he offers her the lizard. She eats it and immediately feels strange and 'scratches her tongue' (that is, puts her finger down her mouth) and vomits. Feeling better, she looks round for him, makes a sign, and runs away: he catches her and they copulate.

Song 25

Churning up dust as she runs . . .

Singing this song, a man causes his sweetheart to run away from the camp through the nearby bush: her running feet raise dust. He follows her in a leisurely way, and finally catches up with her.

Song 26

Collecting paperbark, and making it ready . . .

With this song, a man 'sends' his sweetheart out to collect sheets of soft bark, which she wedges from the trees with her digging stick. Collecting together a large bundle and balancing it on her head, she returns to the main camp. There she makes a paperbark bed. Later, it rains, and she covers herself completely with the sheets of bark. Unobserved by others, the man crawls towards her and joins her under the bark.

Song 27

Rain falls, on the woman sitting there . . .

Rain is falling as a man sings this Djarada. Its power causes his sweetheart to sit with rain streaming over her body. He comes up to her, and they copulate in the rain. (Compare with Song 4.)

Song 28

She is pregnant by me, and the child's spirit has entered her . . .

This Djarada has two interpretations.

The first tells of a man who has 'put a baby' into his wife or the woman with whom he has eloped. He then dreams of the unborn child's Spirit Landing (see Chapter 2). He sees his child's spirit (foetus-animator) in a dream, in association with a particular natural species (usually a fish), and the spirit tells its father that it is ready to enter its mother.

This example underlines the contention that Djarada are not concerned only with illicit love or promiscuous liaisons. While sanctioning (in one sense, legitimizing) pre- and extra-marital relations, they also substantiate traditional marriage patterns.

A man would sing this song, the commentators said, 'because he has been doing it [copulating] with a woman so many times': he wants 'to give her a child quickly [that is, through frequent intercourse], so the spirit child will come and go into her'. When he has sung this, he says, 'I've got my child. I'll be all right now. This is the first time I've had a child. I have my child because I've been doing it with her many times, making that child'. That is, a man's physical and spiritual assistance in the production of a child is emphasized. He is pleased at the prospect of becoming a father and sings about it, giving some of the credit to the power of the Djarada.

In the second interpretation, the commentators added, a man sings this while his wife, or sweetheart, is collecting lily roots in a nearby billabong. The woman squats with legs apart in order to grub out the roots: she wears no loin covering. As he sings, a little *bildu* fish swims towards her and enters her vulva and passes into the uterus. She feels it and, getting up, attempts to shake it out: but she can't. She realizes then that she is pregnant, for the fish is the material representation of a spirit child. Such an experience might occur a month or so after the cessation of her menstrual flow, sometimes much later. The fish, in this case, is said to be sent by the Djarada, which has the reputed power of guiding a spirit child to its physical home, the foetus. It is because of this that words in the song are translated as 'red walls of the vagina' and 'clitoris' (see Appendix 3, page 231): the *bildu*, entering her vagina, tickles the clitoris, making the woman aware of its entry.

(A similar incident occurs in the Djanggawul cycle. There, small fish float into the vulvas of the two creative sisters. A women's version of this same cycle relates that before the sisters could have children the *gabila* fish entered and 'opened' them. That is, the reference is to a spirit child who enters on the back of a fish, in order to animate the foetus: in this context, too, a fish = penis, signifying male fertilization. But also see Chapter 2, in reference to the *dugaruru*.)

Song 29

Smearing herself with red ochre . . .

A man sings about his wife, who has just borne a child. She is lying exhausted, painted all over with red ochre (symbolizing, in this case, the placenta). After having slept and rested, she goes out to obtain wood from the *gudu* 'black' tree. She burns this, and uses the charcoal to draw marks on her shoulders. She also rubs some of it over her newly-born child to 'wash off' its pale colouring, to ensure that it will have a chocolate-brown skin.

Song 30

Ah, the flat pointed boomerang!

Sung by a man, this song refers to the defloration boomerang used in *kunapipi* rituals (see the Rose River song cycle). These boomerangs are thrown into the camp where young girls are singing and dancing, as a sign that the defloration rites will begin soon.

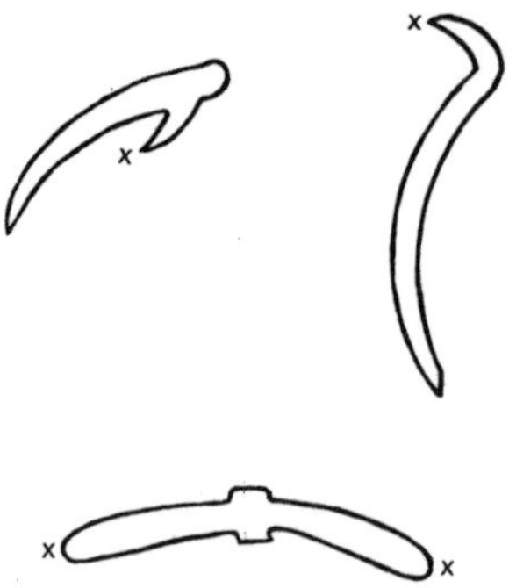

x = the point used in defloration

Diagram 5 Djarada Defloration Boomerangs

Song 31

Chipping and scraping, smoothing the boomerang.

A man sings about the coming ritual defloration of his betrothed. Men have gone to cut wood from which the special boomerang will be fashioned (see Diagram 5, also Diagram 8, page 197). For the significance of this, see the Rose River cycle. In this context, contradictory information was offered. It was said that the girl who was to be ritually deflowered might accompany her classificatory sisters into the bush, and there they would make the boomerang which was later handed over to the men.

Since many girls who took part in these rites would no longer be virgins, the piercing of the hymen might be symbolic or nominal rather than actual. Nevertheless, not all girls would go through the rites, so it was said, even at Rose River: but most were expected to participate in ritual intercourse.

A girl's childhood partners in erotic play might be of her own age, or a little older, and actual insertion might or might not take place. In any case, the penes of older boys are smaller than those of adults, so that although her hymen might have been pierced her vagina would not have been expanded through adult intercourse. If she wanted further sexual experience with men (the commentators said), she might ask an older sister: 'Sister, will you help me to make my vagina larger, for men?' The two would go out into the bush, and make a defloration boomerang. Then the older girl would say, 'I'll try to break you with this boomerang'. The younger would lie back with her legs apart, while the boomerang point was inserted to force an entrance until the hymen was pierced. If this had already been done, the boomerang would be moved up and down at successive intervals in order to enlarge the vagina. A girl might deflower her younger sister in this way, and later hand over the same boomerang to the men for a symbolic performance during the actual rite. The reason given was that this would save her from pain during the *kunapipi*.

Song 32

Blood running down, from her pierced hymen.

A man sings of his sweetheart's defloration; blood from this flows into the sky, where it forms a red cloud (see the Rose River cycle, for example, Song 16).

It was considered desirable that blood should flow, since this demonstrated that a girl had not engaged in pre-marital intercourse. The song overlooks the possibility that she may have been pierced by her elder sister before the rite; but it expresses a conventional attitude. In 'the old days', the commentators said, girls were able to control their desires before ritual defloration and were proud when blood flowed from their piercing. A girl who was not a virgin would feel ashamed by the absence of blood. In such a case, men would say, 'the penis has come before the boomerang', and during ritual coitus she would be subjected to intensive and rough handling by many men, more than she could conceivably enjoy, and more than girls who had conformed with traditional expectations.

Song 33

The native companion bird flew over . . .

It is possible that the commentators here were guessing at the translation of this song (see Appendix 3, page 232), at least in its specific 'bits' if not in its overall meaning: none of its words conforms with those in the native-companion song (15) mentioned above. However, the discussion of it went like this. Two women are walking through the bush, while a man sings this Djarada. This bird materializes and flies over them. Seeing it, they run. The bird follows, skimming over them from time to time, until it sweeps down and plucks some hair from their heads. (This resembles Song 9, where a chicken hawk is also said to swoop down and pluck hair.)

Feeling their hair plucked and seeing the bird flying away, they return to their camp: they know someone has sung Djarada for them. When they see the man concerned (they can identify him automatically through the power of the Djarada), they persuade him to join them, and the three of them go into the bush away from the camp. The women lie down close together, and the man copulates with one, then the other. He moves from one to the other until he ejaculates. He repeats this performance.

(Although this case purports to be an actual one, it is probably based on the behaviour of the two mythic sisters known in the Roper River region, and elsewhere, as the Munga-munga. They were responsible for instituting the Djarada and both are associated also with the *kunapipi*. From a north-eastern Arnhem Land perspective, they are identified with the two Wawalag [see R. Berndt 1951*a*: e.g. 148–52; also C. Berndt 1950*b*]. This song and several others belong to the southern or central-west Northern Territory Munga-munga Djarada. In the process of diffusion into the Rose River area, they have been included in more localized cycles.)

Song 34

They are thirsty for water . . .

A man sings, as two women drink water. They feel its coldness as it 'runs down their throats into their stomachs'. The Djarada is responsible for this. They rub their throats and navels, but soon realize that the Djarada's power has entered them. Turning, they see a man waving to them: they run over to him and go together into the bush.

As in the last song, the two women are probably the mythic Munga-munga. On the other hand, it was quite common in north-eastern Arnhem Land, as in other parts of Aboriginal Australia, for two women to go with one man for sexual purposes. Case histories of various young men in this area tell how they would meet two or more women out in the bush during food-collecting expeditions. The usual procedure was that one would wait for her companion to have coitus, either in front of her, or a little distance away among the bushes: then it was her turn. Or an older girl might be accompanied by her younger sister or 'girl-friend', who merely served as an accomplice in the affair and did not have sexual relations with her companion's sweetheart. Girls going out into the bush in pairs or in groups were not necessarily suspected of having such intentions, as would a girl setting off by herself. But by having a companion or two a girl hoping to meet her lover surreptitiously would always be able to fabricate an alibi, and such a ruse was essential in extra-marital escapades.

Song 35

She is washing her vulva and pubic hair, removing semen.

A man sings while two girls bathe in a nearby stream, cleansing themselves after coitus. The Djarada reawakens their desire. When they have washed, they look round for the man; seeing him, they beckon to him. He meets them, they swim together and have coitus in the water. Again, this song probably refers to the Munga-munga.

Song 36

With the point of the yam stick, digging . . .

After swimming (as in the last song), two women return to their camp, collect their digging sticks and set off once more to search for bush foods. As they dig, a man sings this Djarada. They feel its power enter them and think that their digging sticks are like penes copulating. They look round for the man, and go to him.

Song 37

There in the jungle depression, he sees them . . .

Hunting in a jungle, a man finds two women collecting root foods in a moist depression. He hides himself and sings this Djarada. The women feel it and look round for him. Seeing him, they ask: 'What's wrong with you? We want you now!' He replies, 'No, I don't want you, because you two girls already have a husband'. 'No', they say, 'We don't want him now you have sung us. We want you, straightaway. You can take us away with you, because you have been singing us'. 'All right', he agrees, 'I'll take you with me'. The three of them run away together.

(See Song 9 for comments on the implications of elopement. However, this song might also be sung without any reference to elopement.)

Song 38

With their dilly bags full of *ganei* yams . . .

Two women return from a food-collecting trip with dilly bags full of yams, suspended from their foreheads and hanging down at their backs. A man sings this song to make their backs itch. They scratch themselves, moving their bags aside, and conclude that a man must have been singing Djarada for them. In the meantime, he has sneaked up behind them, and while they are scratching they turn round and see him. He waves his hand, beckoning to them, and they go to him.

Song 39

She blows on the sparks, making a fire . . .

A woman blows on the sparks of her fire until a flame flares up. When the blaze burns down, she puts her yams in the hot coals. At that juncture a man sings this song, concentrating on her. She removes the yams and begins to eat one, but a piece catches in her throat. She gets water to wash it down.

After swallowing it, she looks around and sees a man coming towards her. She knows then what has happened: she gets up and goes with him into the bushes.

Song 40

She is sitting there shyly . . .

A man sings Djarada in praise of his sweetheart. He tells how the two of them were 'playing together' among some bushes not far from the camp. Afterwards she sat up and saw another man coming towards them. She was 'shy', and remained seated demurely with head bowed until he had passed by. In contrast, an immodest female might remain lying down, or jump up, drawing attention to what she had been doing.

Song 41

She is showing her teeth as she laughs . . .

A man sings about his sweetheart. Later, he 'looks at her' (that is, they look into each other's eyes in a special way): the girl winks or flutters her eyes and laughs, showing her white teeth. This means, the commentators said, that they are attracted to each other. That night, the girl surreptitiously comes to his sleeping place. Sneaking up close, she throws a pebble or two, or some bits of cold charcoal, hitting him on the body. He knows at once who it is. 'That's my girl there', he thinks. He gets up and moves quietly towards her, and they go out together into the nearby bushes.

Song 42

He grapples with her for coitus . . .

During the night, perhaps, a husband wants to copulate with his wife and attempts to pull her on to his thighs—only to find she resists. The same thing might happen with a sweetheart: it is not that she dislikes the man, but she is not in the mood. To stimulate her, he plucks a tuft of hair from his head and attaches it to a twig, as if it were a brush. To the accompaniment of this song, he puts this brush into her vagina and twirls it around. This was said to 'open' her vagina and make her receptive: she opens her legs, and is stimulated to such an extent that she calls again and again for the man's penis. The couple play together until both are exhausted.

Song 43

Semen pours from her . . .

A man sings about his relations with his wife. After intercourse, she stands up and finds that seminal fluid has run down her legs. As she attempts to wipe it off, she turns to her husband and scolds him. 'What are you, a dog? A man doesn't ejaculate like you do. If a man does it, just a little semen comes out. But you! Perhaps you want to make my vagina flow all the time! Perhaps your penis is too large!' 'Everyone does it that way, not only me', he replies. 'I can put a lot of semen into you, and that will make a baby grow up in you.' But she keeps on scolding him. 'You can't do that to me, not in that way, all the time. You make me angry. If you do it that way next time, I'll beat you with my stick'. (This is a general rendering. The original dialogue is more detailed and far more colourful.)

The discussion following this song centred on the belief that repeated intercourse with the same man will make a woman pregnant—that 'she is storing up the same semen to make a child'. The song implies that the man is giving his wife more semen than normally in order to make her pregnant, while, conversely, she does not want a child. The commentators added another point: a woman who neglects her personal hygiene and shows obvious evidence of coitus is talked about by other women; she is regarded as unclean, with an inordinate lust. Also, the discussion illustrates the contention that—in this, as in other Aboriginal societies—women are not (and were not) especially submissive, above all in the context of sexual relations. In this case, the account of a woman scolding her husband was handled in almost a matter-of-fact way, as something not at all out of the ordinary.

Song 44

Turning her round to face him, and opening her legs.

A man sings about his sweetheart: when they sleep together, he turns her towards him and they have coitus.

Song 45

She closes her legs after coitus, and hides her clitoris.

This is a continuation of the last song. After coitus he moves away from her and she closes her legs. The reference to her clitoris implies that it touches his penis as he withdraws it.

Song 46

The clustered fruit of the 'white plum' . . .

Two women (probably the Munga-munga: see above) go out to collect plums. They find some, and begin to eat. A man sings this Djarada. Simultaneously, they feel its magical quality enter their stomachs: its power enters them through the medium of the fruit. They look round for the singer, who is (as usual) within easy reach. They go to him without hesitating.

Song 47

Carrying plums, in their bark baskets . . .

As the same two women collect plums, filling their baskets, a man sings this song. It causes a plum to fall, hitting one of them in the eye. Recovering from her surprise, she looks around and sees a man coming towards her. They meet and play together.

Song 48

Calling out to each other . . .

The same two women have become separated because a man has been singing this song about them. Their calling guides him to one of them. He copulates with her. Later, the two women come together again.

Song 49

She rests on the way, following the creek back to the camp.

A woman is returning to her camp by way of a creek, when this song impels her to sit down and rest. The singer has been following her, and waves as he comes into sight. They meet and play together.

Song 50

Walking along through the last rays of the setting sun.

Wanting his sweetheart to come to him, a man sings this Djarada. Even though she is walking in the opposite direction, as soon as she feels its power, she turns back and goes to where he sits singing. If she is at a far-distant camp, he continues singing each day until she eventually joins him.

Song 51

The periwinkle, with 'cap' securely closed.

The periwinkle signifies a woman's vulva, which is closed (like its cap). When she hears the song, her vulva 'opens' (again, like this particular mollusc). In this case, she walks along the beach, among the rocks, collecting periwinkles. When she has enough, she returns to her camp and cooks them on the hot coals. After eating some, she 'opens her vulva' (for these shellfish dislodge their 'caps' during cooking), and 'looks around for a man'.

Song 52

> The chicken hawk swoops and snatches away her loin covering, showing her long clitoris.

This song was credited with having the power to send a chicken hawk to swoop down and pull off a girl's loin covering—either a narrow strip of cloth, or the traditional pandanus or bark apron. She runs after the bird, but it flies towards a patch of jungle. She suspects that the Djarada is responsible. Nevertheless, she enters the jungle in search of her apron. The man follows her tracks, and joins her.

The song, like a number of others, refers to a 'long' clitoris. There is no reason to suppose that it was abnormally large either in this area, or in the places from which the Djarada came. But this particular aspect was traditionally accorded a special value in north-eastern Arnhem Land mythology. It was regarded as being erotically desirable, with the ability to heighten sexual pleasure, and women were said to pull and finger their clitori in order to enhance their length. Men added that through Djarada singing and erotic play, the clitoris would become erect, or 'hard'. (In reference to the Djang-gawul sisters, see R. Berndt 1952: e.g. 271.)

Song 53

> A fish seizes her as she swims in the water.

A man sings for his sweetheart. She feels his singing, and when she sees him coming towards her, runs to the sea and swims away. He swims after her, and when they return to shallow water they play together. He tells her that his penis is only a fish—hence the word *gwia* (fish) in the song (see Appendix 3, page 234). She asks, 'What are you doing?' 'Nothing', he replies. 'It's only a fish.' 'But what a big fish!' she says, as they begin to copulate.

Song 54

> Beware of the shark, as you scratch your pubes!

A number of Djarada songs are directly coercive in intent. In this case, a man who has been repulsed by a woman tries to change her mind through this song. If she continues to refuse him, he implies, he will cause a shark to attack her as she bathes.

The commentators declared that such a song would be sung only by an unscrupulous man, embittered by a woman's constant refusals or angered by his wife's infidelity.

Song 55

The women are talking together . . .

Women are sitting in the camp, talking. When a man sings this, one among them feels its magic and sits waiting for him when the others have gone.

Song 56

She is eating wild honey, in the sunshine.

A woman goes out to collect and eat wild honey. Afterwards she lies in the sun and feels the power of this song. She is aroused, and looks up to see a man coming towards her.

Song 57

The last rays of the sun will guide you.

A man sings in the evening, while his sweetheart sleeps. She awakens and, feeling the power of the Djarada, looks around for him. The song suggests that she can find her way to him just as easily as if she were following a ray from the setting sun.

Song 58

The girl is wearing her armband . . .

The magic of this song flies over to a man's sweetheart and causes her plaited armband to break. By this sign, she knows that the power has entered her: she looks around for her lover.

Song 59

Covering herself with paperbark, wedged from a tree . . .

This song is similar to Song 26, while the words are the same as in Songs 13 and 16. A woman obtains paperbark and returns to her camp, where she covers herself with it. A man sings Djarada for her. Feeling it, she scratches herself and goes in search of him.

Song 60

Water, running down from a spring.

A woman goes to a spring-water stream to drink. As she does so, a man sings this song. She scratches her navel, feeling the Djarada there. Then she goes to join him.

Song 61

She gets up and runs, as she sees the crocodile crawling.

A group of women are collecting lily roots in a billabong. One of them has a lover who wants to come to her. Unable to attract her attention with so many women present, he sings this song, which causes a crocodile to materialize in the swamp and frighten them. In the confusion his sweetheart runs into the bush to meet him.

Song 62

Looking around for him, she scratches herself.

This song attracts a man's sweetheart. As he sings, he cuts some of his own pubic hair and magically blows it in her direction, scattering it over her body. The hair irritates her skin, and she scratches. Then she sets off to find him.

Song 63

Her pubic covering is blown aside, revealing her vulva.

The singing blows aside his sweetheart's pubic covering. Her genitals tingle with its power, causing her to go in search of him. (See also Song 18.)

Song 64

Jabiru bird among the trees, scratching herself . . .

A man walks through a paperbark and mangrove jungle singing this song, looking for a particular woman. At the same time, she feels his singing and scratches herself, then sets off to look for him. Eventually they find each other. He asks her, 'What's the matter with you?' 'I'm scratching myself', she replies. 'Why?' 'Because you have been singing Djarada for me.' They copulate. The jabiru bird, like the chicken hawk, is also associated mythologically with the Djarada.

Song 65

> The chicken hawk flaps its wings, skimming over their heads, and crying . . .

A man wants to find a particular woman, and so he sings this song. Soon he sees a small chicken hawk skimming towards him. He throws a stone to attract its attention, and then another. The hawk swoops down as he sings, seizes the pebble in its beak, and goes in search of her. It drops the stone on her head. She looks up and sees the hawk and, feeling her head, finds the pebble lodged in her hair. From this she knows that the man has sung her. She goes to look for him. (See also Song 52.)

9

THE PERSONAL FACE OF LOVE

The Djarada complex is substantiated in a very general way by Chicken Hawk (Gargan) mythology, which was traditionally comparatively unknown in north-eastern Arnhem Land. In fact, in the version presented here Chicken Hawk is treated almost as an ordinary bird, without mythic associations. However, in the Djarada series farther to the south and south-west, Chicken Hawk is connected with the Munga-munga, who in turn are often identified with the Wawalag although their travels and adventures differ considerably.

Nevertheless, while at first glance the Djarada songs appear to be unrelated to any religious structure, it can be argued that they are tenuously linked with the fertility cults of north-eastern Arnhem Land. In the south, the Djarada is complementary in a secular sense to the *kunapipi*, and the Munga-munga are the daughters of the Kunapipi Mother (see R. Berndt 1951*a*: Ch. IX-XI). Further, these Djarada, in their different versions, extend through much of the Northern Territory. In the central-western region, the women's Djarada include rituals that are basically religious with strong love-magical overtones. It is in this last capacity that we find them here, their religious qualities considerably muted.

While the Rose River cycle conforms, structurally, with the accepted local pattern of poetic song presentation, the Djarada does not. Its compressed verbal style has never been totally acceptable to north-eastern Arnhem Landers, but that style has not proved very accommodating to 'outside' (other Aboriginal) attitudes and influences, perhaps because of its magical aura. As we saw in the last chapter, the singing of these songs was believed to release almost automatically the magical power of the Djarada: that power being contained in each individual song, each able to influence a person or persons in relation to the singer or possessor (or activator) of the Djarada. This contrasts with the kind of power that was said to be inherent in the other two song cycles we have been discussing. In their case, the power is depersonalized, diffused and social, and environmentally directed, being projected, as it were, into the sacred world of which man is part.

There are also other contrasts. Farther south, the Djarada are arranged to form fairly consistent and coherent cycles, in much the same way as the Goulburn Island and Rose River songs are. In their present setting the Djarada are presented as individual songs, although some aspects of the 'original' patterning are evident. For instance, we could perhaps identify features which are present in the other two song cycles. However, a Djarada song, as a separate entity, can be employed alone without any connecting thread. Each is virtually self-contained and, importantly, self-explanatory in so far as its intent and purpose are concerned. There are no direct mythic references or allusions in the Djarada, although, as noted, it is possible to identify the Chicken Hawk and the Munga-munga of the southern *kunapipi*. But the songs do not rest on mythic imagery and symbolism. In contrast, north-eastern Arnhem Land song-poetry *is* poetry just for those reasons: it relies on enhancing the 'build-up' of the theme, on a complex interweaving of imagery and symbolism, much of which is mythological in content, even though supposedly *real* situations are used to express it. The Djarada, on the other hand, is matter-of-fact. Shorn of its power (which will be noted again below), or looked at apart from that, it is both mundane and consciously utilitarian—almost, one hesitates to say, devoid of aesthetic merit.

The utilitarian and instrumental nature of the series becomes to some extent obsessional—its focus almost entirely on coitus: not as having implications for something else, of a social or ritual kind, as was the case with the other two cycles, but concentrating on situations through which sexual intercourse may be achieved *as an end in itself* and, moreover, with a minimum of trimmings. The songs sketch the various devices, or ruses, through which men and women may be personally attracted to one another: and the events epitomized in the songs all have but one meaning. And that is *the* basic thread which links all these songs—that, and nothing else, or virtually nothing else. One of the most interesting points about these songs is that explanations are always given. It was obvious that Aborigines themselves felt impelled to comment on each in order to make clear what they understood the words to mean, so that there was considerable scope for personal interpretation, to an extent which would be impossible in the other two cycles.

A further element in common is the individually projected 'power' of the

Djarada. The basic assumptions involved can be outlined quite simply. Djarada power is latent in the words and rhythm of the songs. It is released through the singing and enters a man or woman, compelling him or her to act involuntarily. The commonest medium through which this power may be projected is food. It may be 'sung into' damper (bread), fruit and so on, and when eaten takes possession of the recipient. Or the power may be felt by a man or woman, usually the latter, since this particular series was presented by men. Or it may be communicated through personal contact with some object.

There are numerous variations on this theme, as the songs demonstrate. In the conventional response, the power causes its target to become dizzy or possessed: his or her body and mind are temporarily controlled by it, and the power remains until sexual intercourse with the singer releases it. It was also said to vary in intensity, and to cause a specially-defined feeling of light-headedness, of thinking about coitus and then about a particular person. A particular symptom is extreme itchiness (of the genitals, for instance) which aggravates sexual desire. The actual singing of the song is a rite in itself. It is not usual for additional ritual to be performed—except in the case of singing over excrement-dampened ground from a desired person; or, occasionally, when some physical 'part' of that person, such as a lock of hair or something which has been in close contact with him or her, is used as a charm to increase the effectiveness of singing.

'Improper' use of this power might lead, as in some examples, to socially undesirable results. Conventionally and ideally, men said, it should be used only in moderation to satisfy immediate sexual gratification, in secrecy, ensuring that there were no repercussions or that these were kept to a minimum; for example, it should not be employed to upset formal betrothals, nor used blatantly in such a way that a girl's husband, guardian or accepted lover became so seriously annoyed that the only possible outcome was fighting. Nevertheless, they added, the power of the Djarada was strong, and its influence on the person possessed might be so overwhelming as to be virtually uncontrollable: a woman (for example) might feel impelled to abandon all her other ties and elope with the singer. Generally speaking, according to my information, in areas where the Djarada was fairly well established, a high proportion of all elopement cases was traced to it, or blamed on it. This was not particularly the case in north-eastern Arnhem Land, however, where the Djarada was regarded as something of an innovation.

While there are obvious exceptions, it seems (and Aboriginal opinion suggested this to be so) that, as one of the contributory conditions, the person to be influenced should be in an emotionally receptive state; also for the Djarada to succeed in the love-magic field, those concerned should be willing to engage in a liaison. Little or nothing is heard of those instances where the Djarada fails. People seem to have simply taken for granted that it must eventually prove successful.

A significant point here is that north-eastern Arnhem Landers, in 1946–47, were uncertain of the extent or intensity of Djarada power. They claimed that to be really successful the singing should be done more or less surreptitiously *but* that the subject should be aware it was being, or would be, carried out. One of the crucial questions is whether the Djarada was really needed in that area. Many men and women were said to welcome irregular liaisons, and this would appear to conform with the pattern of unobtrusive pre- and extra-marital relations that was well-developed in north-eastern Arnhem Land (as in some other Aboriginal societies). When men were asked whether they would be responsive to the Djarada, they replied that they didn't need it, because all healthy adults were more or less ready to embark on such an adventure without too much inducement. However, as noted, the Djarada is linked to elopement. But even in that case, some degree of initial conditioning, along with preliminary arrangements, would be necessary to enable an elopement to be carried out in the kind of haste suggested by the commentary to certain of these songs. That, however, did not seem to be recognized. What the north-eastern Arnhem Landers did not say specifically in this context was that they had other ways (for instance, through the Goulburn Island and Rose River songs) of fulfilling or enhancing their sexual desires—and those other ways were usually considered to be more congenial.

It is the contrast between the Djarada and the other two cycles which highlights its significance. The Djarada contains an element that is absent from the Goulburn Island and Rose River songs. The others are stimulatory in a general sense, with no love-magic that is personally directed. Whatever the believed-in source of Djarada power, even though it may be indirectly associated with the *kunapipi*, the appeal is directly sexual.

The symbolism contained in these Djarada is limited. It is mostly confined to direct sexual symbolism of an obvious character: there is no attempt at complexity in this respect. Examples such as a native companion's beak, an upright yam stick, the tail of a blue-tongue lizard or scorpion, a boomerang and a fish = penis; a bark receptacle and a periwinkle = vagina; rain = semen; or twirling firesticks or digging yam sticks = coitus: these provide little opportunity for imaginative exercise. But, of course, this is not what was intended.

Encouraging (as it probably does, at least at the level of thinking about these things) both illicit and promiscuous sexual relations, it also serves to support marriage, although that may be in the guise of elopement. In passing, it is important to re-emphasize that such a sanction was a back-handed one.

The path to marriage through elopement was rarely a smooth one, and the Djarada (if it were involved) served to exacerbate the situation. Often, the guardian or husband of the woman concerned (in north-eastern Arnhem Land perhaps herself the 'abductor', or initiator of an elopement) would know or guess that such an event would take place. In that case his anger and the supporting anger of his kin might be more conventional than real, and directed towards the lover of the eloping wife or, in the absence of that lover, towards his relatives or hers. The degree of bitterness and injured pride involved, its intensity of expression, depended largely on the temperament of the offended husband. Some husbands would go so far as to arrange an avenging party, with the express intention of spearing both runaways—or at least one of them. So, although many elopements seem to have been more or less socially sanctioned, there was always an element of risk, and virtually always a residue of ill-feeling.

In some of the Djarada songs (for example, 28, 29 and 43) reference is made to what can be regarded as routine marital unions in association with pregnancy. These are especially important because they suggest that the Djarada is not entirely erotic or not entirely concerned with short-term sexual liaisons. In other areas, not in north-eastern Arnhem Land, the Djarada does have this broader view, as having to do with marriage and betrothal as well as with general fertility.

Two of these Djarada songs (14 and 54) express desire for revenge, provoked by personal frustration or by unfaithfulness on the part of a wife. Infidelity in north-eastern Arnhem Land society had a special connotation: a wife was exposed to punishment of varying severity if she committed adultery without her husband's knowledge and approval, and was discovered. Long acquaintance with the possibilities in this direction, through observation and hearsay even if not through first-hand experience, provided a background of information and expertise for those who were that way inclined. Nevertheless, they were sometimes 'caught'. On the other hand, sexual intercourse carried out with the husband's full sanction, although out of his sight and hearing, was not expected to cause dissension between husband and wife. But the Djarada was a double-edged weapon. Depending on the song, its projected power might cause (was believed to cause) destruction and injury, or love and physical desire.

Here there was actually a substantial area of common ground, a set of basic premises which was 'built into' north-eastern Arnhem Land culture just as it was (is) into the Djarada. That is, the non-empirical sequence of cause and effect, the acceptance of magical 'causality', which in north-eastern Arnhem Land has been particularly well entrenched in the sphere of beliefs regarding 'black magic', or sorcery.

Finally, regarding the content of these Djarada, reference should be made to Songs 30 to 32 in which ritual defloration is mentioned. This provides a clue to the Djarada's linkage with the *kunapipi*. It also transforms what are regarded as sacred acts into erotic ones—which to some extent is what the Rose River songs do. With the latter, however, defloration retains its sacred significance even though it was also erotic. In the Djarada, it is removed from the ritual context and the act of defloration becomes de-sacralized although it retains (indirectly) a modicum of symbolic expression. It is difficult to measure the extent to which this was north-eastern Arnhem Land interpretation, especially in the light of the Rose River cycle which is fairly explicit in this respect and—to my knowledge—mirrors actual *kunapipi* ritual, or at least some aspects of it. It is true to say that from their point of view this rite was not as important as what followed—that is, ritual coitus. Further, people at Yirrkalla had, in 1946–7, little personal acquaintance with this subject. Not many of them had travelled at that time beyond their own home territories into other socio-cultural areas. Older people did remark that pressure towards conformity was less strong then than formerly: pre-marital (or pre-pubertal) sexual intercourse was increasingly common among girls. They argued that, in these circumstances, it would be difficult to find a virgin who could be deflowered according to the traditional ideal. But this is exactly what some older people are saying today!

It is the secularization of a primarily ritual act—that is, defloration—which points up the dominating focus of the Djarada in this area, whatever its significance may be elsewhere. It is, as I have mentioned, individualistic: or, in its movement into north-eastern Arnhem Land, it has been revamped to emphasize this. While its origins are religious, in this context it has become non-religious and non-social. It is not concerned with other persons except to a limited degree, and in relation to personal gratification.

Before the Djarada's entry into this region, no form of lovemaking (as far as we can judge) took place without the adornment of romantic conventions. I am not, of course, saying that personal considerations were absent. In some cases, they were very obtrusive indeed. Nor am I saying that personal gratification was not sought and achieved in what can be called 'hit and run' or transitory affairs. In any case, routine marital coitus was an expected occurrence, not necessarily accompanied by additional frills. However, traditional forms of approved and valued lovemaking were almost always seen in relation to symbolic patterning, which provided a context that enhanced the physical act of coitus. In other words, the Goulburn Island and Rose River cycles provided romantic settings in which eroticism could be savoured. This was not the case with the Djarada.

10

THE SIGNIFICANCE OF THE SONGS

It remains for me to draw out some general conclusions from the preceding discussion of these three love song cycles. Already, significant elements in relation to their content and symbolic patterning have been indicated. Here, my intention is to focus on the kinds of information which these cycles are intended (seem to be intended) to convey.

At the manifest level, the first two cycles provide a co-ordinated set of related scenes which revolve round a specific theme or themes. It can be said that they convey a story which leads up to the pivotal act of coitus and the implications of this for the completion of this action sequence, with eventual return to a state which existed at the commencement of the cycle. In other words, events run their course, and wind down, but in such a way that the cycle can be recommenced. It is this which expresses its eternal quality, the recycling of social living and of environmental renewal. The Djarada is excluded, because it is essentially piecemeal in structure, and its songs are not necessarily arranged (in this case) sequentially, or as a cycle. In the Goulburn Island and Rose River cycles, each poetic-song rendering, although it can stand alone, having its own internal consistency and its own intrinsic meaning, leads on to something else. The information it contains is extended or amplified when it is placed in relation to other songs within the same cycle. Further, sequentiality is quite strictly ordered, with one event being regarded as an outcome of what has preceded it. This method of verse construction demonstrates ,clearly explicit recognition of a relationship between cause and effect, a relationship that has a significant bearing on the song content. It is demonstrated too, not only in the unfolding of events from song to song, but in the complex cross-referent system between one song and the next as well as within a song, which spells out interconnectedness of past and future events.

This systematic ordering of material provides a cycle, and indeed the songs which constitute it, with an internal rationale which makes the point that no event is complete within itself, or isolable—all must, by their very nature, have implications of some kind in relation to something else. From the standpoint of the Aborigines concerned, this is a basic human psychological process of thinking and acting, emphasizing an awareness of other persons and other things. It is also basic in establishing a system of meaning or an epistemology: seeing facts in relation to other facts, and extracting from them a workable set of assumptions. And this human characteristic is projected on to the environmental and non-human dimension. Firstly, it humanizes and personalizes the whole of nature. Secondly, it attributes to nature an internal rationale or consistency which is not dissimilar to that conceived for man. This correlation emerges remarkably well in the two cycles. Simultaneously, as mutually sustaining themes, there are the actions of man and the permutations of nature, each envisaged as being dependent one on the other, providing a range of actions or events which affect both. These are not so much different 'levels' of experience, as two parallel streams. Both are manifest, and both are *real* in the sense of what people believe can and does happen. Men and women act in socially approved ways, and what they do automatically 'releases' similar forces inherent within nature. Those forces or their attributes are expressed symbolically, as are the actions of human beings. The symbolic becomes the intended meaning of the real—both in human actions, and in nature. One is explained by or through the other at the manifest level, and the songs themselves spell this out.

As far as interpretation is concerned, the two cycles provide this in their detailed content. However, other information is required—information which is not included in the songs or, if it is included there, is only implied. That additional material relates primarily to the relevant mythology, because many of the actions of men and women in everyday living and many natural occurrences are (or were) phrased in mythic terms or reflect mythic allusions. Much of that information is not necessarily esoteric, and may be generally known to all local adults irrespective of moiety and dialectal affiliation, because the great religious cycles do in fact constitute the traditional heritage of the people. What I am emphasizing is that meaning of events and of symbolic referents in the two cycles involves a common understanding and rests on both general and on specific interpretation. It is true that further explanations may be sought by some—but, for these, a deeper understanding is necessary of the main religious cycles or those parts of them which remain restricted or to which (in their ritual manifestations) access is limited.

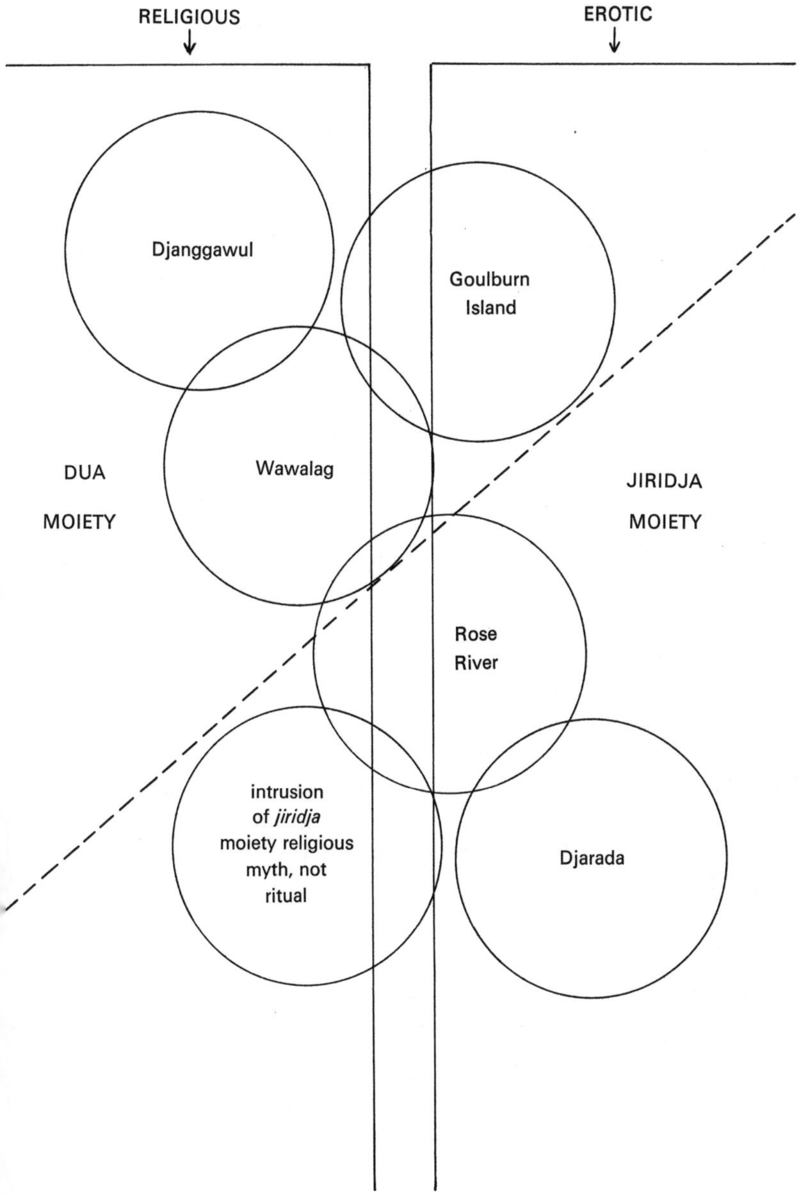

Diagram 6 The Religious and the Erotic

The problem, therefore, concerns broader issues which are latent in the cycles. The three sequences discussed here have something to say about the relationship between religion and sex, and about three aspects of sexual expression.

Religion and Sex

One of the most outstanding features of these songs is their religious significance: even the Djarada is not entirely detached from this. In Diagram 6, I have attempted to demarcate the erotic from the religious. However, it should already be clear that this is not possible, except in a limited way. The great mythic religious cycles of the Djanggawul and Wawalag are linked, on one hand with the Goulburn Island cycle and on the other with the Rose River cycle. They provide the mythic substantiation for these two, and in so doing offer an explanatory frame of reference. The Djarada in turn is linked to the Rose River cycle. One remarkable feature is that the whole belief system which is expressed through these songs—except for a *jiridja* moiety segment in the Rose River sequence—is classified as being of the *dua* moiety. As I mentioned in Chapter 2, there is a substantial body of *jiridja* moiety religious knowledge. However, that has only a marginal relationship to the love song cycles. Nearly all sexual expression of this more or less standardized verbal sort depends on the *dua* moiety, which provides an ideological basis for the two *jiridja* song cycles. The Rose River cycle, especially, makes constant reference to the *nonggaru*, which is the core symbolic ritual representation of the *dua* moiety secret-sacred Wawalag rituals, although included in that cycle are references to the *jiridja* moiety Lightning Snake which replaces the *dua* Yulunggul of the Wawalag. This, however, provides a link with the Laindjung-Banaidja religious cycle. Further, the numerous references to *jiridja* moiety clans and dialectal units place it within that perspective. Nevertheless, it is clear that we are dealing here with a specific religious continuum: the expansion of the *dua* moiety religious belief system and manifestations into the *jiridja* sphere. Of course, I am not referring here to *dua* and *jiridja* moiety participation in one kind of ritual: members of both moieties engage co-operatively in singing and performing. The fact remains that ownership or possession of one cycle in contrast to another is phrased in terms of moiety: so that ownership shifts across moiety affiliation, drawing members of each closer together in terms of common knowledge and providing authority for both to use that knowledge.

The religious continuum which is represented by overlapping circles in Diagram 6 could well be regarded as depicting a process of secularization. For instance, mythology which sponsors secret-sacred and sacred ritual is transformed or used in a context which purports to emphasize sexual expressions. Or, in the case of the Rose River cycle, secret-sacred and sacred topics *and* ritual are treated sexually. However, it would be wrong to interpret that process in this way, when it is really the converse of this. Rather, it is the 'spilling over' of the sacred, investing mundane activity with an aura or a meaning which must be sought at a sacred level and is not to be interpreted solely at the level of physical experience. Physical experience is not denied, nor is it underplayed: but it is seen as a series of acts, among which the sexual act may be located, which provide patterning for religious symbolism.

The themes inherent in the Goulburn Island and Rose River cycles are fundamentally those embedded in or expressed through the great *dua* moiety religious cycles. It is, in a manner of speaking, the other face of religion, turned towards the human participants rather than towards the mythic beings, recognizing that the drama of life concerns both and includes the whole spectrum of social living. Further, the commonalty of theme demonstrates the tremendous influence of traditional religious ideology on all activity and on all institutions in eastern Arnhem Land society (as well as, of course, vice versa). An additional element which draws our two cycles into the sacred sphere, is the emphasis placed on procreation. Both cycles mirror the primary preoccupation of the Djanggawul and Wawalag mytho-ritual systems. In the first, it is *creation*, fertility and procreation in human and environmental terms. In the second, it is *renewal*. Blood and semen and menstruation, in turn, stimulate the forces of nature, causing them to react in a predictable way—a humanized way—to ensure the natural sequence of events upon which man depends.

One explanation concerning the significance of the *dua* moiety mytho-ritual constellations is that the comparable *jiridja* moiety ones do not emphasize fertility and procreation in terms of creation or renewal. It is true that the Laindjung-Banaidja cycles are concerned in part with natural growth, but not in the same way and not in relation to mythic beings who are themselves creative beings. In the Rose River cycle, for example, the *dua* and *jiridja* mytho-ritual sectors combine to bring about the growth of nature. In the songs, reference is primarily made to plants, new shoots, grass, foliage, etc., not to fertility in more general terms, although that is implied when one considers the implications of this cycle's profile (see Chapter 7, Diagram 4). However, the *jiridja* moiety has not personalized its fertility symbols as has the Wawalag—and even more so, the Djanggawul. Also, the Wawalag and Djanggawul, in spite of their male symbolic and mythic representations and characters, are more female-oriented. In contrast, the *jiridja* religious cycles are much more male-oriented.

I said before that the particular religious perspective expressed in these two song cycles is directed towards human beings. It would therefore seem that this is the only way through which a clue can be obtained as to their social meaning. Without that focus, we are faced with a song content which does not appreciably differ from mythic themes that concern spirit beings who act out their eternal roles in pursuance of humanly-defined aspirations.

The Wawalag (and I will not discuss the Djanggawul in this context since the Goulburn Island cycle touches on it only briefly), at the level of myth, provides a set of answers to the question 'why': why menstrual and afterbirth blood of the Wawalag impel Yulunggul to emerge from his sacred waterhole and swallow them (or in the Rose River version, why the *jiridja* moiety Lightning Snake emerges because he smells and eats the blood of the deflowered girls and subincised men); why Yulunggul and other snakes erect themselves; why the monsoonal season comes; and why the Wawalag are eventually regurgitated. The Goulburn Island cycle, at the level of human beings, provides a set of answers to the question 'how'. And the question it poses is phrased in terms of *how* men and women, and not mythic creatures, can cause the monsoonal season to break. Nevertheless, *how* it happens presupposes *why* it happens—and to obtain the 'why' one must return to the symbolic references which are made in the process of how it is done. The same is the case with the Rose River cycle. There the 'how' is expressed through the performance of formal ritual, in contrast to what takes place in the Goulburn Island cycle, where the *ordinary* behaviour of men and women is tantamount to ritual. In the Rose River cycle, the 'why' is implicit. The ritual action paraphrases certain aspects of *kunapipi* ritual, especially in relation to the *nonggaru*. For the symbolic significance of this and its mythic content one must seek the Wawalag on one hand, with the Djanggawul and, on the other hand, southern Arnhem Land mythology which was not available to the majority of north-eastern Arnhem Land people. For the *jiridja* sector of this, one must go to *jiridja* religious ideology, although this is not really necessary because of its identification with the Yulunggul of the Wawalag.

At the human level, it is man and woman, seen as agents in activating a divine plan which is significant to them humanly. They are part of that plan, and must work harmoniously with the forces of nature, symbolized by the mythic beings, so that general fertility may be ensured. In one sense, then, the Aboriginal-categorized 'outside' love cycles virtually perform the same function as the 'inside' (secret-sacred) sacred ritual. But they do this in their own way and within the prescriptions of the Dreaming. It is the Dreaming as an eternal source of knowledge which is especially pervasive. It is worth mentioning again that this is no mystical view but one which is oriented along both practical and spiritual lines. 'Practical' because its associated action (ritual or otherwise) is (was) considered to be necessary to stimulate those forces which lie latent in the Dreaming and can be released or brought to bear only by human beings; and the results which are anticipated are relevant to ordinary, everyday living. 'Spiritual' or super-natural because human action is directed towards mythic forces which, without that mythic intervention, would not bring about the desired results.

It is true, however, that ambiguity does exist in this respect, since there are two contrary views expressed in relation to the Dreaming. I have just mentioned the emphasis on the interdependence of mythic and human beings. But, alongside this is the view that mythic beings are independent of man—that they will continue to exist, eternally, whether or not man is present in the land, and the natural elements of the environment which they represent or over which they have control will do likewise. These two views are less contrary than they seem, and are not really ambiguous. In traditional Aboriginal society, as far as we can tell, it was never seriously envisaged that man *per se* could cease to exist. Man himself is/was inseparable from his culture: and the mythic beings and nature are/were an integral part of it. In the song cycles, as in the great mytho-ritual constellations, this aspect is repeated (as already mentioned) again and again by words which can be translated as 'always there', implying a sense of permanency; expressing a feeling of immutability which is at the basis of the idea of the Dreaming and underlying the belief in the indestructibility of traditional social life. I do not think that it was an awareness of insecurity which led to a reiteration of that principle, although it is likely that their utter dependence on natural resources could have sparked off such a reaction. That aside, what is implied is that this is what *has* taken place, and *is* taking place, and *will continue* to take place—as long as Aboriginal people and their culture exist.

Consistent with the concept of the Dreaming is the view that the past, the present and the future are believed to be one continuum, or in some contexts both simultaneous and eternal. The north-eastern Arnhem Landers were concerned with each of these points of time as such, in relation to their everyday life. However, they also recognized that repercussions from the past were felt in the present and would be felt in the future—that the present inevitably becomes the past, as the future becomes the present. Such a straightforward premise, a *linear* time-perspective, calls for a definite attitude towards processes of cause and effect, of performance and result, and involves recognition that some provision must be made for the future. This element is clear in the cycles we have discussed: they express the need to ensure continuity in life. The basic human requirements of food and sex are used to this purpose. This is especially the case with heterosexual intercourse: only by this means, according to this orientation, may continuity be achieved—whether it be human or animal, vegetable or plant, elemental or seasonal. The assumption is extended to embrace the whole universe as north-eastern Arnhem Landers perceive it, or perceived it in the recent past. Sexual behaviour is, therefore, seen as being central to this general issue.

The Goulburn Island and Rose River cycles express ideas about conventional channels through which the sexual requirements of both men and women may be satisfied. In one sense, sexual activity can be thought of as an entirely natural event, as assuaging a legitimate appetite, like eating, and to a large extent the Djarada expresses that view. With the other two cycles, this is not the case. Mutual attraction and interaction between members of the opposite sex are regulated by prohibitions and obligations which govern all interpersonal association whether or not a sexual element is apparent. Sexual attraction may well rest on a physical (or chemical) basis; but it is, nevertheless, defined and considerably modified or enhanced by cultural trappings. Men and women do not behave individually without relevance to others: conventions, both social and cultural, must be adhered to if satisfaction is to be achieved. It is this lesson which the songs attempt to spell out. To put it simply, men and women do not copulate indiscriminately, irrespective of relationship, as the sexual urge takes them, any more than they consume unthinkingly all available fruits, roots, plants and animals, without paying some attention to such matters as variety, edibility, quality or, for that matter, preparation.

Between eating and coitus, Arnhem Landers recognize a close affinity, and they sometimes use a single word to signify either or both. This attitude towards two basic drives presents us with *a* key, not *the* key, to the question of the need for sexual stimulation. An Arnhem Lander carefully chooses his food and treats it to suit his taste. So, too, he or she selects a sexual partner, and in order to enhance the attractiveness of the situation sings love songs, performs magic and ritual, or participates in erotic pre-coitus play. As in the preparation of food for the climax of eating, so all of these additional elements are regarded as preparation for the climax, coitus.

However, this explanation is far too simplistic. Two elements are essential, within this particular socio-cultural context. One concerns the question of climax, and the other the question of the trimmings congruent with sexual activity. Both fall within the framework of religion, underlining the direct association of sex and religion. In order to follow these two points, we must pass to the three aspects of sexual expression which are symbolized by the three cycles discussed in this volume.

The Three Faces of Sexual Love

It will be recalled that the physical act of sex is approached differently in each of the cycles. Further, I have used the word 'love' in reference to them. In its special meaning here, 'love', in its three different facets, implies something over and above the sexual act itself. It is not 'love' such as, for example, between parent and child or between other close relatives where sexual relations are proscribed or, ideally at least, not explicitly contemplated. Specifically it has to do with an attitude or constellation of attitudes, expressed through particular forms of action which are essentially discriminatory and focused on a desired person or persons. I am not necessarily implying affection, but I am taking into account a special emotional or affective quality. That quality becomes manifest through setting in motion a particular sequence of events. The songs we have presented trigger a response which leads to a sexual act; they create the conditions under which it may be performed.

It is true that Arnhem Land dialects, although they include specific words for coitus and other physical aspects of sexual relationships, also use expressions that can be rendered as 'have' or 'like', among others. There is no separate word which can be translated as to 'love'—except to 'like' (*djaal*). However, a crucial aspect here is sexual receptivity and reciprocity. This is recognized in the Djarada, the most personally oriented of these three cycles. The magic there is designed not only to cause or to enhance desire, but also to provide special conditions under which the sexual act can take place and, importantly, to ensure that attraction exists between the persons involved. The same is the case with other forms of love-magic used to attract a desired partner—not just any partner, but a particular one. For instance, the wooden seagull head with feathered strings attached, referred to in the Goulburn Island cycle, is used to the accompaniment of ritualized action; and it is intended to create a special condition which is conducive to sexual activity. In other words, a suitable atmosphere in such a context is important. It is much more so in the two major love song cycles, where the question of cultural style is significant.

The three faces of sexual love all have this common ingredient, although it is less obvious in the Djarada.

(a) The Goulburn Island cycle depicts what I have called the social face of love. It is social because sexual activity is not regarded simply as a thing in itself, as a private source of gratification between the couple concerned. From the beginning of the cycle, the implications inherent in it are spelt out: the sexual act is paralleled in simultaneous occurrences within the realm of nature. Also, it is seen as having a bearing on other things, as bringing about change and transformation and, by implication, procreation and most certainly general (human and non-human) fertility. Moreover, it is the *ordinary* behaviour of men and women, through their interaction, which is responsible for, or is seen as instigating, elemental (environmental) change—specifically in this cycle, the monsoonal season, which brings fertility to the whole land.

Although this face of love is social, it is also sacred. I do not want to go so far as to speak of 'sacred love', which does have a special connotation relevant to dedication and sanctification: that is not to be inferred from this case. Nevertheless, it *is* sacred, not in terms of a person-to-person relationship, but in the derivations resulting from the actions of those involved. The imagery used to convey socio-cultural messages is couched in mythic terms; it is set within the context of specific religious ideology and, consequently, provides or clothes the whole situation and the events arising from it with what can be called an aesthetic quality. That quality transcends physical elements without destroying them. In fact, the physical dimension is specifically used for that purpose. Further, the network of interrelationships set up between men and women is reflected in relationships between man and nature, and man and the mythic beings—one is seen as being dependent on the other in a divine scheme focused on total environmental fructification.

(b) The Rose River cycle depicts what I have called the ritual face of love. In many respects this cycle resembles the Goulburn Island one. It draws partially on the same mythology, and where it incorporates *jiridja* mythic material, this complements the main theme. The major difference lies in the way it views the sexual act. In the Goulburn Island cycle it is sexual *relations*—the implications of the sexual act for others, in terms of other persons and in relation to a divine scheme involving nature as a whole. In the Rose River cycle, it is the sexual *act* in contrast to sexual relations; it emphasizes the subordination of personal elements to ritual significance. Certainly, we can still speak of it as being social: the songs tell of the participation of different groups (clans and dialectal units) and of persons in association with other persons. However, the fact that, traditionally, coitus occurred between persons of the same moiety, between ordinarily tabued relatives, has the effect of 'destroying' social relations in this context. It was not intended that this kind of relationship should continue normally but that it should be restricted to ritual occasions. Interpreting the ritual breach of tabu as, in effect, a means of reinforcing it in everyday life, for example as a type of catharsis, does not diminish the force of this argument.

This particular face of love is both formalized and ritualized. Personal feelings are subordinated to ritual expediency: it is ritual which counts, and the sexual act assumes the role of a religious (ritual) performance. In this case, the sexual act *is* sanctified—and it is possible to speak of sacred love: but, again, not in reference to the person, and only in relation to the act, although dedication may be relevant in a general way—dedication to ritual and to sacred aspirations, recognition of the significance of the act over and above personal gratification. Of course, as already noted, the Rose River cycle paraphrases some aspects of the sacred *kunapipi* ritual: it is not the actual *kunapipi* cycle. However, although it is a view, from the outside looking in, it nevertheless replicates faithfully the ritual acts themselves (defloration, subincision and ritual coitus), and underlines their significance. In doing this, it attempts to emphasize the sexual, but not necessarily at the expense of the sacredness of the situations in which sexuality takes precedence.

As with the Goulburn Island cycle, the whole cycle is set within a frame of religious symbolism where explanations must be sought from the body of relevant mythology. The emphasis on ritual, with the *nonggaru* as its focus, to some extent circumscribes this; and this is the case, too, with the *jiridja* moiety Lightning Snake. The *nonggaru* symbolizes the ritual acts, providing an explanation of them, and transforming them into mythic acts which influence environmental processes.

(c) The third face of love is to be found in the Djarada songs. These provide an entirely different view of sexual relations, oriented almost entirely in person-to-person terms. It is true that the Djarada was originally a magico-religious phenomenon, composed of a co-ordinated song sequence with mythic referents. Only a part of that has survived in the course of its transference into a new region. Elements of a mythic nature are still apparent in some of the songs (Chicken Hawk and the Munga-munga, for instance): but these have mostly been erased. Even ritual defloration, which appears in the *kunapipi* and in the Rose River cycle, has been secularized. While mythic symbolism can be 'read into' isolated situations, there remains no co-ordinated system of such imagery.

Essentially, the Djarada is an example of self-conscious eroticism. It concerns mundane events which are separated from their social and environmental implications. One exception is the occasional reference to marriage and pregnancy as an outcome of Djarada action: but even there the personal element is dominant, and the broader issues are lost sight of.

The major focus is on short-range liaisons which provide immediate sexual gratification. Social expectations or conventions are subordinated to personal inclination: social factors are limited, and are not necessarily considered to be more important than personal desire. Sexual intercourse is the goal. However, to achieve this, magical action is necessary—otherwise no response is forthcoming. The power of the Djarada is coercive. It forces the man or woman at whom it is directed to respond in a receptive way, irrespective of personal choice, to a compulsive acceptance of the Djarada power.

The sexual ethos

The three faces of physical love may be looked at as a whole in Diagram 7, which is composed of the two diagrammatic profiles set out in Chapters 5 and 7, taking into account the third, the Djarada.

The Goulburn Island and Rose River 'faces' converge (or merge) in their common ends, which are markedly in contrast to those of the Djarada. The ways or means through which those ends are achieved are different, in terms of participation of the sexes and in their varying influence on ritual and mythic symbolism. Space and direction are included, but are not significant

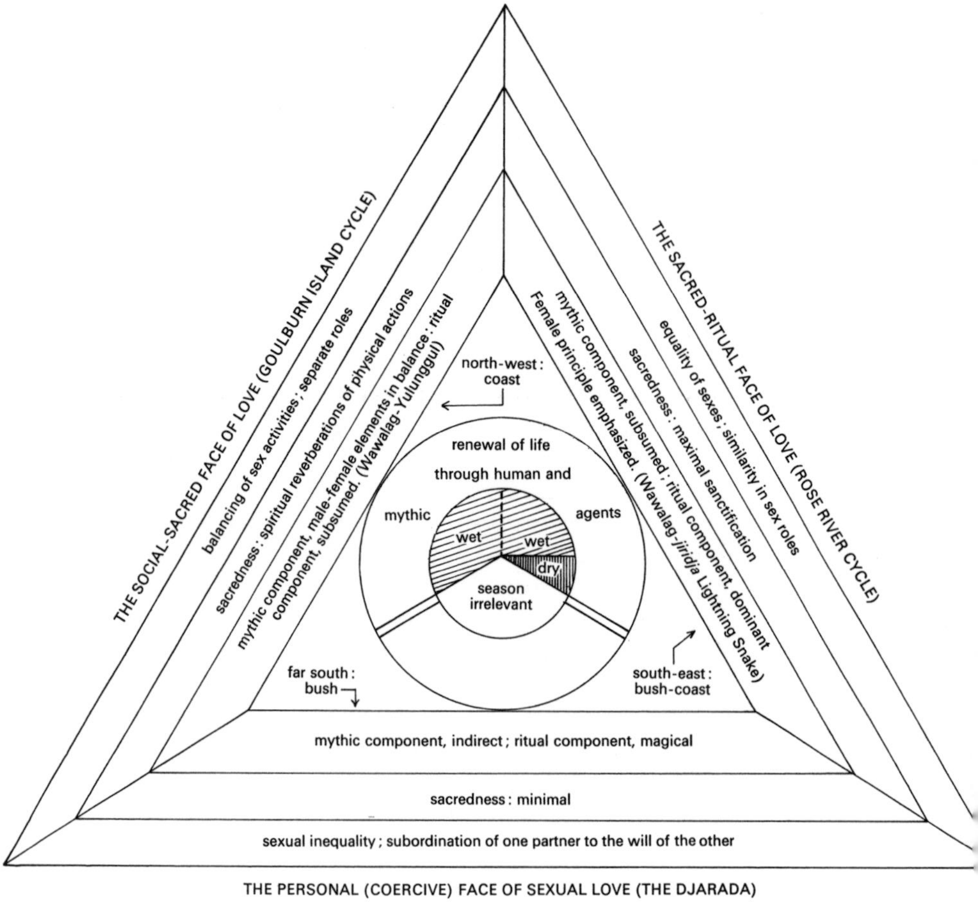

Diagram 7 The Three Faces of Love

in this context. In very general terms, the diagram is saying (or could say, according to my interpretation) that:

1 Where religious ideology is expressed through an equal balancing of male and female human and mythic elements, sexual relations would seem to be concerned not only with personal satisfaction but also with their impact on others and on natural forces.

Conversely, where religious ideology is expressed through the equivalence of male-female ritual action and a dominant female mytho-symbolic principle is present, sexual relations would seem to be sanctified to the virtual exclusion of personal considerations, even though their bearing on natural forces is still relevant.

2 Where the mytho-ritual context has little or no bearing on sexual relations, the emphasis on personal satisfaction would seem to lead to the subordination of one sex in contrast to the other.

At the level of interpretation and *not* of real life, it must be assumed that the two 'sides' of 1 are relevant to the *one* society. One would hesitate to speak of profane and sacred love. Nevertheless, these two stand in relation to each other as does the 'free association of the sexes' to 'the restricted and circumscribed association of the sexes'. Or, to put it another way: on the one hand, where the relationships between men and women are separately defined but complementary, the subordination of one sex to another is less relevant: and, on the other hand, where male-female distinctions are blurred, freedom of sexual expression is less likely to be permitted to or by one sex or the other, with the danger of male or female dominance in other spheres of action. The second statement (2) is really an intrusive one in so far as north-eastern Arnhem Land society is concerned, and the two 'sides' of 1 are really much more relevant in broader socio-cultural terms. It would seem, however, to be not entirely fortuitous that the Djarada is linked with the Rose River cycle. Although it emphasizes, in contrast, personal aspirations, it also leads to dominance by one sex over the other.

Traditional north-eastern Arnhem Land sexuality has been 'caught', as it were, between the social and the sacred. Two features are essential to understand if we are to appreciate these forms of behaviour within their particular socio-cultural setting. One concerns what I have called 'the climax'. In the Goulburn Island cycle, the climax is not necessarily the sexual act as such. Rather, it is what results from it, and this is true too for the Rose River cycle. Second, sexual activity as portrayed in both these cycles is 'enclosed' or wrapped round with a complex patterning of symbolic imagery which creates a special atmosphere. This concerns the aesthetic dimension. It is possible to think of sexual relations, or the relations between the sexes, as having something to do with art, as having a particular quality, as being concerned with particular signals which would enhance sexual activity, *over and above* the purely physical (or biological) stimuli. It would seem reasonable to suggest therefore that traditionally, in this cultural area, the sexual act would rarely be performed without an aesthetic context. Traditionally, that context was as important as the sexual act itself: it was really a question of taste or of preference, at the level of interpersonal relations, a matter of the projection of particular values clustered round particular situational responses. It was, therefore, the implied intention of these songs to create a 'romantic' atmosphere, providing purpose, together with individual satisfaction.

The Djarada, however, whatever it may be elsewhere in Aboriginal Australia, is—in this setting—essentially hedonistic. It is intrusive and antithetical to traditional aesthetic values and partially destructive of them. Furthermore, it subordinates traditionally-defined concepts of beauty to personal inclination and the demands of the moment, so limiting or narrowing relations between the sexes. It is, above all, a secularizing influence.

As Australian-European contact is intensified in this part of Arnhem Land, tastes and aesthetic values change—as they have already done. The great religious cycles are now performed less frequently. The three faces of love become one—and that one can be increasingly identified as a secular face, a face which is concerned primarily with personal physical gratification. The beauty of the disappearing present and the immediate past becomes a romantic mirage which can no longer be recaptured from oblivion.

APPENDIXES

THE INTERLINEAR TEXTS

NOTES TO THE APPENDIXES

Spelling

I have kept the spelling of vernacular words as simple as possible, with a minimum of special symbols and spellings. However, I have adhered to the long-standing convention that in phonetic rendering (and in italics) '*j*' is pronounced as 'y'. And the symbol '*ŋ*' is a convenient way of referring to 'ng' when this is a single sound—whereas English speakers who have trouble with this sound seem prone to splitting it into two, separating the 'n' and the 'g'. In a few words I have retained the glottal stop, shown here by an ordinary inverted comma.

Wherever possible, I have included hyphens to make the words seem less formidable. This is quite straightforward in some cases, for example where the suffixes *-ŋura* and *-lili* make for a reasonable natural division. In other instances it is not really appropriate; nevertheless, here and there I have added hyphens, especially in the Rose River cycle, in words such as *ŋurl-marŋ-marŋ*.

Still on the matter of spelling: since these are 'sung' words, they do not necessarily conform with the shape they would take in ordinary speech—and I have not tried to 'correct' them to that shape. And I have left some variants in this respect, such as *ŋulbur* (for *ŋulbur*[*u*]) and *ŋulbru*.

Translation

The Goulburn Island and Rose River cycles present no real difficulties because, notwithstanding 'singing' and 'inside' words, they are in local dialects which the singers knew and which could readily be translated. It is true that I have not gone into details about the translations. That would have meant too much discussion, especially where words have multiple meanings, or where tense or completed action are involved: for example, *bidjan*, 'thus', refers to present action, whereas *bidjara* conveys a 'past' perspective; and either of these can stand by itself. Also, *bili* can mean 'because', but in other contexts it is a past-indicator, or completed-action indicator. In regard to number: the translation shows some flexibility, as between singular and plural, because mostly the distinction rests on context and not on differences in word form.

In the Djarada, although there are a few local words, the majority were not familiar to the Aboriginal commentators, including the singer. In translation, I have followed what they said they understood the songs to mean. I suspect that in some cases where words appear almost identical but are translated differently, one clue may lie in the tunes which also distinguish one song from another. Such problems are common where songs travel outside the area where their original language is known. But the main thing for our purpose here is what the Yirrkalla people concerned took to be the meaning —i.e. what songs meant to them.

APPENDIX I

THE GOULBURN ISLAND SONG CYCLE

Song 1

bili	*ŋaii*	*bunbuwam*	*milgari*	*njinadugan*	*djamurbunara*
because	it	make	forked stick	put	rafter
gururuɾu	*bugu-damalajuman*				
floor post	make roof like sea-eagle nest[1]				
baima	*malwi*	*ŋaiiŋa*	*guruwilin*	*jalmaŋa*	
always there	Place[2]	it (camp)	Place[3]	Place[3]	
njinadugan	*geindja*	*gwiaŋin*	*galameimei*	*didjiwuru*	
put	force (of rain)	think of	west rain	west rain	
mugali	*waidbargŋa*				
west wind	come up[4]				
njinadugan	*djimdjimdun*	*ganbi-ganbi*	*gadalwuru*	*milgari*	
put	put along[5]	top rail (rafter)	rail	forked stick	
gumur-naŋal	*djimalgan*	*dalaidjŋu*	*burulian*		
chest saw	(invocation)[6]	(invocation)[6]	(invocation)[6]		
gumur-naŋal	*dunaraŋ*	*gaiwiniaŋ*	*gundjul-gundjulna*		
chest saw	(invocation)	(invocation)[6]	(invocation)		
ŋamaŋamaiun	*daa*	*galmag*	*galwin*	*ŋuruduan*	
make	mouth[7]	entrance	middle of camp[8]	hut[9]	
geindja	*gwiaŋir*	*warei-wareina*	*gandalilna*	*balwalunda*	
(rain)	think of	west wind and rain	rain and wind	come up	
dud-dudunda	*ŋambaljunda*				
noise of storm	spread over				
ŋuwarlgaŋ	*njinaduga*	*milgari*	*gadalwuru*	*djamalbunara*	
carefully	put	forked stick	rail	side post	
gumur-naŋal	*marei-mareina*	*mandalboina*	*ragwarina*		
chest saw	clan[10]	clan[11]	clan[11]		

buguweima	*malwi*	*mialmir*	*guruwilin*	
always there	Place	Place	Place	
gabu-digdig	*dambarŋa*	*jalmaŋa*	*ŋuwarlgaŋ*	*gadalwuru*
open expanse of water	Place[3]	Place	carefully	rail

1 Putting on a roof of branches and paperbark with sheets of stringybark. This is likened to a sea-eagle's nest among the trees. *Bugu* means 'face', 'forehead'. The bird is the *damala* (one of its main names).

2 These stilted houses are built in and around a large billabong in the bush, on the mainland south-east of Goulburn Islands.

3 A place with an open billabong edged with bamboo. From these plants, shafts were cut for spears, and bundles traded into north-eastern Arnhem Land.

4 Clouds come from the west, across the sea. Reaching the mainland, they spread over the billabong where the houses are being built.

5 Covering the sides or walls of the hut.

6 Invocation (*bugali*, or power name) associated with Goulburn Islands; referring to clouds rising from the west.

7 Entrance or door of hut.

8 Inside of hut.

9 'Inside' name for the whole hut, both outside and within. The term 'inside' refers to its sacred, sometimes secret-sacred name in contrast to its 'outside' or ordinary name. A large number of such words are used in these songs, together with special 'singing words', which express different qualities or attributes of the creature or object referred to.

10 Yirrkalla version of name belonging to the local clan living in these stilted huts; Maiar'maiar.

11 This clan comes from the mouth of the Woolen River, on the mainland south-east of the Crocodile Islands (Milingimbi), not far from the billabong where the Wawalag sisters were swallowed by Yulunggul. Sometimes it is said to refer to the Goulburn Island people.

Song 2

guruwulu	*djamurbunara*	*galmag*		
forked stick	rafter	entrance		
gumur-naŋal	*dawiliŋun*	*buraran*	*bunbumnaruŋ*	
chest saw	Goulburn I. people[1]	tribe[2]	make along	
bunbumnaruŋ	*bugu-damalajuman*			
make along	make roof like sea-eagle (nest)			
gumur-naŋal	*durlulŋan*	*waranbagalin*	*djalbieian*	*malin-malin*
chest saw	(invocation)[3]	(invocation)[3]	(invocation)[4]	(invocation)[5]
gumur-naŋal	*bunbumnaruŋ*	*bunbarabarŋa*	*guruwulgamin*	
chest saw	make along	snake coiling up	Snake entrails[6]	
djalbieian	*garaŋam*	*bunbuwam*		
(invocation)[4]	all over[7]	make		
ŋamaba	*burulima*	*darial*	*garaŋala*	*djiririwuruma*
Place[8]	Place[8]	Place[9]	all over	Place[10]
garaŋam	*ŋuruŋiwa*	*damala*	*gulaiibei*	*garaŋam*
all over	Place[11]	Sea-eagle Place[12]	Place[13]	all over

bunbuwam *buwaringa*
make Place[14]

bilin *njagu* *ŋuwaidjin* *ŋaii*
because for me (mine) become good[15] it

guruwulu *bugu-damala* *gadalwuru* *galmag*
forked stick roof like sea-eagle (nest) rail entrance

ganbi-ganbi *guruwulu*
top rail forked stick

bili *malwi* *baima* *mialmir* *guruwilin*
because Place always there Place Place

gabu-digdig *jalmaŋa*
open (expanse of) water Place

ŋaii *ŋuwaidjin* *garaŋam* *bunbuwam* *gunumba*
it becomes good all over make Place[16]

waial *waiduwan* *jaljalani* *garaŋam* *dawal-dawal* *ŋagadadba*
clouds[17] pass over[18] line up[17] all over Place[19] Place[19]

bidjandawul *ŋaii* *bunbuwam* *gumur-naŋal* *maŋan-naŋ*
this way/like it make chest saw clouds saw

bandi *djimdjimdunda* *ŋaga-ŋaga* *bandigura*
west clouds[20] lie along west clouds[21] clouds[22]

gumur-naŋal *muluna* *didjiwurun* *galameimeiŋa*
chest saw black cloud[23] raining sheet of rain

birwirunda *ŋambaljunda* *dud-dud-dunda*
thunder[24] spread over noise of thunder

ŋaiam *bunbuwam* *njaguwei* *ŋaii* *guruwuru* *gadalwuru*
I make for myself it forked stick rail

ganbi-ganbi *milgari*
top rail forked stick

baiaŋaŋu *njagu* *birwirljuwa* *durbuliwa*
leave for me noise of thunder thunder along bottom of clouds[25]

dambar *jalmaŋ* *gabu-digdig* *malwi*
Place Place open (expanse of) water Place

ŋaiam *bunbum* *bugu-damalajuman* *dambal* *gabul*
I make make roof like sea-eagle (nest) in water

waiduwan *malwiu* *gurulwindu*
swim along[26] Place open (expanse of) water

ŋaiam *jalala* *bunbum* *baiaŋuŋu* *njagu* *madei-madajuwa*
I later on make leave for me tongue flickers

bili *nunu* *mada-wirmeiba* *durbuliwan*
because you tongues twist to one another[27] thunder along bottom of clouds

jabei-jaba *guruwana* *mainbunara* *miraunjina*
Place[28] Place[29] Place[29] Place[29]

ŋaiam *nuŋgu* *jalala* *djimdjimdun* *darba* *milgari*
I for you later on lie along post forked stick

gadalwuru *guruwuru*
rail forked stick

nunum *njagu* *maŋan* *jararejuwa* *daiimimduwa* *bunbum*
you for me clouds line up along lie along make[30]

25 *ŋaga-ŋaga* *jiridja* *dugaia* *mambulbul* *gurgarwir*
clouds *jiridja* wind[31] wind[31] clouds[32]
rulbu-rulbu *malagara* *njinaduga* *djiŋgana* *djiŋgalwulba* *djamalaŋani*
wind wind[33] put in clouds[34] small clouds west wind[35]
duan *durbulijuwa* *birwirjuwa*
that thunder along bottom of clouds make thunder noise
gunduwirjuwa *madajuwa*
make noise and lightning tongue flickers
ŋaiam *nuŋgu* *jalala* *ŋamaŋamaiun* *daa* *galmag*
I for you later on make mouth entrance
duan *gawinma*
that middle of hut
bili *ŋaia* *djimagaiu* *burulian-ŋaiu* *dalaidjŋuju*
because I (invocation)[36] (invocation)[36] (invocation)[36]
meialwudun-naiu
(invocation)[36]

30 *waidun* *njaguwei* *ŋaia* *bunbum* *dambal* *gabul* *malwiu*
swim[26] for myself I make in water Place
jalmaŋli *balaŋureiu* *djuduli* *guruwilindu* *mialmandu*
Place Place[37] Place[37] Place Place
gabu-digdigli *bugu-damalajuman* *waiduwan*
open (expanse of) water make like sea-eagle (nest) swim along[26]
gumur-naŋal *duŋaran* *geiwiŋian* *gundjul-gundjulna*
chest saw (invocation)[36] (invocation)[36] (invocation)[36]

1 *Babaru* group of the Goulburn Island people: i.e. the original paternal clan. For a description of the use of the term *babaru* see R. Berndt (1965 : 79).

Descent in eastern Arnhem Land being predominantly patrilineal in emphasis, the composers of these songs tend to project this feature on to other societies as well. Most of the western Arnhem Land tribes emphasize matrilineal descent. This term refers, then, to the father's group or tribe, not clan as in the eastern region. Moreover, such terms are in the eastern Riradjingu dialect, and would not necessarily be known to the western people.

2 The Burara 'tribe' living near Cape Stewart. These people and their immediate neighbours serve, in a sense, as a buffer between the two dissimilar cultures of western and eastern Arnhem Land. From them came most of the painted skulls which were in 1946–47 well-known along the north coast.

3 This invocation refers to the male (and female) Yulunggul python(s) who swallowed the Wawalag Sisters (see R. Berndt 1951*a*).

4 This invocation refers to the sinuous twisting of the Yulunggul.

5 This invocation refers to Yulunggul's belly dragging on the ground as it moves.

6 This refers to the *gundaru* rock python, digesting food. When Yulunggul swallowed the two Sisters and child, this snake swallowed a *djandil* wild cat. Later, the two stood erect and spoke to each other.

7 Stilted houses are being erected all around and in the billabong.

8 From this place, on the mainland opposite Milingimbi, emerge (according to Yirrkalla belief) the clouds that rise in the west.

9 The place where the clouds are 'standing'.

10 Situated on the mainland west of Milingimbi, and so named because of its association with the Djanggawul, who put *lindaridj* (or *lindiridj*; parakeet) feathers there. These

feathers may still be seen, metamorphosed as rocks radiating red and blue colours in the sunlight, or as coloured reflections in the water of the swamps.

11 In the bush on the mainland south of Milingimbi; its name was interpreted as meaning 'all clouds there'.

12 This place is on the eastern bank of Milingimbi creek, on the island itself; its name refers to clouds resembling the sea-eagle (*damala*).

13 Milingimbi Point, east of the mission station; its name refers to clouds.

14 A sandpoint (or spit) east of Goulburn Islands.

15 'Becoming good', or 'rising up'—i.e., the stilted hut is nearing completion.

16 A place north-east of Milingimbi Island.

17 Clouds form a bank along the horizon; they are said to 'line up along, standing'.

18 Clouds coming from the west pass over Milingimbi Island. The word used here means that the clouds 'swim' over the island.

19 'Inside' names for the north-eastern part of Milingimbi Island.

20 These clouds, although of the *dua* moiety, are similar to a yellow variety classified in the north-east as of the *jiridja* moiety.

21 They are all coming up.

22 'Inside' name for these clouds; 'younger' or small clouds rise from the horizon and form larger ones, banking across the sky.

23 Black lowering rain clouds.

24 Explained as 'lightning makes noise'.

25 Thunder rolls along the bottom of the clouds, 'pushing the rain away' so that it falls.

26 Referring to a floating hut: see page 52.

27 The flashing of lightning, its 'play' along the horizon on the edge of clouds. *Mada* is the 'tongue' of the snake, which makes lightning as it flickers.

28 Clouds rise from this Place, translated as 'Two Sisters' (*jaba*, sister), where Yulunggul swallowed the Wawalag sisters. The word also refers to the clouds ('sister' clouds) which hover above this place.

29 Same place as 28: names refer to banking clouds.

30 Banking up.

31 The north-west *jiridja* moiety wind, blowing up *jiridja* clouds (see note 20).

32 Clouds blown up by the north-west winds: literally 'like penes', referring to the rain which they hold, 'ready for urinating'.

33 A cold gust of wind bringing relief from the intense humidity of the wet season, and said to 'blow like a cloud'. Now people feel refreshed, for it is 'good wind time', and 'you are ready for anything; you feel fresh from that wind'. At this time, too, young sharks are born, and it is fairly easy to obtain large quantities of food. The people throw themselves with added vigour into hunting and lovemaking, dancing and singing.

34 Small clouds appearing above the horizon.

35 The word *djamalaŋani* refers to the sacred *djamalara* singing of the *kunapipi*; its sound is carried on the western winds.

36 Invocation referring to clouds rising from Goulburn Islands.

37 Places located on the mainland, south-east of the Goulburn Islands. *Djuduli* refers to a sacred tree-emblem place.

Song 3

1	*bili*	*maiaŋan*	*dunba*	*waribum*	*djalubi*
	because	get	beating sticks[1]	another	drone pipe (didjeridu)

bili *wogal* *ŋaruŋan*
because fun[3] feel[3]

ŋaraga *ŋuban* *malwarin* *raguwaiu*
beating sticks[1] beat[4] singing (rhythm) Goulburn Island people

dawiliŋoiu *mandalboiu*
Goulburn Island *babaru* clan

mirigin *djaljalju* *wuŋanŋiwu* *lul'lulŋa* *woŋan* *guluwuru*
chest cold wind west wind didjeridu 'speaks' sound[5]

ŋuban *banal* *naiiŋa* *bugu-damalaŋa*
beat in there it roof like sea-eagle (nest)

guruwuruŋa *garaŋam* *malari*
floor posts (forked sticks) all over sound[6]

ŋuban *buwariŋga* *ŋamaba* *darial* *damala* *ŋuruŋiwa*
beat Place Place Place Sea-eagle Place Place

dunawari *djiririwuruma* *burulima* *gulaiibei* *ŋubannan*
Place[7] Place Place Milingimbi Point beat

guruwulu
forked stick

ŋuban *wogal* *ŋaruŋan* *djimalguwal*
beat fun feel (invocation) of the western clouds

dalaidjŋu *burujunawul*
(invocation) of west clouds (invocation) of west clouds

meialwudunŋawul *djimalguwul*
(invocation) of west clouds (invocation) of west clouds

garaŋam *waidun* *woŋa* *gunumba*
all over[8] swim[9] sound Place

waial *dawal-dawal* *ŋagadadba* *balumara* *bumurwumir*
clouds line up Place Place Place Place (Island of Clouds)

mirigin *ŋuban* *wadarwul* *djalijalwul* *wuŋaniwul* *maladarawul*
chest beat with wind cold wind west wind west wind

ŋan *ŋaliŋgum* *djinagwi* *malwawiri* *jalwiun* *boiu*
it ours from within from singing[10] blows blows

miwulgdun
moves branches

wadar *djalijal* *ŋuru-miwaidj* *bii-ŋuru*
wind cold wind 'stranger' from somewhere

darial-ŋuru
from Goulburn Islands

1 Clapping sticks for beating time while singing, usually termed *bilma*: *ŋaraga* means 'bone'.

2 Literally, 'play'.

3 I.e., for enjoyment or pleasure.

4 Specially used for women's part in beating ('following') the rhythm.

5 Yirrkalla people use this word to refer to the sound of the didjeridu when blown by Goulburn Island men, which differs from its sound when blown by north-eastern Arnhem Landers. In the former case, it is said the Goulburn Islanders 'twist their tongue all the time' as they blow. The word *guluwuru* refers to this 'tongue twisting' in playing, and also symbolically refers to 'foreskin' (see R. Berndt 1952).

6 The combined sound of didjeridu, beating sticks and singing.
7 A large sandhill, opposite Milingimbi settlement.
8 'Drift right over': the sound from the singing and the instruments comes over from the huts, like clouds.
9 The sound of the singing, didjeridu and beating sticks is wafted across the waters ('swimming') to the various places mentioned in the text.
10 As soon as they begin to dance and sing, the wind rises.

Song 4

bili *mindji* *maiaŋan* *bumbuŋa* *maleigara* *bili*
because colour get coloured clay[1] coloured clay because
njinadugan
put on

mindji *gabu* *binji-binji* *barwula* *waribum* *mindji*
colour water water mark on chest[2] water mark another colour

rarjum *madamada* *gurulbu* *boiumin*
put on dilly bag[3] dilly bag[3] dilly bag[3]

mindji *ŋugan* *raguwariu* *bareiu* *mandalboiu*
colour put on Goulburn Island people clan[4] clan

baima *malwi* *ruruwilin* *balaŋuru*
always there Place Place Place

waribum *rarjuwan* *darba* *gwalala* *muŋguli*
another put on paint[5] fighting stick fighting stick
madil *ŋugan*
fighting stick put on

mindji *waribum* *ŋalduma* *babi* *dugmundor* *gwoiwil*
colour another put on top snake snake[6] snake
gawul-gawul *jalwadbad*
black freshwater snake snake[7]

waribum *djarwuli* *ŋugan* *maliguŋu* *bumbuŋa*
another boomerang put on coloured one coloured clay
durlmin
coloured clay

waribum *rarjuwan* *mindji* *gwoiŋja-lili* *galiwali*
another put on colour on to small boomerang boomerang
djarwuli *djarwilgwilg* *durlmin* *njinadugan*
small boomerang small boomerang clay put along

dunarawa *gaiwiniarawa* *gundjul-gundjulruwa* *garaŋam*
(invocation)[8] (invocation) (invocation) all over
mainbunara *jabei-jaba* *guruwana*
Place Place of Two Sisters Place

garaŋam *mindji* *ŋugan* *gulaiibei* *darial*
all over colour put on Milingimbi Point Place

ŋamaba *burulima* *ŋuruŋiwa* *damala* *buwariŋga*
Place Place Place Sea-eagle Place Place
dunawari *baraŋal* *djiririwuruma*
Place Place Place

1 This particular clay resembles ant-hill (termite mound) earth.

2 The design painted on the men's chests represents 'water': i.e., water that will eventually fill the swamps where the stilted huts have been built.
3 This particular 'dilly bag' is really a padded ball.
4 *Mareimarei, mala* (clan) at Goulburn Island.
5 A type of ochre; the word itself means 'tree', or 'stick'.
6 The men paint snake designs in ochre on their chests.
7 This is the Yirawadbad snake which figures prominently in the important *ubar* rituals of western Arnhem Land.
8 Referring to Goulburn Island clay. In Song 1 the same invocations refer to clouds rising from the west. There is said to be a 'singing' association between these and the clay.

Song 5

bili	*goŋ*	*galginan*	*badjil*	*gurulbu*	*maiaŋan*	*djinaŋ*
because	hand	put close	basket	basket[1]	get	within
gu	*ŋalma*	*mariunna*	*judriun*	*djinaŋ*	*guluboiu*	
come on	we	dance	step along	within	dilly bag	
madamadaiu						
dilly bag						
boiu-mirwulgdun	*mirwulgdun-ŋanjin*					
sway branches	sway					
buguweima	*wonjumiŋalji*	*buwariŋga*	*darial*			
always there	Place[2]	Place	Place			
ŋalma	*mariunna*	*mirwulgduna*	*wadarwul*	*djalijalwul*	*wuŋaŋoiwul*	
we	dance	sway	wind	cold wind	west wind	
mirigin	*naŋal*	*munoi-munoina*				
chest	saw	clan[3]				
raguwarina	*mandalboina*	*daludboidjna*				
Goulburn Island people	clan	long penis[4]				
darwuliŋun	*gurga*	*munmunna*				
clan[5]	penis	long foreskin				
bidjan	*mirigin*	*boiu-mirwulgdun*	*ŋuruŋiwaiu*	*dunawariu*		
this way	chest	sway branches	Place	Place		
baraŋali	*damaleiu*					
Place	Sea-eagle Place					
bidjan	*mirwulgduwa*	*mirigin*	*gulaiibaiu*	*darialju*		
this way	sway	chest	Milingimbi Point	Place		
ŋamabal	*burulimaiu*					
Place	Place					
mariunna-judun	*djimalga*					
dance along	(invocation) of Goulburn Island west clouds					
meialwuduna						
(invocation) of Goulburn Island west clouds						
dalaidjŋu						
(invocation) of Goulburn Island west clouds						
mariunna-judun	*burulijuŋa*	*balwadgad*	*njinbaruŋa*			
dance along	(invocation) west clouds	(invocation)	(invocation)			
mirigin	*naŋal*	*duŋaran*	*gaiwiniaŋ*			
chest	saw	(invocation)	(invocation)			

bili	*buguweima*	*ŋaiiŋ*	*bugu-damalaŋa*	*wunuŋulŋa*
because	always there	it	roof like sea-eagle (nest)	hut[6]

1 A ball bag or fighting bag. Men hold these by the teeth.
2 Wonjumi Island, near the Goulburn Islands.
3 Meaning 'new paperbark sapling': referring to people who are short in stature.
4 This refers to the uncircumcised western Arnhem Landers.
5 A *babaru* of these western people.
6 An 'inside' name.

Song 6

bili	*dubduwanan*	*mandja*	*didjuwan*	*ŋoiŋuban*	
because	throw away	branches	throw back	push back (wind)	
marin	*gandalili*	*gadalwulwulju*			
cabbage palm	into cabbage palm[1]	cabbage palm[2]			
djarma	*baiaŋ*	*njaguŋ*	*duriun-ŋan*	*gabu*	*ragaram*
branches[3]	leave	for me	blow along it	water	tell
malwi	*gabu-digdig*	*mialmir*	*jalmaŋa*	*guruwilin*	
Place	open water	Place	Place	Place	
duriu-ŋanjin	*birariuwan*	*wururuŋ*	*munaŋin*	*galada*	*mareiiŋga*
blow along	twist and turn[4]	branches	branches	branches	branches
wagmin	*bidjan*	*dubduwan*	*didjuwan*		
branches	this way	throw away	throw back		
dau-ragaram	*gabu*	*ŋoibanŋu*	*djaniŋarŋu*		
news tell	water	Place	Place[5]		
gabu-ŋuban	*mirigin*	*dubduwan*	*wadarwul*		
water rushes	chest	throw away	wind		
djalijalwul	*ŋan*	*djinagwoi*	*dubdunda*		
cold wind	it	from within	thrown away		
ŋaliŋguŋ	*wadar*	*ŋaruŋan*	*djalijal*	*wuŋani*	
ours	wind	feel	cold wind	west wind	
waribum	*boiu-mirwulgdun*	*ŋaliŋguŋ*	*wadar*		
another	sway branches	ours	wind		
jiridja	*manbulbul*	*dugaia*			
jiridja	north-west wind	north-west wind			
ŋalma	*gurgawiri*	*rulbu-rulbu*	*baiaŋan*		
we	north-west wind[6]	north-west wind	leave it		
dubdunda	*ŋaliŋguŋ*	*duriuŋin*			
thrown away	ours	blow along[7]			
dau-ragaram	*wururuŋdu*	*mandjarju*	*burmaŋa*	*garalwarlŋa*	
news tell	branches	branches	Place[8]	Place	
dau-ragaram	*dilibuma*	*jabei-jabam*	*guruwanan*		
news tell	Place[9]	Place of Two Sisters	Place		
mararŋinaŋun	*guruwanan*				
Place[9]	Place				

1 This word, translated in Song 1 as 'rain and wind' from the west, here refers to the cabbage palm which is associated with them.

2 This word, translated previously as 'rail', here refers to the stem or trunk of the cabbage palm.
3 Branches are blown by the wind into the cabbage palm.
4 Branches blown 'round and round' by the west wind.
5 An inland or bush place, on the mainland opposite Milingimbi; this is the supposed birthplace of the Wawalag sisters, but the exact location of *Djaniŋarŋu* is unidentified.
6 This word in Song 2 refers to clouds, and here to the wind bringing these clouds. It is derived from *gurga*, penis, i.e. the cold wind retracts the men's penes.
7 Float along in the wind.
8 Wind blowing through the branches is calling the name of this place.
9 The place where the Wawalag were swallowed by Yulunggul. There are several alternative names for this site.

Song 7

bili *badji* *ŋaldumanan* *gurulbu* *rarjuna-naruŋ*
because basket hang up[1] ball bag put on along
dambal *darbal*
on to post
milgarin *ŋaiil* *guruwulul* *gadalwurul*
forked stick it (camp) forked stick rail
galŋan *maligin* *boiu-mirwulgdundeiu* *gunjaŋan*
skin (body) tired from swaying branches put on
badji *madamada* *gurulbu* *jelagandja*
basket ball bag ball bag ball bag
waribum *rarjun* *galamba* *waribum* *gunja* *ŋaiil* *galmagli*
another put on headband another put on it (camp) at entrance
duan *mudbu* *djindgal* *marabin* *rarjuna* *munmunba* *ŋaiili*
that headband[2] wear headband put on headband it (camp)
guruwulul *milgaril* *djamurbunarar*
forked stick on forked stick rafter
mirigin *naŋal* *rarjunda* *munoi-munoina*
chest saw put on clan (new paperbark saplings)
ragwawarana *darwuliŋun*
Goulburn Island people clan
gurga *munmunna* *daludboidjna*
penis long foreskin long penis
mirigin *naŋal* *badjil* *rarjunda* *madamadal*
chest saw basket put on ball bag
gunja-naruŋ *gurulbu* *madjindji* *madamada* *jelagandja* *dambal*
put along ball bag ball bag ball bag ball bag on to
ŋaiil *galmagli*
it (camp) at entrance
daŋgarŋaramiŋgan *milgaril* *guruwurul*
hang up forked stick forked stick
mirigin *naŋal* *dalaidjŋun* *burulijuŋan* *meialwudun-ŋan*
chest saw (invocation)[3] (invocation)[3] (invocation)[3]
bawadgadŋa *njinburuŋan*
(invocation)[3] (invocation)[3]
buguweima *malwi*
always there Place

[1] The dancers hang their bags on the wooden posts of the huts.
[2] Made from possum fur and belonging to the *dua* moiety.
[3] 'Clouds rising from the west' (see Song 1).

Song 8

bili *badji* *gialaraŋan* *mindjal-wulgduwan* *buman-ŋin*
because ball bag get ready[1] split it make it
gurulbu *badji* *boiumin* *madamada* *jelagandja*
ball bag ball bag ball bag ball bag ball bag
buguweima *malwi* *djuduŋa* *ŋaiiŋa* *bugu-damalaŋa* *wulnuŋa*
always there Place Place it (camp) roof like sea-eagle (nest) hut
mirigin *naŋal* *wirgulna* *manawinna* *buraran* *mandalboina*
breast[2] saw girl(s) girl(s) tribe[3] clan
raguwarwaŋa *djinani-djinaniŋ* *marei-mareina* *buman-ŋin*
Goulburn Island clan clan clan make it
gwuwalum *badji* *mindjal-wulgdun* *gelaram*
move hand basket split split
buguweima *darial* *ŋamaba* *burulima* *garaŋala* *ŋuruŋiwa* *bilmiri*
always there Place Place Place all over Place Place
gumur-naŋal *gialaraŋara* *gumur-woŋa* *buma*
breast saw[2] soften and tease pandanus strips[1] breast moving make
mindjal-wulgdun *gurulbu* *madjindji* *madamada*
split ball bag basket ball bag
bili *ŋaiiŋa* *rabaŋa* *guruwilin* *djuduŋa* *mialmir*
because it (camp) middle of hut (or camp) Place Place Place
buguweima *malwi* *gabu-digdig* *balaŋura* *dambarŋa*
always there Place open water Place Place
buman-ŋin *ŋaiiŋa* *galmagna* *bugu-damalaŋa* *gurururuŋa*
make it it (camp) entrance roof like sea-eagle (nest) floor posts
djamulbunaraŋa
side slats, wall, coverings of brush, etc.
buguweima *malwi* *darial* *damala* *wariŋga*
always there Place Place Sea-eagle Place Place
djiririwuruma *ŋamaba* *burulima*
Place Place Place

[1] Splitting and preparing pandanus leaves.
[2] These words can mean 'chest' or 'breast(s)', depending on context.
[3] See Song 2, note 2: referring in this case to a group of girls belonging to this tribe.

Song 9

bili *maiaŋan* *wadjar* *gwaljumŋin* *wirgulju* *nawiŋgwiu*
because get string[1] make it young girl tribe[2]
laŋarumŋin *wirgulju* *guniŋgwiu* *burareiu*
move strings[3] young girl tribe[2] tribe
maidga-wulunŋin *wadjarwun* *mirigin* *naŋal* *ragwarina*
breast girdle[3] twist string breast saw Goulburn Island people
marei-mareina
clan

buguweima *ŋaiiŋa* *malwi* *wunurlŋa* *ŋaiiŋa* *malwi*
always there it (camp) Place Place it (camp) Place
gwaljumŋin *djinalaŋa* *milgariŋa* *bugu-damalaŋa*
make it inside on forked stick[4] roof like sea-eagle (nest)
mirigin *naŋal* *mandalboina* *ragwarina* *gwaljumŋin*
breasts saw clan Goulburn Island people make it
gidilaiun
move hands
mirigin *djaljalwul* *wadarwul* *milju* *ganidjuman*
breasts cold wind wind with eye wink[5]
bili *durbu-wogal* *dawaliŋu*
because buttocks move[6] Goulburn Island *babaru*[7]
laŋarna *ŋaliŋgu* *djinagwoi* *baima* *malwi* *maidga-wulunŋin*
string ours within always there Place breast girdle
naŋal *julŋun* *ragwarina* *gurga* *munmunna*
saw people Goulburn Island people penis long foreskin
dawiliŋum
Goulburn Island *babaru*
milju *ganidjuman* *wirgulju* *burareiu* *guniŋgwiu* *nawiŋgwiu*
with eye wink young girl tribe tribe tribe
buguweima *jalmaŋa* *guruwilin* *malwi* *gabu-digdig*
always there Place Place Place open water
mirigin *naŋal* *marei-mareina* *djinaniŋ-djinaniŋ*
breast saw clan clan
bili *ŋaliŋgu* *wogal* *ŋaruŋan* *ŋali* *gwaljumŋin*
because for us play feel we make it
wadjarwun *balaŋaniŋura* *buman-ŋin* *maidgalwun*
twisting string Place make it breast girdle
bili *wirgul* *durbu-wogal* *nawiŋgu* *marei-marei*
because girls buttocks move tribe clan
ragwarina
Goulburn Island people
bidjan *wadjarwun-ŋin* *nama* *daludbudna* *gurga-munmunna*
this way twist string see long foreskin penes with foreskins
dawiliŋun
Goulburn Island *babaru*
milju *ganidjuman* *ŋali* *waidjarwun-ŋin*
with eye wink we twist string
djinal *radjiŋa* *gunbululna*
in cabbage palm[8] cabbage palm
ŋaiiŋa *damalaŋa* *gururuŋa* *milgariŋa* *ganbi-ganbiŋa*
it (camp) sea-eagle (nest) floor posts on forked stick top rail
bili *buguweima* *darial* *ŋamaba* *burulima* *garaŋala*
because always there Place Place Place Place all over
buwariŋga *darial* *gulaiibei*
Place Place Milingimbi Point
mirigin *naŋal* *ragwuwarina* *buraran* *mandalboina*
breast saw Goulburn Island people tribe clan
guniŋgun *nawiŋgun*
tribe tribe

mirigin *naŋal* *guniŋgum* *buguweima* *wunurlŋa* *balaŋura*
breast saw tribe always there Place Place
jalmaŋa *guruwilin* *mialmir*
Place Place Place
mirigin *naŋal* *laŋarwunara* *gwala-wunara*
breasts saw move string make it
waidjar-wunara *ŋaiiŋa* *gadalwuru-ŋura* *ganbi-ganbiŋa*
twisting strings it (camp) on rail on top rail
milgariŋa *gugururuŋa*
on forked stick on floor post

1 I.e., cat's-cradle's, or string figures; more usually played by girls before the birth of their first child.
2 A western tribe, probably the Gunwinggu (now centred at Oenpelli).
3 The *maidga*, in eastern Arnhem Land, is a special girdle of twine formerly worn by girls; it is passed over the shoulders, crossing in front between the breasts. Girls take them off to use in making string figures.
4 Girls lean against the forked sticks of the hut as they play at string figures.
5 Girls are 'eyeing' men as they play their string games. To wink one's eyes at a sweetheart in order to attract him is widely used throughout Arnhem Land, by both men and women.
6 'Buttocks play': girls undulate their buttocks to attract lovers.
7 They speak in 'Goulburn Island language'.
8 Girls hide in the cabbage palm foliage, awaiting their lovers.

Song 10

bili *waragandu* *naŋal* *wirgulna* *buraran* *waidjar-wunara*
because bird[1] saw girl(s) tribe twist string
gwala-wunara
make it
ruwaŋ-ruwaŋduan *mil-manawun* *waragan* *ŋari-ŋariuwan*
looks at that (bird) eye looks[2] bird cries out
biawiig *ŋalgudja* *gumawuru* *naŋal* *waidjar-wunaral*
pigeon pigeon pigeon saw twist string
nawiŋgun *guniŋgun*
tribe tribe
waragandu *gidilwaiulwan* *ruwaŋduan* *naŋal* *daba-jalgdunda*
bird move hands looks at that saw heel taken away[2]
mil-waruŋgal
see (blood)
mil-manawun *biawiig* *mara-mara* *ŋalgudja* *darugma*
eye looks pigeon wings (flap) pigeon word[3]
ŋari-ŋariun *ŋunugwi* *jururuŋ* *wunurdarlbiŋ* *munarlgaŋ*
cries out from there Blue Mud Bay[4] Blue Mud Bay[4] Blue Mud Bay[4]
darugma *waragan* *juwe-juweiun* *garaŋariŋ* *wibunbaŋ*
word bird cries out Blue Mud Bay[4] Blue Mud Bay[4]
ŋalduwan *dambal* *radjiruŋ* *gulwiril* *marimunugli*
up on top on cabbage palm[5] on cabbage palm on cabbage palm

wunaŋiwul
cabbage palm
gadanan *darariu-wudun* *darba* *radjiŋ* *wunaŋia*
seize strike with claws limb cabbage palm cabbage palm
gunbulul
cabbage palm
ŋari-ŋariun *mil-waruŋgan*
cries out see (blood)
naŋal *gwala-wunara* *waidjar-wunara* *laŋar-wunara*
saw making them twist string move string
wirgulna *guniŋgun* *nawiŋgun*
girl(s) tribe tribe

1 This is a female bird, a pigeon, generally called *biawiig* (sometimes condensed to *biwi*). *Waragan* is an inclusive term for birds and animals generally.

2 The pigeon is said to be always looking for, and at, adolescent girls as they sit modestly with one heel against the vulva; it is waiting to see their menstrual blood.

3 The bird's cry on seeing the menstrual blood.

4 This pigeon is calling out from Blue Mud Bay, on the eastern coast of Arnhem Land. It belongs to the 'bottom' Djabu dialectal unit, and lives in the paperbark swamps among the new shoots. It leaves its home, and flies over towards western Arnhem Land and Goulburn Island country.

5 The pigeon perches on the cabbage palm, viewed here as a tabued tree.

Song 11

bili *naŋalan* *julŋuju* *dawiliŋoiu* *mandalboiu*
because saw people Goulburn Island *babaru* clan
wirgulna *waidjali* *gwala-wunaral*
girl(s) twist string make it
maidga-wunaral *nawiŋgun* *buraran* *marei-mareina* *guniŋgun*
twist breast girdle tribe tribe tribe tribe
dambal *radjil*
in that cabbage palm
meindjinan *gadanan* *gulwiri*
sneak along grab cabbage palm[1]
djurabduwan *rumdjinaŋ* *mardjin* *gulwiril*
sneak along bend down go (hide) among cabbage palm(s)
wunaŋial *mareimunugli*
cabbage palm(s)[2] among cabbage palm(s)
bili *gurga-minmin* *ragwarina* *dawaliŋu*
because penis long[3] Goulburn Island people Goulburn Island *babaru*
durbu-wogal
buttocks move
bili *baima* *ŋaiiŋa* *rabaŋa* *malwi*
because always there it (camp) Place Place
buguweima *gabu-digdig* *guruwilin*
always there open water Place
wogalna *ŋaruŋan* *naŋal* *wirgulna* *marei-mareina* *djinaniŋ-djinaniŋ*
play feel[4] saw girl(s) clan clan

buraran | *nawiŋgun* | *guniŋgun*
tribe | tribe | tribe

mardjinaŋ | *naŋal* | *laŋar-wunara* | *waidjar-wunara*
go (hide) | saw | move (string) | twist string

banabal | *maidga* | *maidga-wunara* | *gwala-wunara* | *julŋuju*
in that | breast girdle | twist breast girdle | make it | man

daludjbudŋa | *gurga-minmindu*
long foreskin | penis long

ragwarina | *dawiliŋoiu* | *durbu-wogalju*
Goulburn Island people | Goulburn Island *babaru* | buttocks move[5]

1 A man grasps a cabbage palm as he sneaks along in search of his sweetheart and then hides in the foliage.
2 A young woman sits under cabbage tree foliage awaiting her lover.
3 Translated as either erect penis or long foreskin.
4 Erotic play accentuates desire (*ŋaruŋan*, feeling) for coitus.
5 Movement of the girls' buttocks.

Song 12

bili | *gadanan* | *wirgulna* | *nawiŋgun* | *guniŋgun* | *buraran*
because | grab | young girl(s) | tribe | tribe | tribe

durbu-wogalju | *ragwawariu*
buttocks move | Goulburn Island people

gurga-minmindu | *jeidjawonan* | *jagejiwon* | *wirgul*
penis long | cry out[1] | cry out in pain[1] | girl(s)

marei-marei | *wogal* | *ŋaruŋan* | *druroiwonan* | *dambal*
clan | fun | feel | push over[2] | in that

gulwiril | *radjil*
cabbage palm | cabbage palm

gunjanaŋ | *nuganaŋ* | *bili* | *niniŋu* | *durbu-wogal*
put down[3] | have coitus ('eat') | because | always there | buttocks move[4]

dawiliŋu | *ragwawa* | *gurga-minmin*
Goulburn Island *babaru* | Goulburn Island people | penis long

gadanan | *mareiinna* | *wirgulna* | *buraran* | *nagaran* | *nawiŋgun* | *guniŋgun*
grab | 'pretty'[5] | girl(s) | tribe | tribe[6] | tribe | tribe

bili | *buguweima* | *malwi* | *dambarŋa* | *guruwilin* | *djuduŋa* | *mialmir*
because | always there | Place | Place | Place | Place | Place

durbu-woŋanan | *nuganaŋ* | *djiaŋan* | *julŋuju*
buttocks make sound[7] | have coitus | moving penis (in vagina) | people

dawiliŋuju
Goulburn Island *babaru*

bili | *ŋana* | *bana* | *wirgulna* | *mareiinna* | *buraran* | *guniŋgun*
because | it | they | girl(s) | 'pretty' | tribe | tribe

nagaran | *nawiŋgun* | *guniŋgun*
tribe | tribe | tribe

bili | *durbu-wogalju* | *daludjbudju* | *ragwariu*
because | buttocks move | long penis skin | Goulburn Island people

buguweima | *darial* | *ŋamaba*
always there | Place | Place

druroiwonan *gunjanaŋ* *gulwiril* *radjil* *gunbululi*
push over[2] put down cabbage palm cabbage palm cabbage palm

wunaŋial
cabbage palm

1 A girl cries out in alarm: i.e., a man comes up from behind and grabs her, pulling her squealing back towards him. She is hurt by the initial insertion.
2 'Push the girl over' on to her back.
3 Into position for coitus.
4 In this case, buttocks moving during coitus.
5 This refers to the girl, and is also translated as 'look nice'. The same word is used generally for anything or anyone sacred. See main text.
6 Evidently a reference to the Nagara tribe of western Arnhem Land, near the mouth of the Liverpool River.
7 Sound made by the girl's buttocks during coitus.

Song 13

bili *djalgdun-ŋanjin* *wirgul-lil* *mareiingul* *nawiŋgun* *guniŋgun*
because ejaculate it[1] into girl(s) into vagina[2] tribe tribe

djalgduwonan *gabu-gargululg* *mareiin* *gunbulwol*
ejaculate 'water' semen (vagina) sacred semen

wirgul-lil *burarawol*
into girl(s) tribe

dawiliŋuju *ragwawariu* *gurga-minminju*
Goulburn Island *babaru* Goulburn Island people penis long

djalgduwan *riala* *galwinbin* *luriŋanjin* *mareiingul* *burarawol*
ejaculate flow[3] semen runs down (from penis) into vagina tribe

bili *niniŋuju* *durbu-wogalju*
because always there buttocks move (in coitus)

buguweima *malwi* *ŋaiiŋa* *rabaŋa* *mialmir*
always there Place it (camp) Place Place

djinal *djalgdun-ŋin* *meiaŋa* *radjiŋa* *gunbulwuŋa*
into ejaculate it branches cabbage palm cabbage palm

bili *jeidjawonan* *wirgul* *nagara* *marei-marei*
because call out girl(s) tribe clan

ŋanma *nanŋu* *djalgduwan* *gargululg* *galwinbin* *gunbalol*
it for her ejaculate semen semen semen

meiaŋa *gulwirina* *marimunugna* *wunaŋiana*
branches cabbage palm cabbage palm cabbage palm

djalgduwonan *marei-mareiwul* *ragwawul*
ejaculate clan Goulburn Island people

baiali *gurga-ŋuru* *gurga-minmin-ŋuru* *dawiliŋuju*
from that from penis from penis long Goulburn Island *babaru*

ragwaiu
Goulburn Island people

buguweima *wunurlŋa* *gabu-digdig* *damalaŋa* *malwi*
always there Place open water Sea-eagle Place Place

bili *djalgduwonan* *gabu* *barwala* *galwinbin* *gargululg*
because ejaculate 'water' semen semen semen

baigul *wirgul-lil*
into them into girl(s)
marei-mareiwul *mareiingul* *burarawul* *nawiŋgul* *mandalboiul*
clan into (vagina) tribe tribe clan
djalgduwonan *gargululg* *guniŋgul*
ejaculate semen tribe
bili *bidjan dawul* *ŋan* *ŋaliŋgu* *gwalawan*
because this way it ours make it (string figures)
waidjarwian *laŋar-wulan*
twist string move string
ŋali *nanŋul* *bidjania* *djalgdun* *dambal* *mareiin-lil* *wirgul-lil*
we for her this way ejaculate into (vagina) into girl(s)
barwala *gabun* *gunbululna* *djinal* *meiaŋa* *radjiŋa*
semen 'water' semen into branches cabbage palm
gulwirina
cabbage palm
bidjan dawul *ŋali* *ŋana* *druroiwon* *meial*
this way we her push over (for coitus) (among) branches
wunaŋia *marimunugli* *wolariarlgul*
cabbage palm cabbage palm cabbage palm
ŋali *nanŋul* *djalgdun-ŋanjin* *gargululg* *mareiin* *djinagul*
we for her ejaculate it semen (vagina) within
wirgul-lil *nawiŋgul* *nagarawul* *guniŋgul*
into girl(s) tribe tribe tribe
djalgdun-ŋanjin *gabu* *binji-binji* *duwal-lil* *mareiin-lil*
ejaculate it 'water' semen[4] into that (vagina)
wirgul-lil *burarawul*
into girl tribe
bili *durbu-wogalju* *dawiliŋuju*
because buttocks move Goulburn Island *babaru*

1 'Throw (it) out'.
2 I.e., ejaculating semen into her during coitus. In this context, *mareiin* was translated as 'vagina'. The Aborigines themselves translated it as 'inside her hole' or simply as 'inside woman': probably it also means 'inside (her) uterus'.
3 This word is often used for flowing water. Here it means that semen goes 'all over inside the vagina, just like water running': i.e., it flows into the vagina, 'filling' it.
4 This same word in Song 4 means a design referring to water or to the mark made by water.

Song 14

bili *luriuwonan* *baiigwi* *gurga-minminboi*
because runs down[1] on that (penis) penis long foreskin
dawiliŋul *ragwaŋul*
Goulburn Island *babaru* Goulburn Island people
bili *wurulŋgalna* *luriun* *mawiari* *djabin-djabin*
because blood runs down blood blood[2]
bili *gaidjululu* *djululuwonan* *meial* *gulwiri*
because runs down[3] runs all over branches cabbage palm

radjil
cabbage palm
bili *wurulŋgal* *duwan* *mareiin* *randaga* *girariŋ-girariŋ*
because blood that sacred[4] blood runs down
ŋaraga *gulgduwan* *wirgul*
bone cut[5] girl(s)
nawiŋgu *nagara* *guniŋgu* *burara* *ruŋgalna* *jalguwan* *gabun*
tribe tribe tribe tribe blood (looks like) water[6]
luriun-ŋin *galwinbin* *barwala* *bili* *durbu-wogalwun*
runs down blood[7] blood[7] because buttocks move
dawiliŋuwuŋ *ragwawuŋ* *djinaniŋ-djinaniŋwuŋ*
Goulburn Island *babaru* Goulburn Island people clan
wurulŋgal *gaidjululu* *galwinbin* *mareiin* *mawiari*
blood runs down blood sacred blood
djabin-djabin *ŋaraga* *gulgduwan* *wirgul* *mareiin* *luriun-ŋin*
blood bone cut young girl sacred runs down
buguweima *malwi* *rabaŋa* *ŋaiiŋa* *damalaŋa* *wolŋuna*
always there Place Place it (camp) Sea-eagle nest Place
bili *bana* *mareiin* *wirgul* *nawiŋgu* *guniŋgu* *mandalboi*
because that sacred girl(s) tribe tribe clan
guniŋgu *djabin* *wurulŋgal*
tribe blood blood
bili *niniŋ-ŋuwoŋ* *durbu-wogalwun* *ragwawuŋ*
because always there buttocks move Goulburn Island people
dawiliŋuwuŋ *ragwawuŋ*
Goulburn Island *babaru* Goulburn Island people
bili *mareiin* *marei-marei* *djinani-djinani* *burara* *luriun-ŋin*
because sacred clan clan tribe runs down
buguweima *ŋaiiŋa* *milgarina* *djamurlbunaraŋa*
always there it (camp) forked stick[8] rafter
bugu-damalaŋa *gururuŋa* *luriun-ŋin* *ŋaiiŋa*
roof like Sea-eagle nest on rail[9] runs down it (camp)
dagal-jagalŋa *milgariŋa*
forked stick[10] forked stick
bili *ŋaraga* *gulgduwan* *mareiin* *wirgul*
because bone cut sacred girl(s)
marei-marei *ragwawa* *mandalbi* *nagara* *nawiŋgu*
clan Goulburn Island people clan tribe tribe
mareiin *guniŋgu*
sacred tribe
luriun-ŋin *jalgguwan* *gabun* *riala* *barwala*
runs down (looks like) water blood flowing blood
niniŋu *gunbulul* *dambal* *meial* *radjil*
always there blood on to branches cabbage palm
gulwirilil *wunaŋial*
cabbage palm cabbage palm
luriun-ŋin *wurulŋgal* *wurandaga* *gaidjululu* *djulululu*
runs down blood blood runs down runs all over
mareiin *wurulŋgal* *mawiari*
sacred blood blood

djabin-djabin	*ŋaraga*	*gulgduwan*	*wirgul*	*mareiin*
blood	bone	cut	young girl	sacred

1 After breaking the girl's hymen during coitus, the man withdraws his penis and finds blood on its foreskin—i.e. 'there is blood on his penis because he has for the first time broken through the girl'. See Note 5.
2 Menstrual blood is likened to kangaroo blood running from a spear wound. See main text, page 28.
3 This word implies that menstrual blood is mentioned: *gaidjululu* means to 'flow spasmodically or intermittently' (i.e. 'run and stop') for two or three days.
4 This blood is sacred: men are not supposed to see it. However, as is noted in the song, men find blood on their foreskins.
5 The penis 'goes through' the girl's vagina until its apex strikes a bone, and with the force of coition 'cuts' or breaks it: thus 'breaking', so it is said, causes the menstrual flow, for the 'wall' separating vagina and uterus is pierced and blood flows from the uterus. See main text, pages 62–3.
6 That is, the blood runs freely, resembling water.
7 In Song 13 this word refers to semen.
8 Girls lean against the forked sticks.
9 Women sit under the hut's rails (or rafters).
10 Menstrual blood drips through the floor of the hut into the water below. This is also the name of an important site.

Song 15

bili	*woŋanan*	*julŋu*	*darug*	*ŋagul*	*wudumbul*	*gurabibi*
because	talked	people	word	heard	language[1]	language[1]

waŋanubdun	*ragwawa*	*dawiliŋu*	*djaŋgulul*
talk along	Goulburn Island people	Goulburn Island *babaru*	language[1]

ŋagul	*ririr*	*gurabibi*	*darug*	*marei-marei*	*ragwawa*
heard	word	language	word	clan	Goulburn Island people

buguweima	*ŋaiiŋa*	*bugu-damalaŋa*	*milgariŋa*
always there	it (camp)	roof like Sea-eagle (nest)	forked sticks[2]

gururuŋa
forked stick

darug	*ŋagul*	*djimalgan*	*meiawudunan*	*burulian*	*darug*	*ŋagul*
word	heard	clan	clan[3]	(invocation)[4]	word	heard

mandalboiŋa
clan

nagaran	*nawiŋboi*	*wudambul*	*ŋagul*	*guniŋguŋ*
tribe	tribe	language	heard	tribe

djalgduwan	*darugma*	*meia*	*radjil*	*gunbululi*	*wunaŋial*
throw out	word	branches	cabbage palm	cabbage palm	cabbage palm

waŋanubdun	*buguweima*	*ŋaiiŋa*	*rabaŋa*	*guruwili*	*malwi*
talk along	always there	it (camp)	Place	Place	Place

mialmir	*waidun*
Place	'swim'

waŋa	*damalaŋa*	*bii-ŋagul*	*djaŋgulul*	*gurabibi*
Place	Sea-eagle Place[5]	indeed heard	language	language

darug *ŋagul* *damalaŋa* *mandalboi* *djinani-djinani*
word heard Sea-eagle Place[5] clan clan

waŋanubdun *julŋu* *dawaliŋu* *ragwawa*
talk along people Goulburn Island *babaru* Goulburn Island people

gurga-minmin *daludboidj*
penis long long penis

buguweima *rabaŋa* *jalmaŋa* *ŋaiiŋa* *wunulŋa* *dambarŋa*
always there Place Place it (camp) Place Place

darug *ŋagul* *marei-marei* *djaŋgulul* *gurabibi* *wudumbul* *waŋan*
word heard clan language language language talk

nawiŋguŋ *nagara* *guniŋgu* *burara* *mandalboi*
tribe tribe tribe tribe clan

1 Language or dialectal unit of western Arnhem Land, known in the east by these terms.

2 Girls lean against the walls and posts.

3 Invocations associated with the Goulburn Islands, meaning 'cloud'.

4 Employed as an invocation, but usually a place name (see Song 2, note 8).

5 In one version of this song, this word is replaced by *gamalaŋga*, which is the name of a language group of western Arnhem Land: in this case, the language spoken by several clans mentioned in the song.

Song 16

bili *gara* *maiaŋan* *wogal-ŋaruŋan*
because spear get play feel

baima *ŋaiiŋa* *guruwilin* *djuduŋa* *balaŋura*
always there it (camp) Place Place[1] Place

bili *dubduwonan* *ŋadil* *wogun* *jirainjinaŋ*
because fling first[2] play[3] spear with bamboo shaft

wagminja
spear with bamboo shaft

ŋanma *wombal-warareiwaŋ* *gulumba* *meiarlwul* *dubduwan* *ŋoiŋuban*
it move shaft[4] shaft thin shaft throw throw back[5]

didjuwan *marir* *gandalili* *ŋurum* *gara*
back cabbage palm into cabbage palm[6] point[7] spear

duwagduwan
throw up that (spear)

gwoii *duwagmundu* *wombalna* *meiarlwul* *gulumba* *ŋadil*
'snake'[8] point upwards shaft thin shaft shaft first

djalgduwan *dubduwan* *wogun*
throw fling play

dawalwulul *miwoidj-guwan* *jirainjinaŋ*
another country[9] different language[10] spear

wagmin *mirigin* *naŋal* *marei-mareina* *durbu-wogalna*
spear chest[11] saw clan buttocks (move) play

ragwawarina *dawiliŋu*
Goulburn Island people Goulburn Island *babaru*

ŋaiiŋa *baima* *rabaŋa* *wunulŋa* *dambalŋa* *mialmir* *guruwilin* *malwi*
it (camp) there Place Place Place Place Place Place

wogal *ŋaruŋan* *ragwawarina* *mandalboiu* *dubduwan*
fun feel Goulburn Island people clan fling

gulumba *meiarlwul* *wombalma*
thin shaft shaft shaft

wombal-warareiun *ŋurum* *gwoii* *dubmundur* *ŋurum*
move shaft point 'snake' point[12] point

galwul-galwul *gara* *jeladbad*
point spear spear[13]

wogal *ŋaruŋan* *ŋaiiŋa* *gururuPuŋa* *milgariŋa*
fun feel it (camp) forked stick forked stick

djamulbunaraŋa *gadalwurulŋa*
rafter rail

1 Place of the sacred *rangga* tree, emblem of the Djanggawul.
2 I.e., before throwing the second: one after the other.
3 To 'throw as a child does': i.e., without any feeling of enmity.
4 Twisting it around: making throwing actions without releasing it from the grasp.
5 Interchange of spears, throwing in play.
6 I.e., the wind catches the light bamboo spear in flight, and blows it into the middle of the cabbage palm foliage.
7 The wooden point or 'nose' of the spear, fitted into a bamboo shaft.
8 The spear is likened to a snake: this probably refers to its flight through the air, when the shaft sways 'like a snake', or to the point of the spear thrusting at its quarry like the dart of a snake's head. Also of phallic significance.
9 Referring to spears travelling 'in spirit form' to far places, or to the difference between the spears themselves and those made in north-eastern Arnhem Land: i.e., they are obtained through 'trade' from a 'stranger' tribe.
10 I.e., having a language dissimilar to the north-eastern Arnhem Land dialects, that are known collectively by Yirrkalla people as the Miwoidj or Miwaidj language.
11 The movement (or swinging) of shoulders and chest as a spear is thrown.
12 Special 'singing' name for the spear's wooden point.
13 The whole spear, so named because its bamboo shaft is hollow.

Song 17

bili *waragan* *ŋadinan* *ŋaiiŋa* *gadalwurulŋa* *galmagna*
because bird[1] cries it (camp) rail entrance[2]

djaŋgaweima
pheasant

ŋawaliŋa *ŋadinjin* *ŋaiiŋa* *galmagna* *grudurmura*
pheasant cries it (camp) entrance pheasant[3]

ŋawaliŋa *bugbug* *geindja-ŋagul*
pheasant the sound of its cry (rain) heard

galameimei *didjiwuru* *mugali* *waidbargiŋa*
west rain west rain west wind comes up

ŋadinjin *milgarina* *gururulna* *ganbi-ganbina*
cries forked stick forked stick top rail

buguweima *wunulŋa* *malwi* *rabaŋa* *ŋagulan* *dajimjimdunda*
always there Place Place Place heard lie along[4]

gandalilŋa *wurulminja* *ŋadinjin* *waragan*
west rain and wind west rain and wind cries bird

grudurmura *djaŋgaweima*
pheasant pheasant

ŋawaliŋa *djinalaŋa* *ŋaiiŋa* *gururuuse* *milgarina*
pheasant within it (camp) forked stick forked stick

ganbi-ganbiŋa *galmagna* *geindja-ŋagul*
top rail entrance (rain) heard

warei-warei *durlmindi* *didjiwuru* *mualal-na* *gandaljalŋa*
west rain and wind heavy rain west rain darkness from rain west rain

ŋan *njaguŋ* *darugwoi* *balwalun* *ŋambaljun*
it for me from word comes up spreads over

10 *dud-dud-dun* *birwirjun* *durbuliun*
noise of wind and rain noise of thunder thunder along bottom of clouds

dambar *rabaŋ* *wigaran*
lowering clouds[5] lowering clouds[5] long spreading lines of cloud

ŋadi *ŋawaliŋu* *grudurmura* *djaŋgawogbog* *ŋawaliŋa* *ŋaiiŋa*
cries pheasant pheasant pheasant pheasant it (camp)

djamulbunjarara *milgariŋ* *galmagna* *gururuna*
rafter forked stick entrance forked stick

buguweima *guruwilin*
always there Place

1 The pheasant cries at the beginning of the wet season, 'because it feels the rain'.

2 This pheasant constructs a covered nest. When the rains come it enters the 'door' of the nest, leaving its tail feathers protruding, exposed to the weather. The nest is likened to the 'watch houses' mentioned in Songs 1 and 2.

3 A 'singing' name for this bird.

4 'Hear the clouds, thunder and rain coming up'.

5 I.e., 'bottom clouds'. In other songs these words refer to places on the mainland, opposite the Goulburn Islands, which have this meaning.

Song 18

1 *bili* *darba* *njinadugan-naruŋ* *darba* *gwalala*
because club[1] put along[2] club fighting club[3]

rulbu-rulbu *muŋguli* *madir*
club[4] club[5] club[3]

gumur-naŋal *meialwudunan* *dalaidjŋun* *burulianŋa*
chest saw clan[6] clan[7] (invocation)[7]

ŋuwarlgaŋ *njinaduga* *bili* *darba* *duan* *djiŋgana*
carefully put along because club that 'clan'[8]

djiŋalwulba *madir*
'clan'[8] club

ŋuwarlgaŋ *djimdjimduwa*
carefully put along[9]

5 *buguweima* *ŋaiiŋa* *rabaŋa* *mialmir* *balaŋura*
always there it (camp) Place Place Place

gumur-naŋal *dunaran* *geiwiniaŋ* *gundjul-gundjulŋa*
chest saw (invocation)[7] (invocation)[7] (invocation)[7]

garaŋam djimdjimduwan darba gwalala
all over put along club club

darial ŋamaba burulima ŋuruŋiwa garaŋala
Place Place Place Place all over

garaŋam waiduwan ŋaiiŋa damalaŋa bugu-damalaŋa
all over pass over it (camp) Sea-eagle Place roof like Sea-eagle (nest)

rabaŋa guruwilin
Place Place

ŋuwarlgaŋ djimdjimduwa darba muŋguli madir gwalala
carefully put along club club club club

rulbu-rulbu djiŋgana
club 'clan'[8]

ŋan djinagwoi darbawoi djimdjimdunda managaman
it from within club put along[9] come up

waidbar didjiwuru
come on west rain cloud

ŋalim djimdjimdun rulbu-rulbu gwalala madir djiŋgana darba
we put along club club club 'clan' club

1 The usual word for tree or post. Here it refers to a wooden club.

2 Clubs are placed in the ground, standing upright: they are 'ready for fighting', and men pick them up for use.

3 This is the long black ironwood club, flat on either side and tapering at the handle. It is primarily used for hand-to-hand fighting in, say, camp brawls. Its ordinary name is *gwula*, or *gwala*.

4 Alternative name for *gwula* club: in Song 2 this word means wind.

5 A short, rounded and knobbed throwing club, not used in hand-to-hand fighting. It is ordinarily called *mulgawoŋa* or *mulawol*.

6 Used also as an invocation, meaning 'cloud'. It may further refer to the Maiali 'tribe' in south-western Arnhem Land (see R. and C. Berndt 1970: 10).

7 Or an invocation to the rising clouds at the Goulburn Islands.

8 I.e., *mala* ('clan') of the clubs. In Song 2, this refers to clouds appearing above the horizon—i.e., 'club clouds'.

9 I.e., lining up the clubs, placing them in rows in the ground. The word is also used to refer, for instance, to clouds 'lining up', along and above the horizon (see Song 2).

Song 19

bili baiigwi darbawi njinaduganda gwalalawi managamana
because from that club[1] put along club come up

naruŋ waidbalgŋa
along spread over

didjiwuru galameimei mualal mugali bandi
west rain cloud west rain cloud dark rain cloud west wind west clouds

bunbuwan ŋaliŋguŋ djinagwi darbawi gwalalawi
make for us from within club club

bunbuwonan maŋan
make cloud

bandigura garaŋam dajijimdum waiduwan
clouds all over spread along pass over

5 *gunumbal balumareiu ŋagadadbal jirjirlnanili waiali*
Place[2] Place[2] Place[2] Place[2] Place[2]
garaŋam maŋan djimdjimduwan buwariŋgaiu damaleiu
all over cloud lie along Place Sea-eagle Place
dunawariŋgal
Place[3]
maŋan naruŋ jararaiun garaŋam burulimaiun ŋamabal darialju
cloud along stand up all over Place Place Place
garaŋalil ŋuruŋiwaiu bunbuwam ŋaiiaŋa rabaŋa wunulŋa guruwilin
all over Place make it (camp) Place Place Place
malwi mialmir jindi bandi bandigura
Place Place big clouds clouds
10 *mualal mugali galameimei didjiwuru*
dark rain cloud west wind west rain cloud west rain cloud
wareiwarei
west rain cloud
durlmindi bidjandawul ŋali darba njinadugan
coloured clouds this way we club put along
gwalala madir rulbu-rulbu wonawondurlba muŋguli djiŋgana
club club club clan club clan

[1] When fighting clubs are placed in the ground (see Song 18), clouds come up, 'taking part for' (i.e. symbolizing) them. These are called 'message' clubs because of their power to attract clouds and rain.
[2] Places in the Crocodile Islands. Some clouds 'standing' above the islands join and merge with those above the mainland opposite.
[3] On the mainland, opposite Milingimbi.

Song 20

1 *bili muriuwonan durbuliwan*
because make thunder noise thunder along bottom of clouds
dambar malwi
Place Place
gundrujuwan birwirljuwan maleialgdumin
make thunder noise make noise and lightning[1] lightning breaks clouds[2]
dugmundur
snake
guruwilin mialmir babi jindi malimali guruwulgamiŋ
Place Place snake big snake's belly[3] belly skin
bunbaragba djawalu
snake's back snake
birwirljuwan ŋaiiŋa rabaŋa mialmir
make noise and lightning it (camp) Place Place
5 *gundrujuwan buralma mawugduan miraunjinaiu*
make thunder noise sound comes up that Place
jabei-jabal mainbunaral galiwali
Place of the Two Sisters Place Boomerang Place
burlmaŋaŋ jarlwonli dilibumal
Place Place Place

ŋaiam birwirljun gundrujun dambaljijun
I[4] make noise and lightning make thunder push cloud
guruwilin malwi jalmaŋa
Place Place Place
ŋaia daŋurwalgala ŋjaŋaru njaguŋ gwigdunda
I make crashing sound it (came) from me spat[5]
gundrujunda barwaljun ŋambaljun dud-dud-dun
make thunder noises came up spreads over noise of storm
ŋuru-miwoidj bii-ŋawul
stranger from somewhere
dalmidbiwiŋul geialmaŋguwul balwudul-wudulwiŋul duliŋuruwul
to Caledon Bay[6] Place[6] Place[6] Place[4]
ŋan ŋambaljun bugudjbiwoiŋu dararalwiŋu walga-walgawul
it spreads over Place[6] Place[6] Place[6]
luwandiwiŋu
Place[6]
ŋaia gundrujun birwirljun malwi rabaŋur
I make thunder noise make noise and lightning Place Place

1 'Shaking the clouds'; the noise of thunder shakes the ground and stilted huts.
2 The 'lightning' snake goes up and down in the clouds: it is this snake which makes thunder.
3 Its 'inside' name.
4 The snake speaks.
5 The flashing lightning is the ejaculated spittle of the snake.
6 The wind from the storm reaches these places, at Caledon Bay, eastern Arnhem Land.

Song 21

bili gwoiii mada-junanjin mada-wirmeiba
because snake tongue flickers tongues twist to one another
ŋulina raidjuman ŋulinbam meian radjil gulwiril
flash flashes flashes branches cabbage palm cabbage palm
maleialgdumin gawul-gawul dugmundur dunjin
lightning breaks clouds snake (lightning) snake snake
mada-junanjin
tongue flickers
buguweima malwi djuduŋa dambalŋa
always there Place Place Sea-eagle Place
bugguŋa burululinaŋuru bugguŋa djimalgaŋara dalaidjŋura
on top of place (clan) on top of place of clan place of (clan)
garaŋam mada-junanjin ŋamaba burulima ŋuruŋiwa
all over tongue flickers Place Place Place
darial djiririwuruma
Place Place
garaŋala mada-wirmeiba madajun
all over tongues twist to one another tongue moves
buguweima ŋaiiŋa wunulŋa balaŋura jalmaŋa
always there it (camp) Place Place Place

garaŋam *madajun* *mada-wirmeiba* *miralŋina*
all over tongue moves tongues twist to one another Place
jabei-jaba *mainbunara* *guruwana*
Two Sisters Place Place Place

10 *maleialgduwan-judun* *dugmundurŋa* *gawul-gawi* *djarim*
lightning breaks clouds along (lightning) snake snake flashes
ŋan *gunbirbijuman* *ŋulinma* *ŋulinbam* *meial* *gulwiril*
it close eyes[1] flashes flashes branches cabbage palm
radjil *meian*
cabbage palm branches
biardan *wunaŋiaŋa* *wolariargu* *marimunug*
shine cabbage palm cabbage palm cabbage palm
gunbulul *meian* *biardan*
cabbage palm[2] branches shine

1 Referring to a vivid flash of lightning, so strong that it is necessary to close one's eyes.

2 Also meaning 'semen': it refers to a flash of lightning revealing semen-stained cabbage palm foliage, which shines in the light. See Song 13.

Song 22

1 *bili* *waragan* *galgin-ŋan* *mulunda* *wargnugan* *gandalilŋa*
because bird[1] close, it bird through wind west wind
galameimei
wind[2]
djuŋbiniŋu *dalbandidj* *djurawul* *barldam* *ginbul* *djeladjela*
bird bird bird wing wing flapping[3]
galgin-ŋan *guraral*
close, it bird
buguweima *malwi* *ŋaiiŋa* *rabaŋa* *mialmir*
always there Place it (camp) Place Place
wargnugan *galameimei* *didjiwuru* *mualalŋa* *gandalilŋa*
through wind wind wind[2] darkness from rain west wind

5 *galgin-judun* *guraral* *mulunda* *djuŋbiniŋu* *guraral*
close along bird bird bird bird
wargnugan *dalbandiu* *galginan* *ŋaiiŋa* *malwi* *balaŋura*
through wind bird come close it (camp) Place Place
garaŋam *galgi* *waragan*
all over close bird
ŋuruŋiwa *damala* *buwariŋga* *gularibei*
Place Place Place Milingimbi Point
garaŋam *djiririwuruma* *ŋamaba* *burulima* *darial*
all over Place Place Place Place

10 *barldam* *waragan* *ginbul* *djeladjela*
wing bird wing flapping
guraral *dalbandi* *djurawul* *mulunda* *djuŋbiniŋu* *wargnugan*
bird bird bird bird bird through wind
djamalaŋani *wuŋani* *rulbu-rulbu*
west wind[4] wind wind
jiridja *dugeia* *manbulbul* *gurgarwir*
jiridja moiety north-west wind north-west wind penis wind[5]

ŋalama *malagara* *wargnugan*
wind wind through wind

1 Possibly a swallow.
2 Wind bringing rain clouds from the west.
3 Or, white feathers sticking out: i.e., feathers disarranged and blown by the wind.
4 These birds fly through the wind. The word *djamalaŋani* refers to the sacred *djamalara* singing of the *kunapipi*—its sound is carried on the western winds.
5 Also clouds from the west—i.e., clouds like penes ready for urinating.

Song 23

bili *wadar* *galgin* *jarwirjuwan* *boiu-mirwulgduwan*
because wind close blows blows branches

djalujal *wuŋani* *durlmundijuwan* *djamalaŋani*
cold wind west wind blows all over west wind

ŋadjil *djujuwan* *dubduwan*
first[1] push over throw over

ŋuru-miwoidjna *wagun* *jiranjinaŋ* *wargminja* *walba-walbadan*
stranger child[2] small cloud cloud cloud

njanma (ŋan) *wadar* *bii-ŋuru* *mirwulgduwan* *darial-ŋuru*
it wind from somewhere blows branches from Place
ŋamaba-ŋuru *burulima-ŋuru*
from Place from Place

djaljalŋa *jalwiun* *djamalaŋani* *gandalil* *wuŋani* *jiridja*
cold wind blows west wind west wind west wind *jiridja*
wadar *gurgari* *ŋalama* *dugeia* *manbulbul*
wind penis wind wind north-west wind north-west wind

njanma (ŋan) *boiu-mirwulgdun* *jurminwulan* *wagalwulan*
it blows branches blows spread over

wuŋani *bii-ŋuru* *ŋaii-ŋuru* *garind-ŋuru*
west wind from somewhere from it (camp) from Place[3]
garaŋala-ŋuru *djiririwuruma-ŋuru* *darial-ŋuru*
from spreading all over[4] from Place from Place

bii-ŋuru *mirwulgduwan* *dunurwari-ŋuru* *buwariŋga-ŋuru*
from somewhere blows branches from Place from Place
gulaiibei-ŋuru
from Place

wadar *julminjulan* *djamalaŋani* *wuŋggur* *wuŋani* *boiu-mirwulgdun*
wind blows west wind wind west wind blows branches

ŋaii-ŋuru *damala-ŋuru* *raba-ŋuru* *malwi-ŋuru*
from it (camp)[5] from Sea-eagle Place from Place from Place
djuda-ŋuru *balaŋurei-ŋuru*
from Place from Place

1 A little cloud goes 'first' before the wind, 'like a sail or a child'.
2 The wind 'pushes over' or tosses the small cloud, here likened to a child; *wagu* is a kin term, 'sister's child' (man speaking), or 'own child' (woman speaking).
3 A place on the mainland, opposite Milingimbi.
4 Also a place name.
5 Or from 'big country' to the west.

Song 24

bili *bunaginaŋ* *wadarwuŋ* *gulwiri*
because rustling branches (cabbage palm) from wind cabbage palm
radji *wunaŋia* *marimunug* *gunbulul*
cabbage palm cabbage palm cabbage palm semen[1] (stained leaves)
buguweima *malwi* *rabaŋa* *balaŋura* *mialmir* *guruwilin*
always there Place Place Place Place Place
gulwiri *wunaŋia* *wolariarlgu* *riragai* *dubduwan*
cabbage palm cabbage palm cabbage palm sound thrown over
didjuwan *djerŋanandu* *raralwal* *gudalial* *durum-durumdu*
go back Place Place[2] Place Place
minbilgli *gumurgalinli*
Place Place
maradumdum *djuŋin-djuŋin* *gulwiri* *waiduwan* *woŋan*
cabbage palm cabbage palm cabbage palm 'swim' 'speaks' (sound)[3]
malwi *guruwilin* *djudaŋa* *balaŋura* *gabu-digdig* *janulŋa*
Place Place Place Place 'open water' Place
riragai *ŋagu* *darialju* *ŋoibanŋu*
sound hear Place Place
garaŋam *woŋan* *ŋamaba* *burulima* *darial*
all over sound Place Place Place
riragai *ŋagu* *radji* *gunbulul* *gulwiri*
sound hear cabbage palm cabbage palm cabbage palm
marimunug *wolariarlgu* *wunaŋia*
cabbage palm cabbage palm cabbage palm
riragai *ŋagu* *buguweima* *damalama* *wunurlŋa* *balaŋura*
sound hear always there Sea-eagle place Place Place
malwi *djudaŋa* *mialmir* *guruwilin*
Place Place Place Place
waidun *woŋa* *ŋaiiŋa* *rabaŋa*
'swim' sound it (camp) Place
gulwiri *wunaŋia* *radji* *marimunug*
cabbage palm cabbage palm cabbage palm cabbage palm
wolariarlgu *gunbulul* *ŋoiwoŋan*
cabbage palm cabbage palm sounds within

[1] Also translated simply as cabbage palm, but still keeping this meaning.
[2] This place, on the mainland opposite Milingimbi, is associated with *djunggawon* circumcision rituals under sponsorship of the Wawalag cycle.
[3] Sound made by strong wind blowing through the cabbage tree foliage.

Song 25

bili *gabu* *luriuwonan* *baiali* *gulwiri-ŋuru* *meia-ŋuru*
because water runs down from that cabbage palm[1] from branches
galwinbin *riala* *djularari* *barwala* *niniŋgu*
rainwater[2] flowing flowing from water[3] (clear water)
gurga-ŋuru *radji-ŋuru* *gunburu-ŋuru* *marimunug-ŋuru*
from roots[4] from cabbage palm from cabbage palm from cabbage palm

wolariarlgu-ŋuru *wunaŋial-ŋuru*
from roots and trunk from cabbage palm
mareiin *gargulug* *djuŋin-djuŋin*
sacred[5] 'clean' water[6] sheet of water

5 *galwinbin* *maralwal-maralwal* *bugulul* *riala* *barwala*
water running water banking up foam banks up flowing water
maradumdum *lurinanjin* *buguweima* *ŋaiiŋa* *wunurlŋa*
sound of water[7] runs down always there it (camp) Place
malwi *rabaŋa* *guruwilin* *mialmir* *djudaŋa*
Place Place Place Place Place
buguweima *dambalŋa* *gabu-digdig* *bili* *mareiin* *gabu* *barwala*
always there in open water because sacred water water
djuŋin-djuŋin *ganabumbum* *djularari* *niniŋgu* *bugulul*
sheet of water foam of water flowing from (clear water) foam banking
riala *maralwal-maralwal*
flowing running water banking up

10 *barwalalwulau* *baiali* *gulwiri-ŋu* *radji-ŋuru*
water from that from cabbage palm from cabbage palm
gunbulu-ŋuru
from cabbage palm
wolariarlgu-ŋuru *wunaŋial-ŋuru* *marimunug-ŋuru*
from roots and trunk from cabbage palm from cabbage palm
lurinanjin *mareiin* *galwinbin* *barwala* *niniŋgu* *gargulug*
runs down sacred water water (clear water) clean water
djularari
flowing from

1 Water running down from or through the roots of the cabbage palm.

2 In this context we find the customary north-eastern Arnhem Land play on words, referring back to the main themes of the song cycle. In Song 13, line 13, this word is translated as 'semen', in Song 14, line 6, as 'blood', and here as 'rainwater (flowing)'. The inference is that the rains have come and washed away the semen and blood lying in the cabbage palm foliage, and these mingle with the waters of the billabong.

3 As note 2: in Song 13, line 13, this word is translated as 'semen', in Song 14, line 6, as 'blood', and here as 'water'.

4 'From penes': the projecting roots of the cabbage palm are likened to penes from which flows water (= semen); the penes, on the other hand, indirectly relate to the girls' blood (= water) which flows after coitus. See Songs 13 and 14.

5 In this context the water itself, from having swept through the cabbage palm foliage (in which has flowed the sacred blood), is also sacred.

6 The translation of this word here should refer to foam-whitened or churned-up water. This whiteness is said to be 'clean', because its colour approximates white calico; clear water, according to this reasoning (influenced by mission contact), would not necessarily be clean. In Song 13, line 13, this word is translated as 'semen', which is compared to the foamy or churned-up state of the water.

7 In Song 24, line 4, for example, this is an 'inside' name for the cabbage palm.

Song 26

1 *bili* *waragan* *ŋoiunaruŋ* *malwurŋia* *niniŋu*
because bird[1] flaps along flaps always there[2]

gamalaŋga *wudambul* *djaŋgulul*
Place[3] Place[4] Place[4]

rirandjir-naruŋ *galejalg-jalgduman* *darugma* *wongulum*
talking along[5] sound thrown on every side word talk

bugŋaii *rareiŋoian* *rareibu*
seagull seagull bird's sound

wiriuman *radji* *gunbulul* *meia* *gulwiri*
circles around cabbage palm cabbage palm branches cabbage palm

jeidjun *darugma* *wonagiŋawi*
cries out word fresh-water

balŋuŋu *balŋuma* *duriwan* *gabu-lariman* *malwi*
seagull seagull dives[6] spreads water out[7] Place

mialmir *gabu-digdig*
Place open water

ŋurum *ŋurum-djambaidj* *wareimu* *mararu* *duriwan*
beak point good beak[8] beak beak dives

djiŋgrurala *gandjululul*
beak beak spreads water

wiriuman *meia* *dulumbulg* *ŋambu-ŋambul*
circles around branches fresh-water grass fresh-water lily

wiriuman *jigawiwul* *ŋurum-mambaru* *djalŋingu*
circles around looks for (leech) beak (catches leech) leech

woŋa-naruŋ *rirandjuŋa* *niniŋu* *djaŋgulul* *gurabibi*
'talks' along sound always there Place clan

gamalaŋga *wudambul*
Place Place

mirim *njagu* *djinagwoi* *malwi*
string for me (from) within Place

waịndjam *grudi* *djagalaŋ* *waragan*
string short[9] string bird

mil-muna *mil-djambaidj* *djarulŋu* *djarumba*
going through night[10] keen eye[11] gull gull

wogaiaru *dalmilmil* *bugŋaii* *darugma* *wongulwan*
wing flaps wing seagull word 'talk'

1 Called *gabu-wuraŋaiimi*, a seagull which frequents the coastal freshwater billabongs.

2 I.e., 'always stays there (at that place)'.

3 Place of the Red (or pink) Egg, referring to seagull eggs.

4 Place of the Red Egg: in Song 15, for example, these words are said to refer to a western Arnhem Land language group.

5 A word meaning the cry of this seagull. Hence the dialectal unit named Riradjingu (the dialect in which these songs were recorded) has speech like the *dua* moiety seagull. This bird is mytho-totemically associated with these people.

6 Swoops in flight.

7 Skimming the surface of the water, and sending out ripples.

8 As the gull skims the surface of the billabong it searches for food. This word means 'its beak never misses a fish or worm': it is a 'good hunter'.

9 A short feathered string attached to a carved wooden seagull head and used in love magic. See *Addendum*, pages 192–4.

10 'Eye night-time'. This refers to the bird flying across the billabong at night in search of food. It also symbolizes the use of the love-magic object at night.

11 I.e., keen eyesight: the gull is quick to see its quarry in the darkness and seizes it in its beak, which is like a spear. This too refers to a lover obtaining a sweetheart.

Song 27

bili	*dugar*	*naŋal*	*waragandu*	*mil-djambaidju*	*dugar-widju*
because	road	saw	bird	with keen eye	small road

meial	*dulumbulgli*	*ŋambu-ŋambul-li*	*jidjidjna*	*bulaŋgar*
foliage	into lily foliage	into lily foliage	mouse[1]	mouse

dalararaŋ	*dudid*
mouse	mouse

bili	*wiriuman*	*djarulŋu*	*djarunga*	*magululwol*	*wongaibu*
because	circles around	gull	gull	gull	gull

dalwulmilmil	*darugma*	*wongulum*	*rirandjun*
flaps wings	word	'talk'	sound

buguweima	*malwi*	*djudaŋa*	*mialmir*	*gabu-digdig*
always there	Place	Place	Place	open water

bili	*bunaginaŋ*	*ŋuroiu*	*muraroiŋa*	*wareimoiu*	*djiŋgruraleiu*
because	dives down	with beak	beak	beak	beak

baŋgul-baŋgul	*dareiŋoiaŋ*	*dareibu*	*biganŋa*	*ŋoi-naruŋ*
flaps[2]	sound of wings	sound	seagull	flaps along

balŋuŋa	*balŋuma*
gull	gull

niniŋu	*waragan*	*djaŋgulul*	*gurabibi*	*wudambul*	*gamalaŋga*
always there	bird	language[3]	clan	language	language

rirandjun	*balei-algduman*	*dawalju*	*wararia*
sound	thrown in that direction	wet season time	new shoots of grass

balwia	*dumralia*	*miraralia*
grass shoots	grass	wet season

bili	*ŋadi-naruŋ*	*jidjidj*
because	cries out along	mouse

bili	*njaguŋ*	*bunaginaŋ*	*dalararaŋ*	*dugar-widju*	*ŋuruŋa*	*muraroiŋa*
because	for me[4]	spear	mouse	small road	in beak	beak

ŋadi-naruŋ	*bulaŋgar*	*jidjidj*	*djerarag*	*dubduwan*
cries out along	mouse	mouse	cry (goes up to the sky)	throws[5]

1 Field-mouse or marsupial rat.

2 I.e., up and down, or flapping wings when 'spearing' mouse with its beak: also, shaking the mouse in its beak in order to kill it.

3 Here the bird is said to belong to these dialectal units (as in Song 15). The terms do not refer to a place, as in Song 26: however, the two meanings are associated.

4 The gull speaks.

5 The gull grabs the mouse: its squeaks resound and are 'thrown up' into the sky, like the cry of the gull.

ADDENDUM:

LOVE-MAGIC OBJECTS

North-eastern Arnhem Landers, in the old days, developed a ritualized technique in the art of lovemaking and in obtaining a wife. This has now virtually disappeared, in this particular form.

The commonest procedure was said to have been as follows. If a woman was of the *jiridja* moiety and the man *dua*, he would arrange for a female friend to leave a white-feathered or possum-fur string in her dilly bag. Should he be *jiridja* and she be *dua*, a red-parakeet-feathered string would be used. The type of string always depended on the moiety of the woman, not of the man. The two would then exchange messages through the go-between, eventually meeting in the bush. It was said that, if these strings were discovered by a suspicious husband who made a habit of hunting through his wife's baskets, this could result in camp quarrelling or fighting (see Warner 1958 : 84-5).

Various objects decorated with lengths of such string were also used to obtain sweethearts. Men of the *jiridja* moiety carved wooden anchors, replicas of 'Macassan' and pre-'Macassan' ones. *Dua* moiety men used stylized carvings of seagull or other birds' heads, one variety of which is mentioned in the Goulburn Island cycle. (Some of these have been illustrated: see A. P. Elkin and R. and C. Berndt 1950: Ch. VI, Plates 18A, 19A and 19B; and R. Berndt and S. Phillips 1973 : 164, 198, Plates 154, 178.) *Jiridja* anchors were used for 'hooking' women, while the beaks of the *dua* birds' heads suggest their swooping after food and, symbolically, 'catching' a woman.

Men of either moiety who have commenced their Djanggawul (*dua*) or Laindjung (*jiridja*) *nara* rituals might make such objects, obtaining the feathered string from secret-sacred *rangga* emblems used in those rituals. This highly-valued string was made by *dua* or *jiridja* women (although they did not add the red parakeet feathers), repeating what was first done by the Djanggawul sisters. As they wound the string, twining in the white feathers, they would roll it into a ball which they kept in their dilly bags. Later, when men needed this string for ritual purposes they would steal it from the women, just as the Djanggawul brother stole sacred emblems from his two sisters in the Dreaming era when they were away collecting shellfish (see R. Berndt 1952 : 38-41). When the women discovered their loss, although they might be annoyed, they should not make this obvious: usually, of course, they would know why it had been taken. (To repeat, this string which was used to decorate *rangga* emblems was also used to make these love charms.)

A girl who had not been betrothed might be approached through her parents and other kin to gauge their response to marriage negotiations being carried out and also to find out her own personal wishes in the matter. If these appeared to be in order, a man would publicly prepare a declaration of his intentions. He would unroll his ball of string (previously taken from a woman) and stretch it from tree to tree across the main camp, while a male companion rhythmically beat his sticks and sang. In the case of a *dua* moiety man, verses were sung from the 'outside' version of the Wawalag cycle or from the Goulburn Island cycle: with a man from the *jiridja* moiety, extracts were sung from the Baiini or 'Macassan' song cycles, especially those that relate to the hauling and weighing of an anchor, or to the string itself. He might also use parts of the Rose River songs, although no reference is made there to anchors.

Singing, the two men would move from tree to tree until they reached the girl's camp, where she sat demurely among her relatives. She would wear a headdress of feathered string, decorated with drooping feathered pendants. Approaching the camp, her prospective husband, if he were a *jiridja* man, would take the anchor and hook it into the ground before her; then, still singing, he and his friend would sit down some little distance away and commence to haul it in. As they dragged it slowly towards them, it was said to bring with it the spirit and the desire of the girl. They would retreat to another tree and haul it farther, repeating the process, until finally the anchor came to rest in the man's camp. That evening, perhaps, the girl might follow it and the couple be acknowledged husband and wife. However, I was told that some men found it necessary to carry out this performance several times before a girl finally consented to come.

The anchor might also be used in other ways. For instance, it might be simply hooked into the ground at a girl's parents' camp. In that way a man's desire was made known publicly, so that it was not long before the girl, her parents and mother's brothers would know all about it. She would eventually come or be sent to him. Alternatively, he might hook it into her hair or through her arm, drawing her publicly towards his camp. Or as noted before, he might unroll the string (relevant to her moiety) without an anchor attached, placing it on the ground so that it stretched from his own camp to hers: once she had seen it, he would begin to draw it towards him, rolling it into a ball. Under these circumstances, so men said, the girl had no alternative: she was bound to come to him.

Wooden birds' heads were used in much the same way. The string was threaded through a hole bored at the neck end, and from the main string (the bird's 'body') which was used for drawing the girl's spirit, a short string was arranged at each side to represent the bird's wings. As it was arranged before her camp, it would appear like a bird in flight. The beak would be slightly open, and holding a leech, grub, flying fish, mouse or some other small creature commonly eaten by the particular bird employed (see Songs 26 and 27 of the Goulburn Island cycle). The head and neck, painted and incised in coloured ochres, would bear a special design associated with the bird's traditional story or songs. The small creature held in the beak symbolized the desire or spirit of the girl which was caught by the bird and brought to her lover. In many cases, it would be obliquely associated with the girl totemically.

These forms of love-magic were socially approved. However, they might also be used surreptitiously in order to accomplish a transitory liaison or even an elopement. In this case the rite was usually carried out at night, when (so men said) the girl or woman would be awakened by its magic. Seeing the object being drawn away from her, she would crawl after it to join the man.

Dua or *jiridja* string (without the object attached) was also used for severing marital or sexual ties. In that case, the string (relevant to her moiety) was fastened about her head, with one loose end stretched out across the ground and held by the man. Gradually he would tighten the string until it became taut: one of his sisters' sons would then come forward and cut or break the fibre, symbolizing the release of both parties from their obligations and responsibilities. The woman would either return to her parents or go to another man.

(Several birds' heads with small wax models of creatures held in their beaks, as well as a Baiini-type anchor, were given to me at Yirrkalla in 1946-47, and deposited at the Department of Anthropology, University of Sydney. Unfortunately, they disappeared from this collection between 1953 and early 1956 when I was overseas. A 'Macassan'-type anchor survives, and other birds' heads have been collected since that time: however, these last differ in style from the earlier ones.)

APPENDIX 2

THE ROSE RIVER SONG CYCLE

Song 1

djalgdun-ŋan-ninana *julŋuju* *niniŋuju*
throw out chips[1] men always there
munalju *rewulwulju* *nundaribei* *damanjalg-miri* *daŋarlgaŋ-miri*
clan[2] clan[3] clan[2] clan[4] with clan[2] with
djalgdun-mabalggu *jilbarindji* *galiali* *guliriliri*
chip for boomerang[5] boomerang boomerang boomerang
gunjaŋinjani *munaruŋ* *jilbarindji*
small boomerang[6] small boomerang boomerang
niniŋuju *duri-wogalju*
always there buttocks play[7]
munaruŋ *djalgdun-midmiddun* *gunjaŋinjani*
small boomerang chip off, cut small boomerang
miraŋil *galiali* *bilidj-bilidj* *damuwaru*
small boomerang[8] boomerang flat boomerang boomerang
lai-widjilg-guma *midmiddun*
flatten sides cut (chip)
gwiaŋiri *waŋa* *ŋurldandur* *ŋurlbu*
think camp *nonggaru*[9] middle of *nonggaru*[10]
bili *niniŋuju* *wadiri* *wadirbalei*
because always there tribe[11] tribe[11]
nuŋbululei *nuŋguluŋundu* *rewulwulju* *nundaribei* *baleiu*
clan[12] clan[12] clan clan clan[13]
jigulju *banaŋagbuju* *daŋarlgaŋ-miri* *damanjalg-miri*
clan clan[14] clan with clan with
ŋamaŋameiun *djalgdun* *lai-widjilg-garu* *galgalgali* *bilidj-bilidj*
make throw out flatten sides boomerang flat boomerang
djama *lia-gulgdun-miriama* *midmiddun*
work point used in defloration[15] cut

gwiaŋina *wogal* *gunabibi*
think play kunapipi
munalju *wuldjamindu* *jigulju* *nargaleiu*
clan clan clan clan
mandiala *gwiaŋina*
mandiela[16] thinking about
bili *mabalggu* *duwali* *ŋamadina*
because boomerang this make good[17]
mugoiwa *munalwa* *ŋari-ŋariwa* *baleiwa* *bala*
spirits[18] clan clan[19] clan subincision
gwiaŋina *midmiddun* *djalgdun* *gunjaŋinjani* *munarug*
think cut throw out small boomerang small boomerang
mirindil
boomerang
lai-widjilg-guma *lia-gulgdun-miriama* *bilidj-bilidjdama*
flatten sides point used in defloration flat boomerang
damanjalg-miriu *daŋarlgaŋ-miri* *bili* *nundei'eiu* *wurdboiŋu*
clan with clan with because clan[2] clan[2]
malaŋari *garldjalulei* *dambul-dambulju* *nargaleiu* *nuŋburindiu*
all the clans clan[2] clan[2] clan clan[12]
waŋan-ŋura *ŋurldandurl-ŋura* *ŋurlbur-ŋura*
in (that) camp in *nonggaru* in middle of *nonggaru*

1 Chipping the special boomerang, mentioned later in the song.
2 Clan belonging to Rose River country; some of its names are mytho-totemically related to the barramundi fish. The Nargala clan is associated with the Dalwongu dialectal unit.
3 Clan belonging to Rose River country; its name is mytho-totemically related to an unspecified 'coloured' fish.
4 Clan belonging to Rose River area; its name is mytho-totemically related to a catfish, and also refers to the bush where (according to north-eastern Arnhem Landers) these people usually lived.
5 *djalgdun* means 'throw out' or 'throw away'. It refers here to chips of wood flying off as a boomerang is shaped.
6 Of the returning variety.
7 'Buttocks play' refers to the movement of women's buttocks. The men think of when these boomerangs will be used ritually on the girls.
8 Or *mirindil*.
9 This is the *nonggaru* (*noŋgaru*) hole of the *kunapipi* (*gunabibi*) ritual. See main text, pages 108–12.
10 The middle of the *nonggaru*, on the sacred ground, where the girls lie in readiness.
11 Also referring to the barramundi fish. Wadiri 'tribal' country lay between that of the Mara tribe and the mainland opposite the Sir Edward Pellew Islands, on the south-western side of the Gulf of Carpentaria. *Balei* or *bala* means a subincisure.
12 Clan names of the Dalwongu dialectal unit, indirectly associated with the Nunggubuyu (Nuŋgubuju) tribe in the Rose River area.
13 Rose River people, so named because of their penis incisures (*bala*).
14 So named because they 'sit down' in the bush: i.e. they are inland rather than coastal people, living at this place of the 'armband' bushes.
15 The point (or 'head') of this boomerang, used for 'cutting', ritual deflowering.

16 The *mandiela* was known but only rarely performed in north-eastern Arnhem Land.

17 That is, almost completed.

18 Rose River people who have died, but continue to live in spirit form; ghosts; the part of a person's spirit which continues to live on in its (his, her) own country.

19 This clan name means that Rose River people talk 'like birds'.

x = the point used in defloration

Diagram 8 The Rose River Defloration Boomerang

Song 2

bili *woŋanina* *julŋu* *munal* *wuldjamin* *jigulju*
because talk along people clan clan clan
buduruna *daa-walwalarurina* *riŋguraŋa* *madandja*
flew (words[1]) moved mouth in speech talking[2] language[3]
buduruna *woŋanina* *dialaŋumi* *waŋa-ŋura*
flew (words) talk along from in here in (that) camp
ŋurlbur-ŋura *ŋurldandurl-ŋura* *ŋurl-marŋ-marŋ-ŋura*
in middle of *nonggaru* in *nonggaru* in *nonggaru*
buŋgul-buŋgul-ŋura *djunmili-ŋura*
on dancing ground in shade of branches
jiguluŋ-ŋubanŋu *ŋari-ŋariuruna*
talk (this dialect) quickly talk like birds
junbalalŋa *mada* *woŋana* *ruŋiiri*
talk to one another[4] tongue talk twist tongue[5]
diwiljun *jigul-ŋuban*
talk like birds talk (this dialect) quickly
ŋari-waidbaidjun *junbalal-ŋuban* *wuldjamin*
talk together talk quickly to one another clan
daa-walwaljun *lilia-woŋa*
move mouth in speech join[6] talk
duandja *mada-gulgdun-maraŋala* *dualgindiu*
dua society tongue separate (cut) got[7] *dua* people
wulgandarawiŋoi *murunuŋdu* *jujululwiŋoi*
people from Blue Mud Bay[8] clan[8] from Rose River
garaŋariwiŋoi *garidjalulu* *mada-gulgdun-maraŋala*
from Place clan[9] tongue separate got
murunuŋdu *nuŋguluŋina* *nargalana* *jigulna*
clan clan clan clan
buduruna *ŋari-waidbaidjun* *woŋa* *ŋari-ŋariun*
flew (words) talk together talk talk like birds
jigulul-ŋuban *daa-wudbrugdun*
talk (this dialect) quickly mouth talk slowly[10]

junbalal-ŋuban *mada-ŋagul*
talk (this dialect) quickly tongue heard

wuldjanuma *bagulbiŋu* *djimin-djiminboi* *jiridja-woŋa*
clan people[11] people[11] *jiridja* moiety talk

damanjalg-miri *daŋarlgaŋ-miri* *rewulwuljul* *mada* *woŋana*
clan with clan with clan tongue talk

bala *nundaribei*
incisure clan

burlgai-ŋuban *lilii* *minidja-mindja* *raminboindja*
talk quickly (go) towards (clan from) Place (clan from) Place

gurundul-ŋoindja *banaŋagbujundja*
(clan from) Place[12] (people from) Place

burlgai-ŋuban *woŋa* *diwiljun* *mada* *lindjun*
talk quickly talk talk like birds tongue twist

ŋari-waidbaidjun *junbalal-ŋuban* *jigulul-ŋuban*
talk together talk quickly to one another talk (this dialect) quickly

galawalŋ-ŋagu *julŋu* *nargalaŋala* *nuŋburindina* *nuŋbulna*
sound hear people clan clan clan

ruŋiiri-woŋa *manjalgama* *daa-wudbrugdun* *garldjalulei*
twist talk talk (as they walk) mouth talk slowly clan

mada *nundeia* *wurdboiŋa* *malaŋari* *dambul-dambul*
tongue clan clan all the clans clan

woŋanar-wondi *burlgai-ŋuban* *jigul-ŋuban* *waŋa-ŋura*
talk along talk quickly talk (this dialect) quickly in (that) camp

barindi *waŋa-ŋura* *gundji-wundji*
Place in (that) camp Place[13]

lilii *balwariŋ* *mareialwirŋu* *balwariŋundja*
towards Place[14] Place[14] Place[14]

mada *woŋa* *julŋu* *niniŋu* *daa-wudbrugdun* *djiliil*
tongue talk people always there mouth talk slowly Place[14]

waidjilil *gumalaŋ-aŋu*
Place[14] Place[14]

julŋu *burlgai-ŋuban* *jigul-ŋuban* *woŋa* *garldjalulu*
people talk quickly talk (this dialect) quickly talk clan

nundaŋ-ŋudbrul *gabulmeii* *djuŋgulul* *madandja*
clan[15] clan[15] clan[15] language

duŋgararwira-woŋa *burlgai-ŋuban*
clan[15] talk talk quickly

bili *laindjara* *daa-wudbrugdun* *jigul-ŋuban* *junbalal*
because clan[16] mouth talk slowly talk (this dialect) quickly clan[15]

ŋari-waidbaidjun *daa-walwalun* *daa-wudbrugdun* *niniŋu*
talk together move mouth in speech mouth talk slowly always there

wadiri *wadirbala* *nuŋguraŋmarawi* *nuŋururlboi* *murunuŋ*
tribe tribe clan[8] clan[17] clan

lilii *woŋana* *ŋalala* *mada* *mada-wilindjun*
towards talk sound tongue twist tongue

junbalal-ŋuban *burlgai-ŋuban*
talk (this dialect) quickly talk quickly

ŋari-waidbaidjun *woŋgainna-mala* *garaŋariwoi*
talk together one[18] clan clan[9]

wulgandarwiŋoi *waguju* *ŋilimuruna*
people from Blue Mud Bay children[19] ours

mada-gulgdun-marama *wulgandarawiŋoi* *diala-ŋumi*
tongues separate get people from Blue Mud Bay from in here

woŋana *waŋa-ŋura* *barindi-ŋura*
talk in (that) camp in Place

ŋurlbur-ŋura *gundji-wundji* *balwari* *gumalaŋan*
in middle of *nonggaru* Place Place Place

gumaidjbar
Place (Gumaidj *mada*)

woŋana *ŋurlbur-ŋura* *djunmili-ŋura*
talk in middle of *nonggaru* in shade of branches

ŋurl-marŋ-marŋ-ŋura
nonggaru Place[20]

ŋurldandurl-ŋura *daa-banrawin-ŋura* *buŋgul-buŋgul-ŋura*
in *nonggaru* at mouth of *nonggaru* in dancing place (shade)

burlgai-ŋuban *junbalal-ŋuban* *ŋari-waidbaidjun*
talk quickly talk (this dialect) quickly talk together

junbalal-ŋuban *diwiljun* *woŋa* *daa-walwaljun*
talk (this dialect) quickly talk like birds talk move mouth in speech

daa-wudbrugdun
mouth talk slowly

bili *julŋu* *niniŋu* *duri-wogal* *bala*
because people always there buttocks play incisure

rewulwuljun *nundariba* *woŋana* *burlgai-ŋuban* *mada-wilindjun*
clan clan talk talk quickly tongue twisting

ŋari-waidbaidjun *junbalal-ŋuban* *diwilwiljun*
talk together talk (this dialect) quickly talk like birds

djuŋgulul-ŋuban *nundeia* *nundaŋ-ŋudbrul* *malaŋari*
clan clan clan all the clans

dambul-dambul *geidjulula* *gabulmeii* *laindjarei*
clan clan clan clan

madeindja *woŋana* *djuŋgulul* *waŋa-ŋura* *ŋurldandurl-ŋura*
language talk clan in (that) camp in the *nonggaru*

ŋurlbur-ŋura
in middle of *nonggaru*

1 Words 'fly' from people's mouths and drift into the air.

2 Related to the clan of this name, associated mytho-totemically with the barramundi fish. In this context, the talking refers to the dialect used by this particular clan.

3 'Tongue'.

4 'Hear one another'.

5 'Go back' or 'turn back': the people speak so quickly that outsiders, even those knowing the dialect, find it difficult to understand them.

6 Sound of different people talking joins together: *lili*, 'hither' or 'towards'.

7 *Dua* moiety people talk together here, where *dua* and *jiridja* moiety groups have gathered for the *kunapipi* rituals. However, *dua* dialects differ from those of the *jiridja*. (*Maraŋala*, 'obtained' or 'took'.)

8 Associated with a *dua* moiety new paperbark tree growing at this place.

9 Related to the barramundi fish.

10 Talking slowly so that strangers can understand them.
11 People who live among the 'armband' bushes, from which they make 'shades' or huts. The 'armband' bush is a species of cane from which plaited armbands are made and worn by both men and women.
12 Referring to a place (Gurundul) where there is a thick jungle.
13 Among the bamboo clumps.
14 At Rose River, home of a certain mytho-totemic snake.
15 People of the barramundi fish.
16 Also associated with a mytho-totemic barramundi. In this case, the term has a deeper significance, being related to the *jiridja* moiety mythic being, Laindjung.
17 A clan of the Dalwongu dialectal unit.
18 I.e., as 'one clan', or 'one group': they all come together for the rituals.
19 The inference here is that if children are *dua*, their mothers must be *jiridja*; or, as *dua* women would say, 'our children are *jiridja*'.
20 Related to the *kunapipi nonggaru*-place.

Song 3

bili duri-wumarana manalgaid manalganjala mabunda
because rub bottom red ochre[1] red ochre red ochre
bili duri-wumara midmid wuddun duri-wuma
because rub bottom (chip off fragments) beat[2] (pound) rub bottom
riragaindja wondina waidjililil balweiu djirmalaŋandu
sound (of scraping) runs along (to) Place Place Place of the Snake
wuddun nina duri-wuma
pound sit down rub bottom
bili mugoiu munalju damanjalg-miri daŋarlgaŋ-miri
because spirit clan clan with clan with
baleiu rewulwulju nundaribei
subincisure clan clan
lia-wondinja midmid
(sound) runs along (chip off fragments)
gumur waramanguŋu wuldjamunguŋu munalwuŋu banaŋagboiŋuŋu
chest (used to it) clan clan Bush clan
riŋguraŋguŋu jiguljulŋu
clan clan
bili manalgan duali manalganjala mabunda
because red ochre this red ochre red ochre
midmid wuddun nina mananŋu
(chip off fragments) pound sit down red ochre
gumur naŋu wuddunara nundeiana nundaŋ-ŋudbrulna
chest saw pounded clan clan
gabulmeiina djuŋgululŋina laindjarana
clan clan clan
riragaindja lia-wondinja waŋa-ŋura barindi
sound (of scraping) (sound) runs along in (that) camp Place
gundji-wundji
Place
ŋurlbur-ŋura daguwal-ŋura ŋurl-marŋ-marŋ-ŋura
in middle of *nonggaru* in Vagina in *nonggaru* Place

wulma-ŋura *lamilablab-ŋura* *lamiarlbiŋa* *ŋurldandurl-ŋura*
in shade[3] in shade[3] shade[3] in *nonggaru*

duri-wuma *nina* *manalgaŋ* *manalganjala* *mananŋu*
rub bottom sit down red ochre red ochre red ochre

midmid *wuddun* *mabunda* *duri-wumara*
(chip off fragments) pound red ochre rub bottom

1 Refers to 'raw' red ochre found as 'rock', and not the processed or moulded lumps. The bottom of the red ochre chunk is rubbed against a flat stone.

2 Preparing it in readiness for smearing over women before defloration, and for painting the boomerangs.

3 I.e., among the branches of the small *kunapipi* shade in which women await ritual coitus. (*Wulma* may also mean cloud, or shadows cast by clouds.)

Song 4

bili *guliriliri* *gwig-gwigdurina* *djanbindu-miriaŋala*
because boomerang[1] sprayed on[2] put kangaroo fat on

ŋuni *ŋamulwarina*
that boomerang

midmiddun *ŋuriŋi* *djanbin-miriaŋala* *galialina*
(chip off fragments) from that put kangaroo fat on boomerang

ralŋin-miriaŋala *gareialju* *gwigdurina* *ŋamina* *nina* *mabundei*
put kangaroo fat on fat spray on smear on (along) red ochre

manalgandu *galgalgali* *bilidj-bilidj* *wudduruna* *banara*
red ochre boomerang flat boomerang pounded all over

mabundeiu *duniu*
red ochre ochre

bili *gwiaŋina* *wogal* *gundji-wundji* *waŋa* *ŋurlbur*
because think play[3] Place camp middle of *nonggaru*

ŋurldandur *ŋurl-marŋ-marŋ* *buŋgul-buŋgul*
nonggaru *nonggaru* Place dancing ground (shade)

munaruŋ *gwig-gwigdurina* *gwunjaŋiŋani* *mirindil*
small boomerang sprayed on small boomerang small boomerang

munalju *garldjalulei* *malaŋari* *dambul-dambulju* *duŋgararei*
clan clan of clans clan clan

laindjareiu *nundaŋ-ŋudbrulju* *gabulmeii*
clan clan clan

gwiaŋina *wogal* *guliriliri* *ŋamadinana* *galgalgali* *ŋamulwoli*
think play boomerang make good boomerang boomerang

bugu-djugunjara *lia-wululum-miriaŋala*
point used in defloration ('forehead' of boomerang) point used in defloration

ŋamaŋameiun *ŋamin*
make smear on

gumur *naŋal* *duagandinja* *ŋaminara* *murunuŋna* *gumur* *mugoina*
chest saw *dua* clan smear on clan chest spirits

nuŋgadwolina *dawulbina* *ŋalaŋalana* *gurlbulana*
invocation[4] invocation[5] invocation[4] invocation[4]

ŋaminara *galiali* *mabalggu* *ŋamulwari* *jilbarindji*
smear boomerang boomerang boomerang boomerang

galgalgali *bilidj-bilidj* *diaŋu* *midmiddun*
boomerang flat boomerang from this (chip off fragments)
mabundei
red ochre
mananŋoi *manalgandu* *manalgandjulei* *duniu* *duri-wuma*
red ochre red ochre red ochre ochre rub bottom
ŋamin *gwigdun*
smear spray on
djanbindu *waiindu* *djadjei* *raŋgalmindu* *guraulwalil*
kangaroo fat creature[6] kangaroo kangaroo kangaroo
gandei-gandeiu *djundjungalei* *mawirialaiu* *galwadbalju*
kangaroo kangaroo kangaroo kangaroo
gwigdurina *ŋuni* *mabalggu* *jilbarindji* *ŋamulwari* *galgalgali*
sprayed on that boomerang boomerang boomerang boomerang
ŋamina *nina*
smear on (along)

15 *munalju* *wudjulmundu* *nargaleiu* *nuŋguluŋundu*
clan clan clan clan
nuŋburindi *guraggurei-mala* *nargaleiu* *njaŋbulu* *waŋan-ŋura*
clan name clan clan clan in (that) camp

[1] Red ochre is smeared on to the boomerang.

[2] Prepared red ochre, put into the mouth and sprayed over the boomerang.

[3] I.e., on the ritual ground, referring to coitus.

[4] Invocations to the south-west *dua* moiety hurricane wind. Also referring to a clan in the vicinity of Rose River.

[5] As note 4: screeching, like talking.

[6] The word *waiin* is used as a general term for animals, birds and insects, in much the same way as *waragan*: the distinction between the two, usually ignored in everyday speech, is that *waragan* should be edible, whereas a *waiin* is not.

Song 5

1 *bili* *daranana* *munal* *jarareianina*
because stand[1] clan line up
mardji *waŋa-lili* *ŋurldandur-lili* *ŋurl-marŋ-marŋ-lili* *daguwal-lili*
go into camp into *nonggaru* into *nonggaru* into Vagina[2]
bili *darana* *garldjalula* *nundaŋ-ŋudbrul* *nundeia* *dambul-dambul*
because stand clan clan clan clan
darana *mala* *malaŋari* *djibdunmina* *lugundja*
stand clan all clans poised on toes[3] foot
waŋa-lili *barindi* *gundji-wundji* *ŋurldandur-lili* *ŋurlbur-lili*
into camp Place Place into *nonggaru* into middle of *nonggaru*
daguwal-lili *gumur-lili* *manbrilg-lili* *djunmili-lili*
into Vagina into branches[4] into branches[5] into branches
mandjar-lili
into branches

5 *dara-mardji* *munal* *rewulwul* *niniŋu*
stand go clan clan always there
bala *wudjulman* *goŋ-walgina* *ŋamulwara-lili*
incisure clan put hand on[6] on to boomerang

durbu-wogal *gumur-lili* *malmalin-lili* *buwagan-lili*
buttocks play (moving) into branches into branches into branches
dara-mardji *jarareiun* *mandjar-lili* *wumidjidji-lili* *manbrilg-lili*
stand go line up into branches into branches into branches
wogalna *gwiaŋina*
play think

10 *niniŋu* *duri-wogal*
always there buttocks play (moving)
niniŋu *bala* *nundariba* *rewulwul* *dambul-dambul*
always there incisure clan clan clan
garldjalulul *nundeia* *nundaŋ-ŋudbrul* *djuŋgulul* *laindjarei*
clan clan clan clan clan
dara-mardji *ŋuniwola* *mandjar-lili* *lugundja* *bunbuŋala*
stand go there into branches foot lined up along
dara *jarareiun* *waŋan-ŋura* *ŋurldandur-ŋura* *ŋurl-marŋ-marŋ-ŋura*
stand line up in (that) camp in *nonggaru* in *nonggaru*
dualandja *waŋa* *munalwa* *wudjulmundu* *gwia-miri*
this camp clan clan fish with[7]
jalŋa-miri *bidji-miri* *munda-miri*
(fish) scales with scales with scales with

15 *barindi* *gundji-wundji* *ŋurl-marŋ-marŋ* *ŋurldandur* *daguwal*
Place Place *nonggaru* *nonggaru* Vagina shade

1 Standing ready, about to throw boomerangs: testing them. This is done before using them for defloration.

2 I.e., the *nonggaru*.

3 I.e., ready to throw a boomerang.

4 Within the *nonggaru*: *gumur* means 'chest' or 'breasts', or generally the front part of a person or thing, here, the front of the branches or shade.

5 The *kunapipi* shade for the women.

6 Grasping the boomerang to throw it.

7 I.e., because the female participants have eaten fish in the *nonggaru*.

Song 6

1 *bili* *gandjar-miriaŋala* *galialina* *ŋamulwari* *gumur* *waramandu*
because shake[1] boomerang boomerang chest[2] (used to it)
munalju *rewulwulu* *dubdurunana* *gandjar-warlmura* *juda* *galgalgali*
clan clan threw shake new boomerang
ŋamulwari *galiali* *jilbarindji* *bilidj-bilidj* *mabalgu*
boomerang boomerang boomerang flat boomerang boomerang
gunjaŋinjani *juda* *mirindil* *juda*
small boomerang new small boomerang new[3]
gumur *waramandu* *munalju* *wudjulmundu* *rewulwulj*
chest (used to it) clan clan clan

5 *bili* *wondinja* *dalaluljunana* *ŋamadaŋala* *wondinja*
because runs along[4] twirl around made well runs along
galiali *ŋuni* *mabalggu*
boomerang that boomerang

gandjar-warlmura *dubduruna* *mainmag-dina*
shake threw make good
dalaljuruna *bidjara* *waidjililju* *balwaiu*
twirled this way Place Place[5]
dawal *lagaraŋala* *dubduruna*
(country) told threw
mugoiu *damanjalgaŋ-miri* *daŋarlgaŋ-miri*
spirits clan with clan with

bidjara *dubduruna* *ramin-lili* *gundji-wundji* *gurundul-lili*
this way threw into bush Place Place into bush Place
bidjara *dubduruna* *nandjalei* *warabarei* *ŋawarabu* *waralgeiu*
this way threw Place[5] Place[5] Place[5] Place[5]
miŋei *madandandu* *djun-lili* *malgiei* *warabareiu* *djun-lili*
Place[5] Place[5] into Place[5] Place[5] Place[5] into Place[5]
madjambali *madjamdulei*
Place[5] Place[5]
wondinja *galiali* *juwuguŋu* *gumur-waramanguŋu* *murunuŋ-guŋu*
runs along boomerang clan chest (used to it) (paperbark) clan
gumur *mugoiuŋu*
chest spirit people[6]
dawulinguŋu *gurlbulawuŋu* *ŋalaŋalawuŋu* *nuŋgadwoliwuŋu*
(invocation)[7] (invocation)[7] (invocation)[7] (invocation)[7]
dubduruna *lili-dubdun* *maŋurju* *barindi* *guminidjawindu*
threw towards throw Place[8] Place Place[9]
minidjau-lili
into Place[9]

dubduruna *djiliili* *mareialwirŋu* *bumbiu* *dagumei*
threw (into) Place[8] Place[8] Place[8] Vagina Place[8]
walwaljunmeiu
Place[8]
galiali *dalaljuruna* *mabalggu* *guliriliri* *galgalgali*
boomerang twirled boomerang boomerang boomerang
ŋamulwari *bilidj-bilidj* *gunjaŋinjani*
boomerang flat boomerang small boomerang
jagu-miri *mirindil* *lai-wildjilg-gunara*
name with small boomerang flattened sides
lia-gulgdun-miriama
point made for defloration
dalaljuruna *bidjara* *dubduruna* *wungareiu* *madadiu*
twirled this way threw Place[9] water[10]
gunjarwondu *waralgei* *ŋawarandjiu*
Place Place Place
bidjara *dubduruna* *ŋoii-lili* *muŋarwol-lili* *maiaŋmagwi*
this way threw into inside into water[11] salt water
banbali *gawuluŋei*
sea water sea water

mugulluwulju *rarambaldji* *daragan-mardji* *banbani*
rough water[12] rough water[12] stand up, go[13] sea water
mugoiu *munalju* *wudjulmundu* *malaŋari* *dambul-dambulju*
spirits clan clan all the clans clan

mananŋeiuna	*wondi*	*galiali*	*dalaljurunana*	*mabalggu*
red ochred	'runs along'	boomerang	twirled	boomerang

1 Shake the boomerang, ready to throw. *Gandjar* (*geindja*) has the primary meaning of 'energy' or 'force', or 'speed', from which are derived a number of secondary meanings such as this.
2 The movement of the chest as a boomerang is thrown.
3 Also meaning 'child' or 'semen'.
4 The boomerang 'runs' or flies fast through the air.
5 At Rose River: these places are related mytho-totemically to the crab, snake and catfish.
6 Of the *dua* moiety.
7 *Dua* invocations to the 'heavy wind' or hurricane: see Song 4, note 4.
8 At Blue Mud Bay, belonging to the *jiridja* moiety Mararba-speaking group.
9 Inland from Rose River.
10 The boomerang is thrown, in spirit, into the water at places mentioned in the song.
11 Skimming the surface.
12 Very rough sea between the mainland and Groote Eylandt, specifically between Connexion and Woodah Islands.
13 The waves 'stand up', in long rows.

Song 7

bili	*gurunina-mardji*	*galiali*	*juldu*	*munalju*	*warejuljulju*
because	put sitting along[1]	boomerang	who[2]	clan	clan
gurunana-mardji	*waŋa-lili*	*bili*	*ŋilimuruŋgu*	*mabalggu*	
put along	into camp	because	ours	boomerang	
ŋamadinana					
made good					
wondinandja	*ŋilimuruŋ*	*gurunana*	*dibala*	*waŋa-lil-nina*	
ran along	ours	put along	here	into camp sit	
ŋurlbur-lilina	*barindijina*	*ŋurldandur-lili*	*daguwal-lili*		
into middle of *nonggaru*	Place	into *nonggaru*	into Vagina		
buŋgul-buŋgul-lili	*djunmili-lili*	*gurunina-mardji*			
into dancing ground (shade)	into branches	put sitting along			
laindjareiu	*gabulmeii*	*nundaŋ-ŋudbrulju*	*nundei'eiu*	*dambul-dambulju*	
clan	clan	clan	clan	clan	
malaŋari	*geidjululeiu*				
all the clans	clan				
ŋarei	*ŋilimuruŋ*	*wogalju*	*galŋa*	*gurunina-mardji*	*duala*
(well)	ours	play	body skin[3]	put sitting along	this
ŋamulwari	*jilbarindji*	*bilidj-bilidj*	*galgalgali*		
boomerang	boomerang	flat boomerang	boomerang		
waŋa-lili	*gundji-wundji*	*barunaŋdu*	*balwari*	*djun-lili*	
into camp	Place	Place	Place	into Place	
djunwiindu	*madandal*	*warabarei*	*ŋaindjuleiu*	*ŋawarabiu*	*waralgeiu*
Place	Place	Place	Place	Place	Place

1 I.e., placing boomerangs in a row on the ground.
2 I.e., the singer asks the question, and answers it himself: 'Who did this? The people of those clans . . .'

[3] Their bodies are tired, from 'playing' with boomerangs.

Song 8

bili woŋana mandjarwul jiguna buduruna ŋari-waidbaidjuruna
because talk branches sound flew out talked together

ŋari-ŋariuna wondi
talk like birds[1] runs along

jigul-ŋubana mada-ŋagu junbalal
talk (this dialect) quickly language hear (sound of talking)

juwejuwa daa-walwalun woŋa daa-wudbrugdun
sound of talking move mouth in speech talk mouth talk slowly

mada lindjun mada-wilindjun diwiljun
tongue twist tongue twist talk like birds

galawalŋ ŋagu riŋgaraŋ julŋu-lilii meiameia
sound hear clan people towards bush people

gurundulwoi woŋana raminboi minidjawindja
bush Place talk bush people clan from bush

lilii bagulboi wulmagboindja woŋa mada
towards clan from bush bush people talk tongue

gulgdun-maraŋala
separate (cut) got

waguju murunuŋdu bilililwiŋoi wagun-dalwiŋoi
children[2] clan clan children Dalwongu[3]

garaŋariwiŋoi ŋari-ŋariun jigul-ŋuban riŋgaraŋ
clan talk like birds talk (this dialect) quickly clan

ŋagu jiridjana daa-wudbrugdunŋara ŋalalejunara
hear *jiridja* mouth talk slowly made sound of talking

woŋana mandjarwul ŋurigi buwagangu womidjidjiu
talk branches from that branches green branches

djunmiiju gililirwaral woŋana burlgai-ŋubara
branches branches in *nonggaru* talk talked quickly

jigul-ŋubana
talk (this dialect) quickly

[1] Said to be like the cry of a morning pigeon.
[2] See Song 2, note 19.
[3] Children of these *dua* moiety mothers are *jiridja*, belonging to the Dalwongu dialectal unit.

Song 9

bili gurunina-mardji mandjarna buwaganna womidjidjina
because put sitting along[1] branches branches of shade[2] branches

womiara wogundur
branches shade

malmalin mudu buwagan gumur-ŋamadaŋala
branches branches branches screen made[3]

gililirwara ŋurldanduriama waŋa gundji-wundji
branches in *nonggaru* put about *nonggaru* camp Place

barindi ŋurl-marŋ-marŋ buŋgul-buŋgul
Place nonggaru Place dancing ground (shade)
buldjan lamarid ŋamaŋameiun buldjanmara gumur-ŋamadama
shade branches make shade screen make
minbrilg gwiaŋina wogal
labia minora[4] think[5] play
niniŋoi duri-wogalju
always there buttocks play
baleiu rewulwulju nundaribei laindjareiu djuŋgululja
subincision clan clan clan clan clan
nundei'ei nundaŋ-ŋudbaru dambul-dambulju
clan clan clan
garldjalulei malaŋari duŋgararwirei gabulmeii wudjulmundu munalju
clan all the clans clan clan clan clan
waŋa-lili djirmalaŋandu waidjililju guŋgareiu meidjambali
into camp Place Place Place Place
ŋawaragboi ŋaindjulei warabarei gundji-wundji
Place Place Place Place
gurunan dagu-walgguma dildjina mandjarna
put along vagina hide[6] at back branches
gumur-naŋal duŋgararnina mandjarwul gurunan-mardji djunmili
chest saw clan branches put along branches
buldjanma magumba gililirwara warinba garawur
shade branches branches (in *nonggaru*) branches branches
mandjar gumur
branches chest
ŋamadaŋala wogundurna djunmililna bugundja numundruna
made good shade branches on top cover over[7]
jiwoŋana mandariwoŋana dalaljuruna ŋuni mandjar bunbunara
shake branches shake shook that branches made
mugoiwoŋa damanjalg-miri daŋarlgaŋ-miri ŋamaŋameiun nina
spirit place clan with clan with make (along)
buldjanma
shade
wogal gwiaŋiri mandiala gunabibi
play thought mandiela[8] *kunapipi*
niniŋuju duri-wogalju baleiu
always there[9] buttocks play subincision clan
wudjulmundu munalju riŋguraŋguŋu banaŋagbuju
clan clan clan clan
ŋamaŋameiun buldjanma malmalin womiara womidjidji
make shade branches branches branches
mandjar wogundu djunmili wudjia dagu-walgguma
branches shade branches branches vagina hide

1 Referring to branches of the 'shade' in or alongside the *nonggaru*.
2 Where ritual coitus takes place.
3 Making a 'chest' or barrier: i.e., arranging branches to form a windbreak or screen.
4 The *labia minora, or* the inner walls of the vagina: colloquially translated as 'red part inside': the 'outside' or ordinary term is *ŋirlgŋirlg*.

5 They are thinking of the *minbrilg*, and of ritual coitus: so they put branches to make a screen.
6 Arranging branches on forked sticks and rails to make a screen.
7 'Blocking', so that the women inside may not be seen.
8 See Song 1, note 16.
9 'Because those people come for this'—they are always there carrying out *kunapipi* ritual.

Song 10

bili	*ŋamadina*	*djunmili*	*ŋurldandur*	*waŋa*	*ŋurl-marŋ-marŋ*
because	make good	branches	*nonggaru*	camp	*nonggaru* Place
daguwal					
vagina					

bidji-miri	*gwia-miri*	*munda-miri*	*djuŋgulul-miri*	*ŋjuwa-miri*
fish scales with [1]	fish with	scales with	fish scales with [2]	fish scales with
binbin-miri	*jalŋa-miri*			
fish scales with	fish scales with			

laindjareiwa	*gabulmeiuwa*	*nundeialwa*	*nundaŋ-ŋudbrulwa*	
clan	clan	clan	clan	
malaŋariwa	*radjalulwa*	*dambul-dambulwa*	*raŋaŋawa*	*nargalalwa*
clan	clan	clan	clan	clan
njaŋbrulwa	*nuŋburindiwa*	*nuŋbululwa*		
clan	clan	clan		

waŋa	*barindi*	*gundji-wundji*	*balwariŋu*	*mareialwirŋu*
camp	Place	Place	Place	Place
dagumeiuŋ	*bumbiu*	*walwaljunmeiu*		
Place	Place	Place		

ŋamadina	*gumur*	*malmara*	*malmalin*	*wugundur*	*mandjar*
make good	screen	branches	branches	shade	branches
djunmili	*gililirwara*	*ŋamadina*			
branches	branches in *nonggaru*	make good			

mugoiwa	*rewulwuljuwa*	*mindaribawa*	*balalwa*
spirit people	clan	clan	subincision clan

ŋamadina	*buldjan*	*buldjanmara*	*buŋgul-buŋgul*	*lamaridj*
make good	shade	shade	dancing ground	shade (branches)
ŋurldandur	*ŋurl-marŋ-marŋ*	*lamiarlbi*	*lamaridj*	
nonggaru	*nonggaru* place	shade	shade	

1 Barramundi fish scales and bones have been thrown aside on the sacred ground after eating. See Song 5, note 7.
2 This word has been translated before as a clan name: here it is used in its more literal sense.

Song 11

bili	*daranana*	*galgira*	*waŋa-lili*	*ŋirara*
because	stand	put close	into camp	(stood) [1]
ŋuniwola	*djunmili-lili*	*wirgulna*	*manawinna*	*manan-ŋuna*
in there	into branches	girl	girl	red-ochred (girl) [2]

gumur-lili
into brush screen
gurunana *bili* *mareiin* *wirgul*
put along[3] because sacred[4] girl
ŋurugoi *waŋawi* *raminboi* *minidjawi* *manawin* *gurundulwi*
from that camp Place[5] bush Place[5] girl Place
5 *gilidjilmaru* *djunmili-lili* *gilidjilmila*
come close[6] into branches come close[6]
bili *manawinnani* *munal* *rewulwul* *bala*
because girl clan clan subincision
niniŋu *duri-wogal*
always there buttocks play
ŋirara *buŋgul-buŋgul-lili* *lamaridj-lili* *bidialbi-lili*
(stood) into dancing ground into shade (branches) into shade
lamilablab-lili *daguwal-lili*
into shade into Vagina shade

1 Girls stand at the entrance to the *nonggaru.*
2 A girl is painted with red ochre.
3 A girl is arranged in position for defloration.
4 Translated also here as 'pretty' or 'beautiful', in relation to the girl. See pages 80, 93 for a discussion of this word.
5 The girl's home camp, away in the bush: i.e., bush people.
6 'Pushing near to doing it'; the point of the boomerang is pushed into the vagina.

Song 12

1 *bili* *galgirana* *guliriliri* *magandja* *gaŋalana* *gumur-lili*
because put close boomerang[1] thighs took[2] on to front[3]
duriuruna *ŋuni* *wirgulna* *manan-ŋuna* *magar* *gaŋala*
pushed down[4] that girl that red-ochred (girl) thighs took
gwiaŋma *guliriliri* *lia-widjir-miri* *ŋamulwari*
think boomerang flattened point[5] boomerang
duriuruna *wirgulna* *gumur-lili* *mandjar-lili* *buwagan-lili*
pushed down girl on to front into branches into branches
5 *manan-ŋumirina* *mabunda* *lilina* *djanbin-mirina*
(girl) red ochre with red ochre on to smeared with kangaroo fat[6]
duriuruna *wurgundu-lili* *djunmili-lili* *mandjar-lili*
pushed down into 'shade' into branches into branches
gililrar-lili
into branches in *nonggaru*
bili *galgirana* *lia* *galiali* *lia-wuluma-miri*
because put close point boomerang point used in defloration
daa-waraŋ-lili
into vagina ('mouth')
mananŋu-wola *manawingala* *wirgulwola* *rewulwulwola* *munalwola*
into (red-ochred) girl into girl girl clan clan
jeidjuraŋala *wirgul* *ŋurigi* *liabwoi* *galialiwuŋu* *bilina*
cried out girl from that point of boomerang finished

bilid-bilidjwuluma *wirgulna* *lia-widjimiriu* *mabalgwiu*
put flat boomerang girl flattened point boomerang

jeidjuru-wondi *gurundulju* *jeidjuru-wondi* *raminboi* *banaŋagboi*
cry runs along[7] Place cry runs along Place Place
jeidjuru-wondi
cry runs along

meiameia *ŋurigi* *wirgul* *ŋawarabuŋ* *waralgaŋ*
clan from that young girl from Place Place
djirmalaŋanŋu *gundji-wundji*
from Place Place

bilid-bilidjrun *ŋuriŋi* *liaju* *galiali* *ŋamulwariu*
put flat boomerang in with that point boomerang boomerang

riragaindja *wondinana* *dudbidju* *madjambari* *waralgeiu*
sound runs along white cockatoo[8] Place Place
madjambalju *nandjaleiu* *gumurlaŋandu*
Place Place Place[9]

ŋuni *wirgul* *manawin* *jeidjuruna* *riragai* *bunjarwondu*
that girl girl cried out sound Place
malumindu *malgieiu* *jagagiŋeiu*
Place Place Place

malmalreiu *malgiei* *miŋei* *waidjililju* *djilili-lili* *riragai*
Place (of branches) Place Place Place Place sound
madanandu *waminŋarei* *jamulgulg-mugoiu* *wadiriu* *geiinbalei*
Place Place Place of spirit people tribe Place

wondina *riragaindja* *jeidjuruna* *ŋurigi* *galialiwi*
runs along sound cried out from that boomerang

riragaina *munal* *jeidjuruna* *rewulwul* *wiŋgaraŋ*
sound clan cried clan women's 'clan'[10]
wudjulmun *damanjalg-miri* *daŋarlgaŋ-miri*
women's 'clan'[10] clan with clan with

jeidjurunana *gumur-ŋura* *mandjar-ŋura* *djunmili-ŋura*
cried out on front part in branches in branches
buwaiga-ŋura *malmali-ŋura* *wogundur-ŋura*
in branches in branches in shade

riragai *jeidjun* *mananŋu-miri* *duni-miri*
sound cries out (girls) with red ochre red ochre with
mabunda-miri *wirgul* *manalgan-miri* *manalgandjala-miri*
red ochre with girl red ochre with red ochre with

riragaindja *waŋa-ŋura* *ŋurlbun-ŋura* *gundji-wundji*
sound in camp in middle of *nonggaru* Place
ŋurl-marŋ-marŋ-ŋura *ŋurldandur-ŋura*
in *nonggaru* place in *nonggaru*

[1] The defloration boomerang.
[2] 'Carried' or held.
[3] The girl's legs are drawn on to the man's thighs or hips, one at each side, in the customary position, ready for coitus.
[4] The girl is pushed backwards on to the ground.
[5] Use in defloration.
[6] The red ochre is mixed with fat.

7 The cries of the girl 'flew over' or drifted across the sacred ground.
8 Actually a place-name: alternatively, Dudadiu, at Rose River.
9 In this context, 'on the man's legs', referring to the girl: they are doing it at that place.
10 I.e., a large group of girls together.

Song 13

bili *luganana* *ŋari-ŋariuruna* *gurgaju* *gurwalwalju*
because 'eat'[1] 'talked'[2] with penis erect penis

daa-ŋarin-ŋarindu
penis ring[3]

ŋari-ŋariun *luga*
talk 'eat'

daa-wudbrugdun *gabu-jaljaljun*
mouth 'talk' slowly 'water' (semen) (comes out)

gurgai *luga* *gurwalwalju* *ŋambuju* *ŋambu-liliun* *djalaljun*
penis 'eats' erect penis penis penis moves forward moves[4]

gabu-jaljaljun *wirgulna* *manawinna* *gumur-ŋura* *mudu-ŋura*
semen (comes out) girl girl within screen[5] in branches

luganana *malmali-ŋura* *buwagan-ŋura* *gurgaju* *ŋari-ŋariun*
'eats' in bushes in branches with penis 'talk'

daa-wudbrugdun *gabu-jaljaljun*
mouth 'talk' slowly semen (comes out)

gurgai *gudunbuju* *daa-ŋarin-ŋarindu* *djuŋguli*
penis[6] penis penis ring penis ring[7]

walwaljun *luga* *gurgai* *djuŋguli* *balindu*
grows[8] 'eat' penis penis ring subincised penis

bili *daa-ŋarin-ŋarindu* *niniŋuju* *duri-wogalju*
because penis ring always there buttocks play

gabu-jaljaljun *ŋuriŋi* *gurgaju* *rananeiu*
semen (comes out) from that penis erect[9]

ŋudjidbei *dambdundara* *wirgulna*
penis big[10] goes into[11] girl

gurgaju *daa-ŋambuju* *walwaljun* *gurgandja*
penis 'mouth' of penis grows penis

daa-ŋarin-ŋarindja *gurgamura-miri* *manawinna* *wirgulna*
penis ring penis smell with[12] young girl girl

gumur-ŋura *mudu-ŋura* *buwagan-ŋura* *gililirara-ŋura*
within screen in branches in branches in branches in *nonggaru*

djunmili-ŋura *gabu-jaljaljur-ŋura*
in branches in (place where) semen came out

maleiu *luga* *nargaleiu* *jaŋbulju* *nuŋguluŋundu* *nuŋburindi*
clan 'eats'[1] clan[13] clan[13] clan[13] clan

malaŋari *luga* *garldjaluleiu* *daŋarlgweiu* *maleju* *garldjaluleiu*
all the clans 'eats' clan clan[13] clan clan

dambul-dambulju
clan

djaljaljuna *luga* *gabu-jaljaljuna*
move[14] 'eats' semen (comes out)

luga *ŋari-ŋariuna* *wirgulna* *manawinna*
'eats' 'talk' girl girl

raminboiŋu *banaŋagboiŋu* *gurundulwoiŋu* *balwaririwoiŋu*
from Place from Place from Place from Place
gunjarwonboiŋu *miŋaroi-ŋura* *dumungalwoiŋu* *waidjililwoiŋu*
from Place at Place from Place from Place
djirmalaŋanboiŋu
from Place

gurga-ŋuna *walwaljunara* *balana* *luganana*
penis that grew subincision 'eat'

rewulwulna *nundaribana* *geidjululnana* *munalna* *riŋgarana*
clan clan clan clan clan

ruŋiiri *luga* *gabu-jaljaljun* *gabundu*
go back 'eat'[15] semen (comes out) semen

bumbiu *mareialwirŋu* *walwaljunei* *dumungalju*
Place Place grows Place

gurgaju *walwaljun* *gudunboiu* *rananei* *djimbari* *djuŋguloi*
penis grows penis-clan penis-clan penis penis ring
balindu *raŋalwondu* *daa-ŋarin-ŋarindu*
subincised penis penis penis ring

1 I.e., 'having that girl'. The word *luga*, 'eat', has the secondary and common meaning, as in this context, to 'copulate'.
2 Others sing on the sacred ground not far from where the couple lie. The word, which means making a noise, may also refer to the sound of the penis in the vagina.
3 Ridge on penis, towards its apex; this ridge becomes more pronounced as the penis erects.
4 Movement of penis during coitus.
5 Alternatively, on man's thighs or loins; see Song 12, note 3.
6 Literally, 'penis like a barramundi fish': the penis is said to 'take part for' (i.e., represent) this fish. It also refers to the subincisure, and is used as a clan name.
7 Also used as a clan name.
8 The penis 'grows', becomes erect: the word also refers to a place name, connected with the snake.
9 'Very erect': the penis is hard and upright.
10 Reference is made to its size and length.
11 The act of insertion: *dara*, 'stands', again refers to the upright penis.
12 Translated as 'smell of woman on the man': i.e., the penis smells from the vaginal juices.
13 I.e., of the barramundi (see previous songs), symbolically referring to the penis; these clans belong to the Dalwongu dialectal unit.
14 Here the girl moves because she feels uncomfortable and sore after having received so many men.
15 Men come and go from the shade: the girl receives them in turn.

Song 14

bili *gaŋgadinana* *gumur-ŋura* *mandjar-ŋura* *wirgul* *manda*
because became weak[1] within screen in branches girls two
manawin *manda*
girls two

bili jaljaljuruna ŋamama dubduruna
because flowed out[2] (make semen flow)[3] threw out
ŋamamali jaljalwondi gumur-ŋura mandjar-ŋura
(make semen flow) flows running out within screen in branches
buŋgal madjina
(branches) dance branches
munalwu mananŋu-wol duni-miriu dubdunna
clan (girl) red ochred (girl) red ochre with throws out
wondi ŋamamali jaljaljun ŋamama
runs along (makes semen flow) flows out (makes semen flow)
wirgulju gurundulwoiul raminboiu minidjawoiu meiameia
girl from Place from Place from Place (Place)
djirmalaŋanboiu bagulboiu
from Place from Place

5 *dubdun wondi jaljaljuruna ŋamamali*
throws out runs along flowed out (make semen flow)
manawindu rewulwulju baleiu wudjulmundu munalju
girl clan incisure[4] clan clan
daŋarlgaŋmiri damanjalgmiri
clan clan
gumur-ŋura djunmili-ŋura buŋgul madjina wirgullul
within screen in branches (branches) dance branches girl
bili dubduruna mandiala ŋamama ŋamamali
because threw out *mandiela*[5] (make semen flow) (make semen flow)
bili waŋan-ŋura ŋurlbur-ŋura ŋuldandur-ŋura gundji-wundji
because in camp in middle of *nonggaru* in *nonggaru* Place

10 *barindiwura wulma-ŋura ŋurl-marŋ-marŋ-ŋura buŋgul-buŋgul-ŋura*
Place in shade in *nonggaru* Place in dancing ground
djunmili-ŋura daguwal-ŋura
in branches in Vagina (shade)
ŋamamali dubduruna wirgulju manawindu ŋamama
(make semen flow) threw out girl girl (make semen flow)
dubdun
throws out

1 The girls feel weak and 'soft' after the ritual.

2 I.e., semen coming from her as she stands up after coitus.

3 The word refers to the pressure applied to the lower abdomen, to dislodge semen.

4 This word, meaning subincised, is often applied generally to the subincising clans. Here, however, it refers to the young girl. She is called *bala* because the defloration rite and subsequent coitus are said to break an 'armband' or bone in her vagina (see pages 62–3). She is, in this context, likened to a subincised man.

5 See Song 1, note 16.

Song 15

1 *gwig-gwig-durunana wirgulna manawinna djanbindu gareialju*
sprayed on[1] girl girl kangaroo fat kangaroo fat
duni manalgandu banara
red ochre red ochre all over

djalulnuŋala *gwig-gwig-durunana* *duri-wumara* *ŋamina*
put all over (her) sprayed on rub bottom (of ochre) smear on
manawinna *wirgulna* *duniu* *banara* *gwigduruna*
girl girl red ochre all over sprayed on
bili *galŋa-ŋura* *bariweidaruna* *ŋigduruna* *djanbin-ŋura*
because on skin (body)[2] red ochre shone[2] shone[2] on kangaroo fat
gwigdun *banara* *wirgulna* *munalna* *rewulwulna* *wudjulwuma*
spray on all over girl clan clan clan
dambul-dambulna *ṅargalana*
clan clan

[1] Red ochre and blood from the girl's vagina, with kangaroo fat, are smeared over her body before she leaves the sacred ground.

[2] The shining body of the ochre-smeared girl is emphasized.

Song 16

bili *warara* *guruŋala* *ramin-ŋura* *minidja-ŋura*
because red cloud[1] hung[2] at Place at Place
warara *bariweidun* *mudbaŋga* *ruŋgul* *daluŋgur*
red cloud shines[3] red cloud red cloud yellow and red cloud[4]
wir'wirun *guruma*
goes all over[5] hanging
gumigumi *malaŋgara* *bala* *gwigdunara* *munalwuŋu*
red cloud red cloud subincision sprayed[6] clan
rewulwuluŋu *nundaribawuŋu*
clan clan
balalwuŋu *warara* *banaŋag-ŋura* *guruŋala*
from subincisure[7] red cloud at Place hung
gumigumi *gumur-ŋura* *nuga* *djilibiriwir* *gamarala*
red cloud at screen Place[8] that Place[8] Place[8]
buŋgarindji *buralwandji* *djelŋanar*
Place[8] Place[8] Place[8]
banara *bulariun* *bili* *gulaŋ* *wirgul* *manawin* *munal*
all over shine because blood girl young girl clan
nargalala *nuŋburindi* *nuŋguluŋin* *nuŋburindi*
clan clan clan clan
wir'wirun *ruŋgul* *daluŋgur*
goes all over red cloud yellow and red cloud
bulariun *djilil-ŋura* *bulariuruna* *dindi-ŋura* *dindi-dindi-ŋura* *waidjilil*
shines at Place shone at bamboo among bamboos to Place
banara *djirmalaŋan* *bawei* *ŋibawei*
all over Place Place Place
guruma *gulaŋ* *niniŋu* *munal*
hangs blood always there clan
duri-wogal *baima*
buttocks play always there
guruma *lia-ŋura* *munalwola* *dialaŋumi*
hang on top of clan from in here
waŋan-ŋura *gundji-wundji* *barindi'indi* *ŋurlbur-ŋura*
in (that) camp Place Place in middle of *nonggaru*

daguwal-ŋura *lamialbi-ŋura* *lamaridj-ŋura* *buŋgul-buŋgul-ŋura*
in Vagina shade in shade in shade on dancing ground

banarana *bulariuruna*
all over shone

wirgul *manan-ŋun* *lidara* *bulariun* *gulaŋ* *munal*
girl (girl) red ochred shone shines blood clan

rewulwul *banaŋagboi*
clan from Place

1 This is the red-tinged cloud of the *jiridja* moiety, seen at sunrise and sunset. It is explained in a number of different ways, and in this case is said to be formed from blood lost by the girls.

2 The cloud is hovering over bush country from which the girls come.

3 The sun's rays light up the red-tinged cloud, like the shining red-ochred bodies of the girls. (See Song 15, note 2.)

4 The cloud is yellow, tinged with red. The redness comes from the girls' blood and the red ochre smeared or sprayed on their bodies: the yellow is from the semen of men who have copulated with them.

5 These clouds spread across the sky: *wir'wirun*, 'go round and round'.

6 See Song 4, note 2. The red clouds are formed by 'spitting' (i.e., 'spraying') fat mixed with blood over the girls: some goes over their bodies, some into the sky to form clouds.

7 This refers both to the ritual status of the women, and to the fact that subincised penes have copulated with them.

8 Near the sacred billabong where the Wawalag sisters were swallowed by Yulunggul. The place mentioned here is of the *jiridja* moiety and the Ridarŋu dialectal unit: its names refer to crab, goose, and running spring water. The inference is that the red clouds float over this place.

Song 17

ninananana *munal* *mauliŋari* *dambul-dambul* *garldjalulu* *nundeia*
sit down clan clan clan clan clan

nundaŋ-ŋudbrul
clan

nina-mardji *waŋa-lili* *bruma-lili* *gundji-wundji* *barindi'indi*
sit down go into camp into camp Place Place

ninana *djuŋgulul* *mala* *dambul-dambul* *garldjalulei* *djuŋgulul*
sit down clan clan clan clan clan

djuŋgarigari *daŋgarawa* *mala*
clan[1] clan[2] clan

ninana-mardji *dibala* *waŋa-lili* *bruma-lili* *ŋurldandur-lili*
sit down along here into camp into camp into *nonggaru*

ŋurl-marŋ-marŋ-lili *daguwal-lili* *djunmili-lili*
into *nonggaru* Place into Vagina into shade branches

ninana-mardji *jarareiun*
sit down along line up

ninana-mardji *jarareiun* *nuŋbulula* *nuŋguluŋin* *njaŋbul* *munal*
sit down along line up clan clan clan clan

nargalal *nina* *jarareiun* *rewulwul* *wudjulmundu*
clan sit line up clan clan

lilii *gundji-wundjiŋ* *bagulboindja* *wulmaboindja* *lilii* *nina* *jarareiun*
into Place Place from shade Place into sit line up

julŋu *niniŋu* *duri-wogal* *nundaribei* *bala*
people always there buttocks play clan subincisure

wudjulman *riŋgaraŋ* *djuŋgarigari* *dungararwa*
clan clan clan clan

1 These people are mytho-totemically related to the frog.

2 Clans associated with the barramundi fish, mentioned earlier in the cycle.

Song 18

bili *wudduruna* *lindjurnana* *munalju* *gara*
because struck[1] flaked[2] clan stone spear

ŋambi *ŋandina*
stone spear[3] mother[4]

wainmulmulna *gwudabin* *wuddun* *lindjun* *gumurndja* *ŋainbuljun*
stone spear stone spear strike flake chest[5] moves

dualandja *gumur* *garamandu* *wudduru-nina*
this chest (used to it) struck sit

daladalei *wirlbumeii* *marlgawoni* *gaiilmiri* *djibaroi*
(invocation)[6] (invocation)[6] (invocation)[6] (invocation)[6] (invocation)[6]

gara *djau'juruna* *lindjun* *wuddun* *gwiaŋiri* *bala*
stone spear broke flake struck think incisure[7]

ranana *gurwalwal* *daa-ŋarin-ŋarindu* *gurgawul* *lindjuruna*
penis erect erect penis penis ring penis flaked

gurwalwalwul *ranan-ŋawul* *djuŋgululul*
erect penis erect[8] penis ring

gwiaŋina *walwaljunara* *gabu-jaljaljunara* *djalaljunara*
think grew big semen (came out)[9] moved

daa-wudbrug-dunara *gwiaŋina* *daa-ŋarin-ŋarindu* *daa-ŋalaŋar*
mouth 'talked' slowly think penis ring penis ring

gurga *lindjun-nina*
penis flake sit

naŋbidu *guŋulumiri* *jidaniŋdu* *gabu-magumiri* *daiwaiindu*
(invocation)[10] (invocation)[10] (invocation)[10] spring water[10] (invocation)[10]

gwiaŋina *gurwalwal*
think erect penis

1 Splitting stone to make a stone spear blade: *wuddun*, 'knock', 'pound' or 'strike', with a number of associated meanings.

2 Tapping the stone and flaking it to make a sharp edge.

3 Also a word used for penis.

4 A *dua* moiety stone spear is called *ŋandi*, 'mother', 'mother of *jiridja* moiety people'.

5 The men's chests move as they flake their stone spears.

6 Invocations referring to a place on the northern side of Blue Mud Bay where there is a high hill from which stone is quarried for spear blades.

7 A stone blade is used to cut the penis incisure.

8 The penis is partially erected before the incision is made.
9 They are thinking of copulating with women, with their 'open' (subincised) penes. The subincision (men said) allows the ejaculation to flow more readily with the minimum of exertion on the man's part.
10 Invocations referring to running spring water, likened to semen being ejaculated.

Song 19

bili *gadara* *gurwalwal* *gurga* *daa-windja* *gadarana* *gurwalwal*
because seized[1] erect penis penis 'mouth'[2] seized erect penis
daa-barawindjal *daa-ŋarin-ŋarin*
penis aperture penis ring
garwagguŋara *dunubaiaŋala*
lifted up[3] straightened up
bili *djanmilwari* *lia-ŋirara* *ranana-lili* *balawunara*
because stone blade point stood[4] on to erect penis to make incision
rewulwulna *niniŋuna* *balana* *wadirina* *wadirbalana*
clan always there incisure tribe tribe
rewulwulna *nundaribana* *wudjulmuna*
clan clan clan
munalna *djaŋgariŋ-garinja* *duŋgararwira*
clan clan clan
gurgal *gurgal-gulgduruna* *balalwulmana* *mardji* *gurga*
penis penis cut make subincisure go penis
ranana *gurwalwal* *dambul-dambul* *daa-ŋarin-ŋarin* *balalwulmara*
erect erect penis clan penis ring made incisure
gwiaŋina *wirgulna* *manawinna* *djanbin-mirina*
think girl girl kangaroo fat with[5]
waŋa-ŋura *bruma-ŋura* *ramin-ŋura* *gundji-wundji* *ŋurldandur-ŋura*
in camp in camp at Place Place in *nonggaru*
ŋurl-marŋ-marŋ-ŋura *ŋurlbur-ŋura*
in *nonggaru* Place in middle of *nonggaru*
midduna-mardji *balalwuma* *gurga* *ŋuni* *djuŋguluna*
cut (incisure) go make subincisure penis that penis ring
dawalmiri *ŋuna* *gabu-maiina*
always there there spring water clan

1 The initiator holds a postulant's penis for incising.
2 Or *ŋin*, penis aperture: the penis is held and the orifice is opened.
3 Lifting the penis in order to subincise it.
4 Placing the stone blade on the underpart of the penis, in readiness to incise.
5 A girl, smeared and 'sprayed' with (subincision) blood mixed with kangaroo fat and ochre (see Song 15).

Song 20

bili *daranana* *maŋan* *giliuruna* *djun-lili* *madjambali*
because stand up cloud bent down into Place[1] Place[1]
madjandulei
Place[1]

wululul *djunabiŋa* *goŋalbun* *widuruna* *galŋamiriun*
yellow clouds[2] yellow clouds clouds[3] shook[4] (take shape)[5]
jarawal-wunuŋala *wunuŋ-darana* *gargarluna*
stood up along stand along stand high
waidjal *waidjalnambi* *meilibin* *giliuruna* *madandandu*
cloud cloud cloud bending down Place
madjambali *djun-lili* *djunwiindu* *ŋawaraboi* *waralgei*
Place into Place Place Place Place
garldalili *garldandandu* *madandandu* *gunjarwondu* *nandjalei*
into Place[1] Place Place Place Place
warabarei *madaulumei*
Place Place
giliun *miŋeiu* *waidjilili* *djililju* *buŋgareiu* *balweiu*
bend down Place into Place Place Place Place
djirmalaŋandu *wagiei* *mudidi* *malgiei*
Place Place Place Place
giliun *widun* *djunabiŋa* *gumur-lili* *waidjal*
bend down shake black cloud[6] on to front[7] breast girdle[8]
waidjalŋabi
breast girdle[8]
galiali *djalgdun* *maŋan-lili* *maduŋgurlna* *rarjaruna*
boomerang throw out into cloud breast girdle[9] put along[10]
dara *giliun* *dumungalju* *miŋurju* *dagumei* *bumbi*
stand bend down Place Place Place Place
walwaljunei *mareialwirju*
Place Place
bii *darana* *ramin-lili* *gurundulju* *banaŋag-lili* *minidjau-lili*
indeed stand into Bush Place into Place into Place
djililili *dindi-lili* *djirmalaŋandu*
into Place into bamboos Place
dara *widun* *bugu-juda-diri* *gargarlun* *galŋamiriun* *minjirama*
stand shake face new becomes[11] stand high (take shape) shakes
ŋungargarlun *wabuljuroiun* *ŋuna* *dara* *garaŋarndja*
there stands high rise up[12] stand stand all over
maiaŋ-maggwi *maŋgarigbalju* *manga-lili* *duri-duri*
Place[13] Place[14] into sea water low down (right in water)
gwiwildjeiu *wonbali* *daragan-mardji* *mugululwulju* *lirin-mardji*
over water water[15] stand (it) along sea water sea water go
gawuluŋei *gumanaumineiu* *gumaneiu*
sea water sea water sea water
giliuruna *goŋalbun* *milarŋabi* *miljalŋarlbunŋira*
bent down clouds clouds clouds stand joined together
darana *wabuljuranina* *maiaŋ-maggwi* *lugu-luriundu*
stand rise up along Place low tide[16]
giliuruna *wunuŋmureiu* *dadarundu* *ŋurun-nineiu*
bent down right on water on water on water[17]
gumur-lili *rarlgan-djalgdun* *gunjanja* *marubiri*
on to chest throw black mark across mark on cloud[18] beach crab
jiniŋeiga
beach crab

djalgdun-mardji   maŋan   lia-juda-diri   gargarlun   garaŋarndja
throw out go   cloud   head new becomes   stand high   all over
marmiei   giliuruna   juguldjigbei   waŋurlboi   badulumboi
Place[19]   bent down   Place[19]   Place[20]   Place[21]
mamindjeiu   wadunmialgei   ŋeiaŋgulju
Place[22]   Place[22]   Place[22]
bargu-lili   wululu   giliuruna
towards far away   yellow clouds   bent down
bili   dawalju   marawudjara   dulu.ljar
because   time[23]   wet season   rains
jindidaŋoi   gandjina   djaŋgalja   boiulwulna
from big (rains)   underneath   new grass shoots   new shoots
maraudaŋgwia
new water (rain)
darana   jarareiun   maŋan
stand   line up   cloud
ŋurumiriaŋala   djaŋgalja   gandjina   boiuwulna
swamp shoots grow[24]   new grass shoots   underneath   new shoots
jimaganda   wundjaŋwuna
new shoots   new shoots
bii-darana   bargu-lili   goŋalbun   wululu
indeed stand   towards far away   clouds   yellow clouds
jadigbei   ŋeliei   jinigamboi   wondranŋeiu
Place[25]   Place[26]   Place[27]   Place [27]
maŋan   widun   gilun
cloud   shakes   bend down
gargarlun   wamaruŋgulju   bugundja   djunabiŋa   meilibin
stand high   at Place[28]   in front   black cloud   cloud
waidjalŋabi   maduŋgur
breast girdle   breast girdle
duriuruna   madandandu   madaulumur   waimunŋarei   dumwondi
feel down   Place   Place[19]   Place[19]   Place[29]
warlgangiu   ŋelieiu   darana   jaranŋiu
'island'[30]   Place[26]   stand   Place[26]
dawul-wudduruna   darana   dawul-wuddun   maŋan   gilun
place struck   stand   place strike   cloud   bend down
jindi-lili   djun-lili   wudureiu   geiinbalei   mulgamulgoiu
into big (place)[31]   into Place   Place   Place   Place
darana   wululu   goŋalbun   maliwiljun   madjandulei
stand   yellow clouds   clouds   bend down   Place
madjambali   jilileiu   darana   djarlgari   miŋeiu
Place   Place   stand   Place   Place
ŋuna   darana   ŋumunieiu   waldarju   miŋeiu
there   stand   Place   Place   Place
bii   dara   lurl-lili   waiingala   waŋa-lili
indeed   stand   into Place[32]   Place[33]   into camp[33]
bugu-juda-dina   giliuruna
'face' new make   bent down
bili   dawalju   gaduragda   maraudaŋgwia   gugarŋoia   dululjar
because   time[23]   wet season   new water (rain)   wet season   rains

1 Clouds 'stand up' across the sky and seem to touch these places, at Rose River. The word 'stand' here refers to their height, to the way in which they seem to loom upward in the sky.
2 'Clan' or *mala* in this case refers to a large number of clouds. See Song 16.
3 Pillars of clouds, like 'hands' (*goŋ*).
4 Translated as 'standing high up, and moving': changing its shape.
5 The 'body' (or main bulk) of the cloud shakes: *galŋamiri* is 'skin' or 'body'/with.
6 Black lowering rain clouds.
7 Bands of black across the clouds, as if on their 'chests'.
8 This word refers back to note 7: the cross-part of the cloud is likened to the breast-girdle (or 'harness') worn by girls: this string passes from the back over both shoulders and under the breasts, and is commonly called *maidga*.
9 A black cloud like a string breast-girdle.
10 'Join together': i.e., the clouds merge with one another.
11 In this context, 'young' clouds emerging on the horizon.
12 'Going up along': i.e., the clouds are rising from the horizon.
13 Above the waters, of a tidal stream (*maiaŋ*).
14 Or Wamaligbalju, at Rose River.
15 Alternatively, Gambali.
16 The 'feet' of the clouds seem to stand in the shallows at low tide.
17 The 'nose' or front of the cloud seems to sit on the water.
18 A little mark on the cloud, or a small black cloud in a larger one: it is said to be the footmark of the beach (or land) crab.
19 Situated near Groote Eylandt mission station; its names are derived from the clouds mentioned in this song.
20 Where the present Groote Eylandt mission station is situated.
21 At Badalumbu, on Groote Eylandt.
22 Near the present Groote Eylandt mission station.
23 Also used for 'place'.
24 The 'nose' of the grass has been formed, above the ground.
25 The whole of Groote Eylandt: the clouds go 'into' that place.
26 The long sandspit, named Djeradbin, near Ambu Kambu (Umbakamba) on the northern side of Groote Eylandt.
27 A barrier of rocky hills in the bush at Groote Eylandt.
28 Sand point near the Groote Eylandt mission station.
29 A place near the old Groote Eylandt mission station, on the Emerald River.
30 Rocks in the sea; Garei ('king') 'Macassan' Rocks upon which offerings were made by Indonesian traders to the spirits of the sea (see R. and C. Berndt 1954: 45).
31 *Jindi* means 'big', in the sense of importance or size; but, as here, it also refers to the mainland as distinct from the islands.
32 Referring to the hole of the snake.
33 Referring to the home of the snake.

Song 21

1	*bili*	*mada-jurunana*	*dalaljun-ŋanana*	*lia-ŋura*
	because	tongue flickers	moves fast along (flashes)[1]	on top
	goŋalbun-ŋura	*maiilibi-ŋura*	*wululu-ŋura*	
	on clouds	on clouds	on yellow clouds	

mainmag-diri-nina *manan-ŋeiun* *wululu-ŋura* *goŋalbun-ŋura*
shining become along[2] go like red ochre on yellow clouds on clouds

wombal-woŋanina *dalaljun* *buguwalmanina* *waŋan-ŋuru*
tail moves[3] moves fast (snake) face comes up along from (its) camp

lur-ŋuru
from (its) hole

jindi *wonduguŋu* *djulgameii* *meimeiun* *djalunaŋu*
big snake snake makes lightning snake

dalaljun-nina *maŋan-ŋura*
comes up fast along (flashing) on cloud

waŋan-ŋuru *lur-ŋuru* *dawal-wudduruna*
from (its) camp from (its) hole place struck

waiin *mundumundu* *geimarana* *gabuwei-garuŋmiri* *marandaldal*
creature snake snake living in salt water thin snake[4]

1 I.e., tongue of lightning.
2 *mainmag* has the general meaning of 'good' or 'nice'; *diri*, 'become'; *nina*, 'sits', or 'is'.
3 The Lightning Snake coming up, with its tail moving: i.e., the flash of the lightning.
4 Like 'thin' streaks of lightning.

Song 22

bili *waiin* *jalwulŋurana* *djurirurunana*
because snake (creature) crawls on belly[1] crawled down, moving along

ganana-ŋuru *lurndja*
from (its) hole hole

ŋurundja *dawal-wudduna* *lur-ŋura* *waiin* *gandjindja*
nose place struck hole in creature nose

djuriririna *jalwuŋuranana* *wudud-bwudub-duranana*
crawled down, moving along crawls on belly smelt blood of girls

barguna
far away

waiin *wombal-woŋana* *jalwulŋuranana* *ganarana* *waŋa* *lurndja*
creature tail moves crawls on belly hole camp hole

dalaljuna-mardji *wombal-woŋana* *jaŋgulg-ŋuranana*
moves fast, goes[2] tail moves swallows along[3]

bili *dawalju* *gaduragda* *maraudaŋgura* *duruda*
because time wet season new water (rain) rain

numara *wirgulna* *gulaŋ* *balana* *rewulwulna*
smelt girl blood incisure[4] clan

lugana-mardji *mananŋeiun* *dalaljun* *wombal-woŋa*
eat goes[5] go like red ochre moves fast tail moves

dibala *ŋara* *bada-lili* *geiaŋla-lili* *mandjigura-lili* *waralga-lili*
here I into intestines into intestines into intestines into intestines

dalaljun *ŋanarmiŋ-woŋa* *wombal-woŋa* *wombalndja* *djirwinbin*
moves fast tongue comes up tail moves tail tip of tail

lugana-mardji *jaŋgulg-lili* *jaŋgulgdja* *milwoiun* *dalaljun*
eat goes swallows into (intestines) swallowing crawls moves fast

gulaŋ *lugana* *waŋa-lili* *gundji-wundji* *barindiu* *dumungalju*
blood eats into camp Place Place Place

rewulwulna *munalju* *wudjulmuna* *ŋari-ŋarina* *jigulna*
clan clan clan clan clan

lugana-mardji *ŋanarmiŋ-woŋa*
eat goes tongue comes up

juda *lugana* *dulul*
new (water) eats rains[6]

15 *jindi* *geigundama* *gabuwei-garuŋ-miri* *wonduguŋu* *geimarana*
big snake living in salt water snake snake

jindi *gandaraŋ* *mundu-mundu* *geigundama* *djalunaŋu*
big snake snake snake snake

dalaljuna-mardji *meimeiun*
moves fast, goes makes lightning

djulgaboi *dildjina* *waiin* *buruldji* *dalaljun*
snake backbone creature back (of snake) moves fast

wudud-bwudubdun *ruŋiiri* *luga*
smells blood of girls goes back eats

dalaljun *ŋanarmiŋ-woŋa* *gurundul-lili* *ramin-lili* *buma-lili*
moves fast tongue comes up into Place into Place into Place

minidja-lili
into Place

20 *gulaŋ* *mananŋuna* *wirgulna* *munalna* *jigulna* *wadirina*
blood (girl) red-ochred girl clan clan tribe

ruŋiina *lugana* *dalaljuna* *mudidi* *wagiei*
goes back eats moves fast snake's place Place

gwunjarondu (*gunjarwondu*) *balwari* *ŋawaraboi* *madjambali*
Place Place Place Place

madjandulei *waralgei* *ŋawaraboi* *minidjawundu* *miŋeiu*
Place Place Place Place Place

dalaljuna-mardji *waiin* *dildjina* *buruldji* *djulgaboi*
moves fast, goes creature backbone back (of snake) snake

djulgameii
snake

dalaljun-mardji *bidjan* *luga* *dumungalju* *miŋurju* *barindiu*
moves fast, goes this way eats Place Place Place

dagumeii *bumbiu* *walwaljunei* *mareialwirŋu*
Vagina Place Place Place Place

dalaljun-mardji *jaŋgulg-lili* *mananŋeiun*
moves fast, goes swallows into (intestines) go like red ochre

25 *wombal-woŋa* *wudud-bwudubdun* *milŋoieiu*
tail moves smells blood of girls Place

dalaljun *luga* *gulaŋ* *numara*
moves fast eats blood smelt

waiindu *gurudjiu* *waidwaiddun* *luga* *marandaldal*
creature snake swims along (under water) eats thin snake

migarama *geigundama*
snake snake

jawulŋura *jaŋgulgŋura* *dawaljul* *jindida* *gugarŋoia*
crawls on belly swallows time big (rains) wet season

maraudaŋgwia *dululjar*
new water (rain) rains

ŋurumiriama *gandjiŋa*
grow up (swamp shoots) swamp grass time (or inside, underneath)
djaŋgalna *boiul-woiulna*
new grass shoot new shoots

30 *dalaljun* *luga* *ŋanarmiŋ-woŋa* *wombal-woŋa*
move fast eat tongue comes up tail moves
gabuwei-garuŋ-miri *wombalndja* *waiin* *djirwinbin* *ŋurundja*
living in salt water tail creature tip of tail nose
daluwir *gandji*
nose (inside)
dalaljun *mardji* *madandja* *mainmagdiri*
moves fast goes tongue shines[7]
dalaljun *bidjan* *gabundu* *mareiawirju* *dagumeii*
moves fast this way (into) water Place Vagina Place
bumbiu *dumungalju*
Place Place
dalalal *milwul* *wudub*!
(lightning comes along) lightning (go down now!)

1 'Belly rests (or lies)': the snake crawls along, smelling the blood (see Song 15). There is a marked resemblance here to the Wawalag cycle.
2 Like lightning flashing along: see Song 21.
3 *Jaŋgulg* may mean the act of swallowing, or the belly into which food is swallowed.
4 The snake smells blood, not only from the girl, but also from the subincised penis. (See Song 19.)
5 That is, 'having' the blood as it moves along.
6 It 'eats' blood mixed with water: the rain has washed down the blood and ochre, and streaks of this are seen in the running water. Comparison should be made here with the Wawalag cycle (see R. Berndt 1951*a*).
7 'Becomes good or nice'.

Song 23

1 *bili* *gurda* *duri-ŋirara* *manalju* *wudjulmundu* *jigulju*
because fire low down stood clan[1] clan clan
ŋirana-mardji *boiul-woiul* *mara*
stand goes new shoots foliage[2]
duri-ŋirara *gandji* *wundjaŋu* *ŋirana-mardji* *jimagan*
low down stood low down new shoots stand goes new shoots
narana *magar*
burning root of swamp grass[3]
djirmalaŋan *lululmara* *dindi* *waidjilil* *ŋurlbu*
Place bamboo foliage bamboo Place (camp)

5 *narana* *duri-ŋirara* *nuŋbululei* *nuŋguluŋundu* *nargaleiu*
burns low down stood clan clan clan
nuŋburindi *nuŋbulju* *wudjulmundu* *rewulwulju* *baleiu*
clan clan clan clan subincision clan
gurda *duri-ŋirara* *djun-narana* *djunwiin* *garldandan*
fire low down stood Place[4] burns Place Place

baruŋaraŋ *madjamdulaŋ* *balundja* *wiin-miri* *madjambaliŋ*
Place Place incisure Place long[5] with Place
mariala
smoke

naldjara *gurda*
how[6] fire

goŋulbindina *maraluŋara* *waidjilil-djilil* *djirmalaŋu*
make clouds like hands[7] smoke rose up into Place Place

dindi *narana* *lululmara* *djirmalaŋan* *ŋawarabuŋu*
bamboo burns bamboo foliage Place Place
gunjarwaŋu *mudadiŋ* *gurda* *walalgalŋu* *balundja* *wiin-miri*
Place Place fire Place incisure Place long with

1 These people light the fire mentioned in the song.
2 Twigs or foliage growing (the word also means 'hair').
3 Also means 'thigh' or 'foreleg'.
4 Fire is burning through that place.
5 I.e., a long bank of smoke hovering in the sky.
6 'How' or 'In what way?' People at the various places mentioned ask why the smoke is spreading over their country and how the fire has started.
7 Long 'hands' of smoke like spreading wind-swept clouds.

Song 24

bili *ŋainbag* *galbira* *muari* *juda* *gaŋal-guŋala*
because spider twisted[1] spider[2] new took round (thread)
bururu *jiginiaŋala* *burur-bururun* *madaŋgi*
web went round and round made web grow spider
miredada *galbira*
web twisted

djirmalaŋandu *dindi-lili* *mari* *burur-bururuna*
Place in bamboos web made web grow

ramdun *goŋdja* *goŋdja-jubduna* *lululmara-lili* *djili-lili*
twist 'hands' moves 'hands' into bamboo foliage into Place
djirmalaŋandu *ramin-lili* *gurundul-lili*
Place into Place into Place

galbina *wondi* *bundjaliama* *mar-luma* *gargarba* *muarindu*
twists runs along make 'string' twists around spider spider

banaŋag-lili *ramin-lili* *garlbawaŋa-lili*
into Place into Place into bushes

burur-burun *guluŋguma* *ramdun* *jiwalgalarama*
makes web grow makes (it) round[3] twists twists
goŋdja-jubdiri
made 'hands' move

burur-burun *mara-lili* *malabuŋala* *jimagan-lili*
makes web grow into foliage made into swamp grass shoots
gandji-lili *boiul-woiul-lili* *wundjaŋa-lili*
underneath (into) into new shoots into new shoots

galbin-wondiri *bidbidjun* *gurulma* *muarin* *midug*
twists ran along makes bigger hang spider mist[4]

wagaluŋgul *geiman*
mist[5] mist

ramdun *galbira* *munalwola* *balawola* *rewulwulwola*
twists twisted clan[6] incisure clan clan

jigulwola *gunaraŋgala* *wadiriwola*
clan clan tribe

galbira *ŋainbag* *bidbidjun* *burur-burun*
twisted spider make bigger makes web grow

1 Spinning its thread, making a web.
2 A spider hides behind a cross it makes in the web.
3 I.e., towards the centre of the web.
4 The web resembles mist or haze from the smoke mentioned in Song 23.
5 Translated as 'spider makes the web through the mist'; i.e., resembling the misty haze of the fire.
6 The spider is seen by the people who live in that country: they 'always see them there'.

Song 25

gudin *djug-djug-duruna* *marawada* *ŋugingara* *ŋigŋig* *djinjul*
mouse hopped along[1] mouse mouse mouse[2] mouse

bulaŋgar *gudeiwarei* *dalarara*
mouse mouse mouse

maramulgana *boiul-woiul* *gandji* *jimagan* *wundjaŋu*
grasps foliage new grass shoots underneath new shoots new shoots

dudid *balana* *lilina* *jugjug-ŋurana* *djarma*
mouse away hither backward and forward[3] message[4]

gunbululu-lili *widiŋali*
into grass shade swamp grass

bili *waiin* *djinju* *dudid* *midug-guru* *galŋa*
because creature mouse mouse through mist skin

wabuluŋgulju *geimandu*
covered with mist[5] mist

djug-djugdun *ŋugingara* *dudid* *djinjul* *wirial* *gurunarana*
hops along mouse mouse mouse message[4] put along

dugar *judu*
road little

djug-djugdun *maramulgana* *waidjilil* *djiliil* *djirmalaŋan*
hops along grasps foliage Place Place Place

dindi *midug-guru* *geiman-guru*
bamboo through mist through mist

dugarndja *gurunarana* *marawada* *dalarara* *ŋugingara* *dudid*
road put along mouse mouse mouse mouse

ŋigŋig *djinjul* *garidjawidja* *maralwoi*
mouse mouse mouse mouse

gunbaluruwoi *widiŋalwoi* *gandjiwoi* *jimaganboi*
swamp grass swamp grass swamp grass new shoots

wundjaŋuwoi *boiul-woiul-woiulwoi*
new shoots new shoots

1 And shaking itself 'from the enveloping mist'. The 'mist' in this case signifies smoke mentioned in Song 23, and also the haze of the web threads in Song 24.
2 Its name is derived from the squeals it makes.
3 The mice or rats run backwards and forwards, men said, like women carrying gossip and causing trouble (see R. Berndt 1948*a*: 29-32, Song 5).
4 This refers to the mice 'gossiping' together: or, alternatively, to 'messages' and 'paw-marks' left along their tracks.
5 Or covered with spider-web thread.

Song 26

bili *wondaba* *burlgululu* *madeindja*
because pigeon[1] pigeon tongue (talk)
waiin *jigul* *gunaraŋ* *burlgan* *ŋari-ŋari*
creature clan[2] clan talk quickly bird language
woŋana *geiman-djau'jun* *midug* *wabuluŋgul*
talk mist breaks through[3] mist covered with mist
djau'juruna
broke through
waiindu *bulalujun* *woŋa* *djalbarura* *djalbruŋgidj* *jumarin*
creature dries itself[4] talk pigeon pigeon pigeon
waŋan-ŋura *barindi* *ŋurl-marŋ-marŋ* *wuddun*
in (that) camp Place *nonggaru* Place strikes
wuddun *ŋurlbu* *wurlmal* *djimin-djimin* *bagu*
strikes middle of *nonggaru* branches branches armband bushes
durabiril
armband bushes
jigulna *mada-djau'jun* *waiindu* *balana* *rewulwuljuna*
clan language break through creature incisure people clan
mada-djau'jun *dambul-dambulna* *malaŋarina* *nundeiana*
language break through clan clan clan
garldjalulana *njaŋbrulna* *nargalana* *nuŋburindina*
clan clan clan clan
waŋan-ŋura *ŋurldandurl-ŋura* *barindi* *ŋurlbur-ŋura*
in (that) camp in *nonggaru* Place in middle of *nonggaru*
daguwal-ŋura *djunmili-ŋura* *ŋurl-marŋ-marŋ-ŋura*
in Vagina Place in branches in *nonggaru* Place
waiindu *mada-djau'juruna* *mugoina* *munalna* *buldjumuna*
creature language broke through spirit people clan clan
daŋarlgaŋ-mirina *damanjalg-mirina* *midug-guru*
clan with clan with through mist
bulgidjun *gulililili . . .* *bulgidj*
goes into nest (sound of its cry) goes into nest

1 Or *wanba*, the 'morning star' pigeon or 'swamp' pigeon.
2 Speaking the dialect used by that clan. This song refers back to Song 2 where certain people are said to 'talk like birds'. The voice of the morning pigeon sounds like the speech of the clans mentioned in the song.
3 The cry of the pigeon 'breaks through' the haze.
4 Ruffling its feathers, making them stand up.

APPENDIX 3

THE DJARADA

Song 1

wogulmanba	*rari-rari*	*bilimanba*	*rari-rari*
breasts	come up	nipples stick out	come up

Song 2

giraraŋ-giraraŋ	*jibarŋa*	*luwandinja-luwandinja*
flicker eyes[1]	sand fly[2]	hit (her) eye

[1] Blink or wink.
[2] A man sends a fly to his sweetheart; it attracts her attention by persistently touching her eyes.

Song 3

gulaŋ	*djaŋi*	*wandjana*	*diragin-dirgilja*	*gulaŋdja*	*na*
blood	comes out	(because of her vagina)	[1]	blood	

wandjana
(because of her vagina)

[1] This word was said to mean 'seeing her and singing at the same time'.

Song 4

wana	*gulari*	*nina*	*gulari*	*ma-gulari-gulari-gani*
rain and hail	runs down	(there)	runs down	keeps running down[1]

jalarni-balmani-gani-jalarni
all spread out[2]

shud	*garg!*	*garg!*	*wirgul!*
spit[3]	[4]		[5]

1 The ‘arms’ or ‘hands’ of rain stream down her body.
2 Spreading over the ground in pools.
3 Used conventionally in the song: referring to the chicken hawk cry.
4 The cry of the chicken hawk.
5 This word was said to be, not the usual word *wirgul* which in the Yirrkalla region means a girl, but a ‘joking’ word, used by small children, referring to sexual attractiveness.

Song 5

reidja-reidja	*waruwarei*	*djubu*
(soaping hair)	washing body	soap[1]
ŋalara-ŋalara	*gaŋgaŋ*	*ŋalara-ŋalara*
2	3	2

shud	*garg*!	*garg*!	*wirgul*!
	4		

1 The soap in this case was obtained from the Roper River mission. The word *djubu* is, of course, ‘soap’. This first word sounds very much like ‘razor’, as in Song 19; but the commentators translated it as it is here.
2 She is washing her pubes: the word refers to her vulva and *labia majora*.
3 ‘Sting’ inside vulva: the soap apparently irritates the flesh. Translated as ‘scratch herself inside’.
4 The conventional ending to many of these songs.

Song 6

jaŋgudju	*mandaniŋ*	*galadju*
handkerchief[1]	blown or flapping in wind	tie around neck

mandaniŋ
blown or flapping in the wind

1 Said to be a coloured one.

Song 7

dibul-dibul-gula	*dibul-dibul-gula*	*gananeindja*	*jabulgali*	*jabulgali*
emu	emu	throat feathers[1]	throw (it)[2]	throw (it)
dibul-dibul-gula	*gananeindja*	*jalwijawul*	*gananeindja*	
emu	throat feathers	go out (to bush)[3]	throat feathers	

jalwijawul
go out (to bush)

1 A small bunch of emu neck feathers.
2 Sending the feathers to a girl.
3 She goes out to the bush away from the camping-place, to meet the singer.

Song 8

bulŋoiu	*ŋadu*	*balala*	*ŋadu*	*boiu-waragara*	*budjuju*	*ŋadu*
twirl firestick[1]	fast	2	fast	smoke spreads out[3]	feathers[4]	fast

1 I.e., making fire by twirling a stick (the stick-in-groove method): the upper pestle signifies the male organ, the groove beneath the female. The pestle twirled in the groove represents coitus.
2 This means the black soot or powder which forms in the firestick groove as the pestle is twirled.
3 Smoke emerges from the groove as the twirling increases in speed, and tinder is applied: the smoke spreads out.
4 The chicken hawk burns or singes its feathers.

Song 9

gargan	*garg garg garg*	*gudjinba*	*rulu-rulu*
chicken hawk	cry of chicken hawk	fly	(a number together)

garg garg garg	*gudjinba*	*rulu-rulu*	*gudjinbalaŋa*
cry of chicken hawk	fly	(a number together)	fly down
rulu-rulu			
(a number together)			

Song 10

dii	*nandjaŋi*	*nandjaŋi*	*dii*	*nandjaŋi*
tea[1]	drink	drink	tea	drink
shud	*garg!*	*garg!*	*wirgul!*	
2				

1 English word.
2 See previous songs.

Song 11

walwanu	*dindjulba*	*dindjulba*
piece of tobacco[1]	rub (it)	rub (it)

1 Cutting a plug of stick tobacco.

Song 12

balŋan-djara-djara	*beibubu*	*balŋan-djara-djara*
roll (it)	paper	roll (it)

Song 13

jabidja	*bidjana*	*jabidjaŋei*	*bidjana*	*jabidjaŋei*	*maluwari-maluwari*
knead[1]	this way	knead	this way	knead	flatten (it)[2]
damba					
damper[3]					

1 Kneading flour with water. Cf. the first word in Song 16, where the basic meaning is similar.
2 Forming the kneaded flour into a flattened loaf.
3 English word.

Song 14

giraŋ-giraŋ	*giraŋ-giraŋ*	*wanu-waŋun*	*wanu-waŋun*
coitus	coitus	get tight	get tight

Song 15

djabana	*guralji*	*didbiu*	*guralji*
native companion	native companion[1]	can send it	native companion

[1] 'Singing' name for this bird.

Song 16

jabidj-jabidjana	*jabidjana*	*jabidj-jabidjana*
hurt herself[1]		hurt herself

[1] A woman strikes or bangs her foot with her digging stick and then complains of being hurt.

Song 17

gandeialgana	*jalanidjbana*
urine	faeces

Song 18

badigudu-gurula	*badigudu-gurula*	*dindjulba*
skirt[1]	skirt	pubic hairs

[1] I.e., 'petticoat', used in this region as another name for skirt. European clothing was introduced by missionaries and others.

Song 19

reisa reisa	*mara-mara*	*gaŋgalaradja*
razor blade	hair[1]	blood runs[2]

[1] A man is shaving his face.
[2] Blood runs from a cut.

Song 20

balmani-gani	*djundulba*	*dja-minidj-minidj*
man's hat	brim turned down	scratch hair

Song 21

wondru-wondrila	*nawiniga*	*djileielga*
break (oyster)	oyster	eat

Song 22

ladaringa	*wombal-ludaid-ladaringa*
blue-tongue lizard	tail

Song 23

djadbari-lilia	*djiria-djiria*
scorpion	tail upright

Song 24

jalwi-jalwiana	*maliangana*	*jalwi-jalwiana*	*maliangana*
blanket lizard	frill sticks out	blanket lizard	frill sticks out

Song 25

wili-jalgana jalgana	*ja-wililgana jalgana*
footmark in dust[1]	make dust

1 This is the footprint of a girl: as she runs she churns up dust.

Song 26

jalŋaidbana	*gawudja-wudjana*
paperbark	wedges from tree

Song 27

wulŋaidbana	*ŋaidja-ŋaidjana*	*wulŋaidbana*
raining	sit down	raining

Song 28

gulunguru	*mana*	*djibidi*	*ganjurala*
pregnant	get	[1]	clitoris

1 The red 'walls' of the vagina.

Song 29

djabinabana	*manimana*	*djabinabana*
red ochre and fat	smear it on[1]	red ochre and fat

1 A woman paints herself with red ochre.

Song 30

gindiari-gandi	*marulbandi-gandi*
boomerang	flat boomerang

Song 31

bi-jalia	*jalina*	*bi-jalia*	*jalina*
chipping	scraping	chipping	scraping

Song 32

gulaŋ	*djabani-jaŋgana*	*gilijiriŋgana*
blood	(blood) runs	from that break [1]

[1] I.e., during ritual defloration.

Song 33

madjas-djiana	*gwi-jelga-jelgana*	*madjas-djiana*	*gwi-jelga-jelgana*
native companion [1]	flew over	native companion	flew over

[1] This sounds like the English word 'matches': but the translators insisted that, with the above suffix, it refers to the native companion bird.

Song 34

ralwiri-ralwiri	*gabu*	*binijalgana*
thirsty [1]	water	drinking

[1] Two women are thirsty.

Song 35

bajelga-jelgana	*bajelgana*	*jelga-jelgana*
wash pubes		wash off semen

Song 36

mabinbrin	*jelganamara*	*mabinbrin*
digging stick	point	digging stick

Song 37

giwiulbana	*waialbana*	*giwiulbana*
jungle	low place	jungle

Song 38

ŋaidjaŋguli	*gana*	*ŋaidjaŋguli*	*gana*	*gawijulgana*
1	2	1	2	dilly bag

[1] The *mawuga* bush yam.
[2] Another name for it, *ganei*.

Song 39

gwiei-jaŋgana	*madei-jaŋganei*
blowing fire	flame

Song 40

gura-njelmi-njelmi	*djida-waraŋ-baraŋ*
woman shy[1]	sits down[2]

1 Not so much shyness, as embarrassment (*gura*).
2 She sits down coyly because she is 'shy' of the man.

Song 41

girara-raŋgana	*jibarŋala*	*raŋgana*
laughing	teeth showing in laughter	

Song 42

mani-mani	*liriŋga*	*mani-mani*	*liriŋga*
pull her[1]	pull back[2]	pull her	pull back

1 A man attempts to pull his sweetheart on to his thighs (i.e., in a conventional position for coitus).
2 She restrains him and pulls back.

Song 43

mululŋgur	*jelgana*	*jelgi-jelgana*
semen	ejaculating	ejaculating[1]

1 This word implies that semen pours from a woman, running down her legs: she 'rubs herself', wiping it off.

Song 44

bidja-bidja-bidjana	*guwaielgana*	*guwaielgana*
this way (turn woman around)	open legs	open legs

Song 45

rami-jelgana	*rali-jelgana*	*rami-jelgana*
close (her) legs[1]	clitoris[2]	close (her) legs

1 I.e., after coitus.
2 Her clitoris protrudes; *rali* indicates 'direction toward' the speaker.

Song 46

gombarelbana	*gombarelbana*	*mada-djidbana*
white 'plum'[1]	white 'plum'	rounded bunches together[2]

1 The wild white 'plum', *gombudaŋar.*
2 The plum's rounded fruit, bunched together and devoid of leaves.

Song 47

minji-jelgana	*rali-jelgana*
1	put into 2

1 A bark receptacle pointed at each end: bark receptacle = vagina.
2 The plums (Song 46) are placed in it. The commentators insisted this was not the same as the word in Song 45.

Song 48

marijelgana	*jalijelgana*
calling out	1

1 Two girls who have been separated call out to each other.

Song 49

giwarungana	*walamundun-gari*	*jandu-bili-bili*
walk up	follow along creek	sit down for a rest

Song 50

ba-raguragu-mana	*ba-ralirali-mana*
sunset	walk along with sun's rays

Song 51

dabalbana-bana	*jelagana*
periwinkle 1	2

1 I.e., sea snail.
2 The 'cap' with which the snail closes its shell.

Song 52

mala-widi-widi	*gulmalain-gulmalain*	*mala-widi-widi*
big chicken hawk	flapping	big chicken hawk
gulmalain-gulmalain	*malawuramangari*	
flapping	removing loin covering clitoris 1	

1 A chicken hawk swoops down and snatches off a woman's pubic covering, revealing her clitoris.

Song 53

gwia-ŋandrudbara	*gwia-rarin-gwingura*
fish grabbing	fish in water

Song 54

manaindjara	*jalwirigara*	*manaindjara*
shark	scratching pubes	shark

Song 55

madjigin	*madjigin*	*balulan-balulan*
words		sound of talking

Song 56

guguna	*waluna*	*lugana*	*banganja*
eat (it)	daytime[1]	eat (it)	wild honey

1 While the sun (*walu*) is up.

Song 57

walu-rurugu	*ban-mani*	*walu-rurugu*	*ban-mani*
sunset	rays of sun	sunset	rays of sun

Song 58

wona	*midaidba*	*wona-midaidba*
arm	armband	arm armband

Song 59

jabidja	*bidjana*	*jandjara*	*djarara*
digging stick	thus	covering herself	*djarada*

Song 60

milamani	*gagalarinja*	*milamani*	*gagalarinja*
spring water	runs down	spring water	runs down

Song 61

balanjari	*gambu-garinja*	*ŋagalana*
crocodile	crawls along	(woman) gets up

Song 62

wolurlma	*lindjilma*	*bugurin-dara*	*bugurin-dara*
pubic hair	scratch herself	looking at	looking at

Song 63

maularin	*diridiri*	*maularin*
labia majora	(grass) pubic covering	*labia majora*

Song 64

rabindi-rabindi	*djinawa*	*wiridji-ridji*
jabiru bird	inside[1]	scratch herself

[1] Among the paperbark trees and mangroves.

Song 65

binji-nanjina-njila	*ragan-boiu*	*djugan-boiu*
small chicken hawk	flap along	skim along

shud *garg*! *garg*! *wirgul*!

BIBLIOGRAPHY

Adam, L. 1952. Review of *Kunapipi* by R. M. Berndt, *Meanjin*, Vol. XI, No. 1.

Ashley-Montagu, M. F. 1937*a*. 'Infertility of the Unmarried in Primitive Societies', *Oceania*, Vol. VIII, No. 1.

—— 1937*b*. (Revised edition, 1974.) *Coming into Being among the Australian Aborigines.* Routledge and Kegan Paul, London.

Basedow, H. 1925. *The Australian Aboriginal.* Preece, Adelaide.

—— 1935. *Knights of the Boomerang.* The Endeavour Press, Sydney.

Berndt, C. H. 1950*a*. 'Expressions of Grief among Aboriginal Women', *Oceania*, Vol. XX, No. 4.

—— 1950*b*. *Women's Changing Ceremonies in Northern Australia.* L'Homme, Hermann, Paris.

—— 1952. 'A Drama of north-eastern Arnhem Land', *Oceania*, Vol. XXII, No. 3.

—— 1965. 'Women and the "Secret Life"', in *Aboriginal Man in Australia* (R. M. and C. H. Berndt, eds). Angus and Robertson, Sydney.

—— 1970*a*. 'Prolegomena to a study of Genealogies in north-eastern Arnhem Land', in *Australian Aboriginal Anthropology* (R. M. Berndt, ed.). The University of Western Australia Press, for the Australian Institute of Aboriginal Studies, Perth.

—— 1970*b*. 'Monsoon and Honey Wind', in *Échanges et Communications: mélanges offerts à Claude Lévi-Strauss* (J. Pouillon et P. Maranda, eds). Mouton, Paris.

Berndt, R. M. 1948*a*. 'A Wonguri-Mandjikai Song Cycle of the Moon-Bone', *Oceania*, Vol. XVII, No. 4; Vol. XVIII, No. 1.

—— 1948*b*. 'Badu, Islands of the Spirits', *Oceania*, Vol. XIX, No. 2.

—— 1951*a*. *Kunapipi.* Cheshire, Melbourne.

—— 1951*b*. 'Ceremonial Exchange in Western Arnhem Land', *Southwestern Journal of Anthropology*, Vol. 7, No. 2.

—— 1952. *Djanggawul.* Routledge and Kegan Paul, London.

—— 1955. '"Murngin" (Wulamba) Social Organization', *American Anthropologist*, Vol. 57, No. 1.

—— 1958. 'Some methodological Considerations in the Study of Australian Aboriginal Art', *Oceania*, Vol. XXIX, No. 1.

—— 1962. *An Adjustment Movement in Arnhem Land.* L'Homme, Mouton, Paris.

—— 1964. 'The Gove Dispute: the question of Australian Aboriginal Land and the preservation of Sacred Sites', *Anthropological Forum*, Vol. I, No. 2.

—— 1965. 'Marriage and the Family in North-eastern Arnhem Land,' in *Comparative Family Systems* (M. F. Nimkoff, ed.). Houghton Mifflin, Boston.

—— 1966. 'The Wuradilagu Song Cycle of Northeastern Arnhem Land', in *The Anthropologist Looks at Myth* (J. Greenway, ed.). University of Texas Press, Austin.

—— 1969. *The Sacred Site: the Western Arnhem Land Example.* Australian Institute of Aboriginal Studies, No. 29, Social Anthropology Series 4, Canberra.

—— 1970*a*. 'Traditional Morality as Expressed through the medium of an Australian Aboriginal Religion,' in *Australian Aboriginal Anthropology* (R. M. Berndt, ed.). University of Western Australia Press, for the Australian Institute of Aboriginal Studies, Perth.

—— 1970*b*. 'Two in One, and More in Two', in *Échanges et Communications: mélanges offerts a Claude Lévi-Strauss* (J. Pouillon et P. Maranda, eds). Mouton, Paris.

—— 1971. 'Social Relationships in Two Australian Aboriginal Societies of Arnhem Land: Gunwinggu and "Murngin"', in *Kinship and Culture* (F. L. K. Hsu, ed.). Aldine, Chicago.

—— 1972. 'The Walmadjeri and Gugadja', in *Hunters and Gatherers Today* (M. G. Bicchieri, ed.). Holt, Rinehart and Winston, New York.

—— 1974. *Australian Aboriginal Religion.* Brill, Leiden, for the Institute of Religious Iconography, State University of Gröningen: 4 fascicles. (Also combined in one volume.)

—— 1976. 'Territoriality and the Problem of Demarcating Socio-Cultural Space', in *Tribes and Boundaries in Australia* (N. Peterson, ed.). Australian Institute of Aboriginal Studies, Canberra.

—— (ed.) 1971. *A Question of Choice: an Australian Aboriginal Dilemma.* University of Western Australia Press, Perth.

Berndt, R. M. and C. H. 1943, 1944. 'A Preliminary Report of Fieldwork in the Ooldea Region, western South Australia', *Oceania*, Vol. XIII, No. 3; Vol. XIV, Nos 2 and 3.

—— 1946. 'The Eternal Ones of the Dream', *Oceania*, Vol. XVII, No. 1.

—— 1951. *Sexual Behaviour in Western Arnhem Land.* Viking Fund Publications in Anthropology, No. 16, Wenner-Gren Foundation, New York.

—— 1952, 1953, 1954. 'A Selection of Children's Songs from Ooldea, western South Australia', *Mankind*, Vol. 4, Nos 9, 10 and 12.

—— 1954. *Arnhem Land, Its History and Its People.* Cheshire, Melbourne.

—— 1964. *The World of the First Australians.* Ure Smith, Sydney. Second, revised edition, 1976.

—— 1970. *Man, Land and Myth in North Australia*: the Gunwinggu People. Ure Smith, Sydney.

Berndt, R. M. and Phillips, E. S. (eds) 1973. *The Australian Aboriginal Heritage. An Introduction through the Arts.* Ure Smith, for the Australian Society for Education through the Arts, Sydney.

Durkheim, E. 1954. *The Elementary Forms of the Religious Life* (J. Swain, trans.). Allen and Unwin, London. First edition, 1915.

Elkin, A. P. 1933. 'Marriage and Descent in East Arnhem Land', *Oceania*, Vol. III, No. 4.

—— 1934. 'Cult-Totemism and Mythology in Northern South Australia', *Oceania*, Vol. V, No. 2.

—— 1950. 'The Complexity of Social Organization in Arnhem Land', *Southwestern Journal of Anthropology*, Vol. 6, No. 1.

Elkin, A. P., and Berndt, R. M. and C. H. 1950. *Art in Arnhem Land.* Cheshire, Melbourne.

Hawkesworth, J. 1773. *An Account of the Voyages undertaken by the order of his present majesty for making discoveries in the southern hemisphere.* London, 3 vols.

Hiatt, L. R. 1971. 'Secret Pseudo-Procreation Rites among the Australian Aborigines', in *Anthropology in Oceania* (L. R. Hiatt and C. Jayawardena, eds). Angus and Robertson, Sydney.

Kaberry, P. M. 1939. *Aboriginal Woman.* Routledge, London.

Lévi-Strauss, C. 1963. *Totemism* (R. Needham, trans.). Beacon Press, Boston.

Malinowski, B. 1913. *The Family among the Australian Aborigines.* The University of London Press, London.

Radcliffe-Brown, A. R. 1951. 'Murngin Social Organization', *American Anthropologist*, Vol. 53, No. 1.

Róheim, G. 1933. 'Women and their Life in Central Australia', *Journal of the Royal Anthropological Institute*, Vol. 63.

—— 1945. *The Eternal Ones of the Dream.* International Universities Press, New York.

Roth, W. E. 1897. *Ethnological Studies among the north-west-central Queensland Aborigines.* Government Printer, Brisbane.

Spencer, B. and Gillen, F. J. 1938. *The Native Tribes of Central Australia.* Macmillan, London. First edition, 1899.

—— 1904. *The Northern Tribes of Central Australia.* Macmillan, London.

Strehlow, T. G. H. 1971. *Songs of Central Australia.* Angus and Robertson, Sydney.

Thomson, D. F. 1936*a*. 'Fatherhood in the Wik-Monkan Tribe', *American Anthropologist*, ns. Vol. XXXVIII.

——1936*b*. *Interim General Report of Preliminary Expedition to Arnhem Land, Northern Territory of Australia, 1935-36.* Department of Interior, Canberra.

—— 1939*a*. *Report on Expedition to Arnhem Land, 1936-37.* Northern Territory of Australia, Department of Interior, Canberra.

—— 1939*b*. 'The Tree Dwellers of the Arafura Swamps: a new type of bark canoe from Central Arnhem Land', *Man*, No. 109.

—— 1949. *Economic Structure and the Ceremonial Exchange Cycle in Arnhem Land.* Macmillan, Melbourne.

Warner, W. L. 1958. *A Black Civilization.* Harper, New York. First edition, 1937.

Webb, T. T. 1933. 'Tribal Organization in Eastern Arnhem Land', *Oceania*, Vol. III, No. 4.

INDEX